THE MANY FACETS OF LEADERSHIP

ISBN 0-13-100533-2

9 790131 005333

FINANCIAL TIMES
Prentice Hall

In an increasingly competitive world, it is quality
of thinking that gives an edge—an idea that opens new
doors, a technique that solves a problem, or an insight
that simply helps make sense of it all.

We work with leading authors in the various arenas
of business and finance to bring cutting-edge thinking
and best learning practice to a global market.

It is our goal to create world-class print publications
and electronic products that give readers
knowledge and understanding which can then be
applied, whether studying or at work.

To find out more about our business
products, you can visit us at www.ft-ph.com

Pearson
Education

THE MANY FACETS
OF LEADERSHIP

MARSHALL GOLDSMITH

VIJAY GOVINDARAJAN

BEVERLY KAYE

ALBERT A. VICERE

FINANCIAL TIMES
Prentice Hall

An imprint of PEARSON EDUCATION
Upper Saddle River, NJ • New York • London • San Francisco • Toronto • Sydney
Tokyo • Singapore • Hong Kong • Cape Town • Madrid
Paris • Milan • Munich • Amsterdam

www.ft-ph.com

Library of Congress Cataloging-in-Publication Data

The many facets of leadership/Marshall Goldsmith...[et al.].
    p. cm.—(Financial Times Prentice Hall books)
    Includes bibliographical references and index.
    ISBN 0-13-100533-2
    1. Leadership. 2. Executive ability. I. Goldsmith, Marshall. II. Series

HD57.7.M38 2003
658.4'092—dc21   2002029270

Editorial/production supervision: *Kerry Reardon*
Cover design director: *Jerry Votta*
Cover design: *Anthony Gemmellaro*
Art director: *Gail Cocker-Bogusz*
Interior design: *Meg Van Arsdale*
Manufacturing manager: *Alexis Heydt-Long*
Manufacturing buyer: *Maura Zaldivar*
VP, executive editor: *Tim Moore*
Editorial assistant: *Allyson Kloss*
Marketing manager: *Bryan Gambrel*
Full-service production manager: *Anne R. Garcia*

© 2003 by Pearson Education, Inc.
Publishing as Financial Times Prentice Hall
Upper Saddle River, NJ 07458

Chapter 13 © 2003 by Peter Koestenbaum
Chapter 31 © 2003 by David Lei

Financial Times Prentice Hall books are widely used by corporations
and government agencies for training, marketing, and resale.

For information regarding corporate and government bulk discounts please contact:
Corporate and Government Sales (800) 382-3419 or corpsales@pearsontechgroup.com

Printed in the United States of America
10 9   8   7   6   5   4   3   2   1

ISBN 0-13-100533-2

Pearson Education LTD.
Pearson Education Australia PTY, Limited
Pearson Education Singapore, Pte. Ltd.
Pearson Education North Asia Ltd.
Pearson Education Canada, Ltd.
Pearson Educación de Mexico, S.A. de C.V.
Pearson Education–Japan
Pearson Education Malaysia, Pte. Ltd.

FINANCIAL TIMES PRENTICE HALL BOOKS

For more information, please go to www.ft-ph.com

CONTENTS

ix

PART II FACILITATING CHANGE: THE LEADER'S ROLE

Chapter 13 FACING THE PARADOXES 151
OF LEADERSHIP: EIGHT RULES
by Peter Koestenbaum

Chapter 14 HUMAN INFLUENCE 157
by Charles E. Dwyer

PART III MAKING THE GRADE:
NEW LEADERSHIP SKILLS

PART IV CREATING COMPETITIVE ADVANTAGE: STRATEGIES FOR SUCCESS

FOREWORD

have been involved in education for a good part of my life, most of which came through the Institute for Management Studies (IMS), founded in 1974 by my father, mentor, and friend, Gordon A. Peters. IMS, his brainchild, was designed to deliver knowledge from cutting-edge business thinkers to managers at large organizations, who might otherwise not have a chance to receive it. In its first year, IMS presented such well-known faculty as Stephen Covey and Ken Blanchard. We also introduced a promising young Harvard professor, Dr. Michael Porter. Since that time, IMS has worked with the best and brightest from academia and consulting to provide management development to over 25,000 managers a year throughout the Western world.

Over the years, I have contemplated gathering together the views of these great minds into a collection of essays that would reach more people than IMS alone had an opportunity to touch. I quickly realized two fundamental truths; it would take several volumes to collect even a small portion of the knowledge that these thought leaders have to offer, and I did not have nearly enough time to devote to the task.

Nothing much happened with the notion of a "Best of IMS" book until an unusually warm winter's day when I received a call from my business colleague and friend, Marshall Goldsmith. He prompted me to once again explore the idea, stating that there "was tremendous upside potential for a book of this kind and almost no potential downside."

Why now? Extremely busy working with two different companies, I knew that it would take more than a few phone calls to put a great book together. However, I had two compelling reasons to accept: the state of management as a practice and my four-year old son.

THE STATE OF MANAGEMENT

During the 1980s and 1990s, organizations were restructuring in order to find new efficiencies. The usual result was that they became flatter and managers were given an increased span of control, usually with a commensurate increase in the length of their workday.

At the turn of the millennium, business entered a new era. The Information Age truly arrived and has since changed the way organizations conduct business. While one could certainly argue that many new business models have been built on shaky foundations in the hope that they would create new economic models, the changes ushered in by this new age are nonetheless far-reaching. Technology has forever changed the way that companies manufacture, market, sell, and ship products and/or services. Technology has also changed the way people manage and work in organizations. People are using technology to communicate, gather information, collaborate with team members, manage personal time and productivity, and learn.

These changes have created tremendous organizational and managerial efficiencies. With technology to fill the void, we can now get more done in less time with fewer people. Organizations can quickly and easily communicate with customers and employees around the world, creating a truly global community. Through technology people can also get a seemingly limitless amount of information with which to make better and faster decisions. Unfortunately there have been some negative impacts as well.

Everything moves faster. With cycle times and product life-cycles becoming increasingly shorter, the ability to create a long-term strategy has become almost impossible. While organizations can find almost any information about their competitors, their competitors are engaged in the same fact-finding mission about them.

Employees have huge amounts of data on which to base decisions, but the enormity of it can induce a state of paralysis. People often forego making a decision rather than make one without all the information that is available, or soon will be.

Communication, now constant, has suffered in some significant ways. Face-to-face conversation is frequently replaced by e-mail or voicemail in instances of employee praise, reprimand, or even termination. In an effort to drive support costs down, customer service has been reduced from personal interaction to voicemail and now to e-mail.

Leadership, and the skills required to be a leader, have changed dramatically in our new digital world. Leadership used to be driven by knowledge and expertise in a given area. Now, it is virtually impossible to know it all. Instead, leaders must rely on managing knowledge workers. Thus, people skills have become the key to successful leadership, which may seem ironic given the tremendous dependence we all have on rather impersonal technology. So, the time was right for a book that explored these changes and challenges while giving insight on how to leverage them to our benefit.

TUBEROUS SCLEROSIS

The second reason that I wanted to help with this book is my son Mitchell, who at birth was diagnosed with Tuberous Sclerosis. TS is a debilitating genetic disease. Sixty percent of those affected are unable to live independently. The disease affects multiple organs and can cause tumors in the skin, kidneys, brain, heart, eyes, lungs, teeth as well as other organ systems. TS is the leading genetic cause of epilepsy and can also cause retardation, autism, or renal failure. An estimated 50,000 people in the US are affected with Tuberous Sclerosis.

When our son was born, the doctors found several tumors in his heart and numerous tumors in his brain. Fortunately, we have been lucky. For the most part, our lives have been normal. Many others have been far less fortunate. For the past several years, I have felt powerless against the progression of this disease. It is my sincere hope that the awareness generated by this book may, in some small way, help Mitchell and others like him.

Jon V. Peters
President, COO
The Institute for Management Studies

INTRODUCTION

No book of collected works happens overnight. This one took a good two years of labor and then some. Perhaps the best way to provide you with an overview of its contents is to tell you a bit about its name. The subject of leadership is clearly multifaceted. The depth and breadth of the subject itself allows thought leaders everywhere to rethink it through their own lens. It is by adding a unique lens that the old becomes new—or at least worth exploring in new ways. In each chapter of this book you will see the distinct lens of its author, as each presents the cutting edge of his or her own subject matter.

For most of the authors of this book, this was *not* a two-year project. Rather, it was the distillation of their thinking over a much more extended period of time. In some instances, the thinking shaped itself throughout their professional careers. The authors come from varied backgrounds. Some are academicians and have spent the bulk of their careers in business schools, colleges, or universities. Others have had long consulting careers and now direct their own firms. Still others gained their experience in private or public sector organizations. And many have done all three.

Diverse as they are, they have several things in common. All have served as IMS faculty, and many still do. All have been leaders in organizations in one way or another. All believe that the education of managers in organizations is critical and that learning to be a good leader is a lifelong process.

Here's what you'll find.

Part I, "Forging Ahead: The Quest for Knowledge," suggests that the quest for learning and knowledge is key to great leadership and provides a variety of perspectives. Tony Buzan looks at learning in the context of improving techniques for management, and employs his Mind Mapping technique in "Intelligence on Intelligence and the Development of Intellectual Capital." Paul J. H. Schoemaker discusses a useful way to understand the barriers to internal change in "Organizational Renewal: Overcoming Mental Blind Spots." In "The Creativity and Commitment Connection" Amarjit Chopra focuses on the ability to create buy-in for new ideas and how to motivate people to implement better ways of interacting.

William Ury shows us that eight out of ten decisions are not self-made—they are negotiated. He believes that "networks of negotiation" are taking their place in "The Negotiation Revolution." John J. Scherer suggests that chaos plays a vital role in birthing fundamental change and innovation in "The Role of Chaos in the Creation of Change." Russell L. Ackoff, in "Fundamentalism and Panaceas," describes his concept of how leaders look for simple solutions to serious problems.

Part II, "Facilitating Change: The Leader's Role" provides insights to the vital role of the leader. In "Leadership in the Networked Economy" Albert A. Vicere describes four key roles necessary for effective leadership. In "The Organizational Change Leader" W. Warner Burke provides a phased system of viewing organizational change and the role of leadership within each phase. Joel R. DeLuca proposes a working model for development of successful leaders in "Entrepreneurial Leadership: Building Capacity for Speed, Risk, and Continuous Innovation."

In "Leadership: Reflections and Learnings" Robert Terry shares a series of learning's that have challenged his own understanding and practice of leadership. Michael M. Lombardo and Robert W. Eichinger describe four kinds of experiences related to learned skills in the workplace in "Experience Is Still the Best Teacher." In "Polarity Management: One Tool for Managing Complexity and Ambiguity" Barry Johnson illustrates the way in which leaders deal with dilemmas. Peter Koestenbaum consolidates insights about the structure of human existence in "Facing the Paradoxes of Leadership: Eight Rules." Charles E. Dwyer summarizes the essential elements in a successful approach to human influence in "Human Influence."

Part III, "Making the Grade: New Leadership Skills," suggests several critical leadership qualities that are essential for leaders. In "Help Them Grow or Watch Them Go" Beverly L. Kaye provides a series of practical tips to leaders for effective (and non-time-consuming) career coaching. Randall P. White and Phillip Hodgson, in "The Newest Leadership Skills," offer interesting insights on leadership styles of the past and the changes in new leadership styles. In "When Good People Do Bad Things" Ronald M. Green analyzes the causes of the Ford Explorer/Firestone tire disaster to understand why business managers sometimes make ethically poor decisions. Marshall Goldsmith talks about how to be coached and includes some helpful questions to ask when engaging in a coaching relationship in "Recruiting Supportive Coaches: A Key to Achieving Positive Behavioral Change."

In "Global Leadership and Global Emotional Intelligence" Stephen H. Rhinesmith correlates Daniel Goleman's ideas about emotional intelligence with global leadership. Larraine Segil offers her ten essential traits in "Is Your Organization Driven By Dynamic Leaders?" Idalene Kesner examines how organizations should prepare for potential future crises and provides helpful tools for examining current preparedness in "Effective Crisis Management: Now More Than Ever."

Part IV, "Creating Competitive Advantage: Strategies for Success," provides an array of useful strategies. Fons Trompenaars and Peter Woolliams present a methodology for developing marketing strategies based on cultural differences in "Marketing Through Reconciliation: Global Brand, Local Touch." In their article "The Effective Use of Scenario Analysis to Support Research and Development" Peter Schwartz and Gerald Harris identify six best practices useful to companies applying scenario analysis to R&D planning.

James M. Hulbert and Pierre Berthon address the movement away from a material to an information economy and its impact on marketing in their article "Morphing Marketing: Dissolving Decisions." Chip R. Bell provides a framework to understand the customer relationship process as circular in his article, "Creating Obnoxiously Devoted Customers." In "The Strategy of Bundling" Barry Nalebuff provides understanding of the mechanisms that underlie this strategy with examples of when it works and when it doesn't.

Finally, Part V, "Taking the Lead: Organizations of the New Millennium," speaks to the rapidly changing business environment and the need for flexibility, speed, and strategic agility. In "Anatomy of an Innovation Machine: Cisco Systems" Vijay Govindarajan and Chris Trimble provide a natural progression of the innovation process utilizing their four-step process and organizational design. In "Achieving Best Fit" Judith M. Bardwick describes borderless and stable organizations and how they attract and appeal to different individuals in the job market today. Maurice Saias and Olivier Tabatoni describe their definition of strategy in today's environment and outline the discontinuities corporations face in "Strategy for the 21st Century: Portfolio Is Back."

Homa Bahrami and Stuart Evans, in "Organizing for Strategic Flexibility," define three core dimensions that are utilized in the architecture of a flexible enterprise. David Lei introduces value confederations and the way in which these groups of firms will reshape industry in "Competitive Dynamics, Strategy, and Competence Development: The Rise of Value Confederations in Fast-Change Industries." Thomas Monahan and Stephen A. Stumpf, in "New Measures of Prosperity," suggest a means to value and to measure an organization and its employees' performance beyond the standard financial measurements currently in place. Charles Handy discusses the different types of leadership needed within organizations during different stages of the organization's lifecycle in "A World of Fleas and Elephants."

We hope you will use this collection of articles as a guide. Turn to the subject you need when you need it. Scan the material, ponder the suggestions, talk it over with peers, and test these ideas in your own organization. Let these thought leaders mentor you.

Marshall Goldsmith
Vijay Govindarajan
Beverly Kaye
Albert A. Vicere

ACKNOWLEDGMENTS

All of the authors have donated their time, expertise, and profits to the Tuberous Sclerosis Alliance *(www.tsalliance.org)* to fight this horrible disease. I thank each one of them for their gracious contribution. I would also like to thank the books editors, Marshall Goldsmith, Vijay Govindarajan, Beverly Kaye, and Al Vicere. I have had the pleasure of working with all of these great management thinkers over the years and can think of no finer team to edit the first book of this kind with the Institute for Management Studies.

I would like to acknowledge the tremendous work and dedication that Sarah McArthur has committed to this project. Her tireless efforts are what made this book possible. Lastly, I would like to again thank Marshall Goldsmith for his time, effort, friendship, and for living up to his promise to do almost all of the work on this effort. Mostly though, I would like to thank him for helping me do something about an idea whose time had clearly come.

Jon V. Peters
President, COO
The Institute for Management Studies

THE MANY FACETS
OF LEADERSHIP

FORGING AHEAD: THE QUEST FOR KNOWLEDGE

1

INTELLIGENCE ON INTELLIGENCE AND THE DEVELOPMENT OF INTELLECTUAL CAPITAL

Tony Buzan

I n the middle of the modern era in which we still exist, computers did not. They burst into existence, and within a few decades, have multiplied faster than the human race itself. Computers have taken over the world's business operations systems, its information systems. Calculating at billions of operations per second, computers have made significant contributions to many of humankind's most prized intellectual disciplines.

So powerful and important has all this become that business spending on knowledge management, information technology (IT), and leadership development is becoming the largest item in many capital-spending budgets. This trend is predicted to increase for the foreseeable future.

Imagine, now, that within the next few years computer research comes up with the next generation supercomputer, which by comparison would make the best computers we have today the equivalent of a pea in relation to the size of our planet.

Imagine that this new supercomputer could, in addition to being fundamentally competent in mathematical calculation, learn three languages fluently, each language with a vocabulary of 25,000 words (equivalent to Shakespeare's vocabulary in English); memorize multiple gigabytes of knowledge in general (rather than only in specific) areas, and recall them by random rather than linear access; learn from its own experience, thus self-developing its own programs; program other computers to a high level; operate those same computers; read books and incorporate the newly assimilated knowledge into existing and relevant data bases; think creatively, in a goal-directed manner, without external input; and organize its own work schedule on the basis of its externally and internally generated goals.

Imagine that this supercomputer could also communicate in its various languages with human beings; could move independently, safely, and with purpose in a local office environment; and could move similarly in a national or international environment.

Imagine even further that this incredible new computer operated on a mere 10^{12} chips aligned in multiple parallel; that this configuration allowed it to function normally in most of the sense areas of sight, hearing, smell, taste, touch, and kinesthesia; imagine that it could operate independently of an electrical power source; and finally that its multiple parallel processing system gave it the ability to generate functionally infinite patterns of thought for instances of intelligence.

What would be an appropriate name for your masterwork? *The human brain!*

Why, then, with over six billion copies of the super-bio-computer "in production," is the sum total of its interactions so grossly inadequate, and why did each one, as surveys over the last 40 years have confirmed, experience in some deep degree the following problems:

■ Memory
■ Concentration

- Communication: presentation skills (public speaking)
- Communication: presentation skills (written)
- Creative and innovative thinking
- Reading speed
- Reading comprehension
- Decision making
- Thinking
- Organization
- Planning
- Problem solving
- Boredom
- Analytical thinking
- Strategic thinking
- Time management
- Stress
- Fatigue
- Assimilation of information
- Decline of mental ability with age

INTELLECTUAL CAPITAL AND MENTAL LITERACY

The answer to the above conundrum lies in the nature of what we have been taught, how we have been taught, and what we have not been taught.

In their academic careers, those who have become business executives have spent, on average, between 1,000 and 10,000 hours each on the learning of literature, mathematics, the sciences, economics, geography, history, and languages. In other words, their brains have been confronted with what to learn for tens of thousands of hours.

What about "how to learn"—the development of intellectual capital and mental literacy?

To our race's credit, we pour hundreds of billions of dollars worldwide into completing our mastery of literacy—the verbal and the numerical alphabets. To our discredit, we ignore the most basic and most important "alphabet" of all—the alphabets of the brain, both physiological and behavioral. If we possessed this one fundamental literacy, we would be able to master all other literacies with ease.

Most of us are by definition both literate and numerate, but what about our mental literacy? Consider the following as a guide to your MLQ (Mental Literacy Quotient):

EXERCISE 1 Mental Literacy Quotient

IN YOUR ENTIRE SCHOOL CAREER, WERE YOU TAUGHT MORE THAN TWO HOURS ABOUT	YES	NO
1. The number of your brain cells and how they function?	❑	❑
2. The difference in your memory functions while you are learning and after you have learned?	❑	❑
3. How to apply your creativity to any subject?	❑	❑
4. How your thinking affects the growth of your brain cells?	❑	❑
5. How to "ride the waves" of concentration?	❑	❑
6. How to raise your I.Q.?	❑	❑
7. The relationship between physical and mental health?	❑	❑
8. How to apply learning theory to your own learning?	❑	❑
9. The different functions of your left and right cortexes?	❑	❑
10. The rhythms of memory?	❑	❑
11. Your eye–brain relationship and how to control it for improving the intake of information?	❑	❑
12. How to take notes that increase both your memory and your creativity?	❑	❑

DO YOU THINK THAT	YES	NO
13. Memory naturally declines with age?	❑	❑
14. The brain loses brain cells with age?	❑	❑
15. Children learn languages faster than adults?	❑	❑
16. Each alcoholic drink costs you 1,000 or more brain cells?	❑	❑

HAVE YOU EVER CAUGHT YOURSELF SAYING
ANY OF THE FOLLOWING?   YES   NO

17. I'm not creative.   ❏   ❏
18. I have the world's worst memory.   ❏   ❏
19. I'm not very good at mathematics.   ❏   ❏
20. I can't sing.   ❏   ❏
21. I can't do art.   ❏   ❏
22. I'm stupid.   ❏   ❏

CIRCLE THE CORRECT ANSWER:

23. The percentage of the brain we consciously use is approximately
    A. 50 percent   B. 20 percent   C. 1 percent

EXERCISE 2 Creativity Exercise

1. In 1 minute, jot down all the possible uses you can think of for a safety pin.
2. In 1 minute, jot down all those things for which you *cannot* use a safety pin.

You would be truly mentally literate if you answered yes to questions 1 to 12, no to questions 13 to 22, 1 percent to question 23, and you found eight or more uses for a safety pin and zero ways in which you cannot use one. A score of even 30 percent on these questions would place you in the top 1 percent of the mentally literate!

THE AWAKENING OF A SLEEPING GIANT

Why do we have this enormous lack of knowledge about that sleeping giant we carry around with us all our lives? Because the science of the brain is truly in its infancy. Ninety-five percent of what we now know about the human brain has been discovered in the last 5 years. The brain itself has only existed in its present form for some 45,000 years—a mere twinkling of an eye in the context of evolutionary history. And, it is only in the last 500 years that scientists have come to recognize that our mental skills are located in our heads.

THE REVOLUTION

Indeed, the revolution has already begun! In the brief span of the 1990s, the following epoch-changing and epoch-making changes in global behavior have occurred:

■ Stock market analysts have begun to watch, like hawks, the "brains" of Silicon Valley and other intellectual capital-intensive areas. When there is even a hint that one might move from company A to company B, the world's stock markets shift.

■ Skandia, the multinational insurance giant based in Stockholm, changed its standard annual report format to include a major supplement entitled "Intellectual Capital—An Accounting for the Intellectual Power of its Company and its Customers." Now, more individuals and companies request the intellectual capital supplement than its main report!

■ Singapore recently stated that it is to be known under the slogan "Thinking Schools; Learning Society; Intelligent Island." It also initiated a vast program of public events and learning festivals to promote thinking skills and the development of intelligence in all levels of society, especially the professional.

■ The English Manpower Services Commission publishes a survey in which it is noted that in the top 10 percent of companies, 80 percent invest considerable money and time in people development; in the bottom 10 percent, no money or time is invested. National Olympic squads devote as much as 40 percent of their training time to the development of thinking skills, memory training, "mental setting," psychological stamina, and imagination/visualization training.

LEARNING ORGANIZATION OR EXTINCT ORGANIZATION

The business world is swinging irrevocably from a manufacturing orientation to one in which information processing and systems, creative and strategic thinking, and other intelligence-driven factors are the norm. Where manual labor and routine activity once ruled, brainpower and creativity now begin to reign supreme. Brainpower is the new driving force in the accumulation of wealth. In these contexts, consider the following points:

1. On average, executives spend 30 percent of their time reading and sorting through information, 80 percent of which is forgotten in 24 hours.
2. Executives spend, on average, 20 percent of their time solving problems and thinking creatively, and over 90 percent have had no training in these areas.
3. Executives spend 20 to 30 percent of their time communicating in writing or in speech, and most find it arduous, distasteful, boring, and even frightening.
4. Companies that spend $1 million on training lose $900,000 of that investment within two weeks of the completion of the training, because they do not understand the nature of brain functions or the methods of guaranteeing that the training will be learned, remembered, and applied.

The fact that we use a small percentage of our brains contains some interesting and apparent contradictions: In the 1950s the proportion was thought to be about 40 percent. Each decade has seen a dramatic decline in this estimate, from 40 down to 30, then to 20, then to 10 in the 1980s, and today 1 percent or even lower. This might suggest that people are becoming stupider rather than smarter. But, in actuality, the reason for this decline is that recent research has revealed the human brain to be much more powerful than was once thought. These findings tell us that there are immense opportunities for personal and organizational development.

Professor Anokhin, Pavlov's most brilliant student and one of the world's renowned neurophysiologists, declared, "No human being exists who can use all of the potential of his brain." This is why we don't accept any pessimistic estimates on the limits of the human brain. The human brain's potential is unlimited.

The past few years have seen an increasing number of traditional market leaders toppled by more mentally literate and creative-thinking newcomers. It is no coincidence that the leading companies are those who spend the highest proportion of their income on developing their employees, and it is similarly no coincidence that the leaders among these leaders are those who are "front-ending" such learning: teaching their employees to think, create, remember, concentrate, plan, and communicate before they embark on any other personnel development. This ensures that all subsequent training is absorbed and applied appropriately and that it is at least two times more effective than average. It also makes it more likely that all employees will use their vast intellectual resources to gain competitive advantage.

To dramatize this competitive advantage, consider the following scenario: Your company is suddenly cloned, and there are two identical organizations with identical staff, identical buildings, identical equipment, and identical objectives. Your current organization remains as it is, while the "twin" is identical in all ways with the one exception that every member of the staff is deeply skilled in learning how to learn, in memory function, in creative and strategic thinking, and in communication skills on all levels.

The two organizations go into direct competition with the ultimate goal of completely dominating the market. For your own amusement and entertainment, jot down the advantages you think each organization would have over the other, which organization you think would win, and how long you think it would take the winning organization to accomplish victory. In surveys done during the last 5 years, 100 percent of executives and managers chose the mentally literate organization, and they predicted complete victory within 5 years. The reality in the open marketplace is now beginning to reflect this scenario.

Solutions

A quick overview of a few cornerstones from state-of-the-art research on the functioning of the human brain gives an indication of how the super-bio-computer's momentary problems can be solved by the intelligent application of the brain's research on its own intelligence! I shall touch on seven major areas:

1. Left and right brain research
2. Mind Mapping[1]
3. Super-speed reading/intellectual power packs
4. Mnemonic techniques
5. Memory loss after learning
6. Decline of mental abilities with age
7. The brain cell

Left and Right Brain Research

It has become common knowledge that the left and right hemispheres of the brain deal with different intellectual functions. The left brain handles logic, language, number, sequence, analysis, listing, and words. The right brain deals with rhythm, color, imagination, daydreaming, spatial relationships, and dimension.

Recently, we have found that the left brain is not the so-called academic side, nor is the right brain the so-called creative, intuitive, emotional side. We now know that both sides need to be used in conjunction for academic and creative success. The Einsteins, Newtons, Cezannes, and Mozarts of this world, like the great business geniuses, combined their linguistic, numerical, and analytical skills with imagination to produce their creative masterpieces.

Using this basic knowledge of our functioning, it is possible to develop personnel in skills relating to each problem area, often producing incremental improvements of as much as 1,000 percent. One of the modern methods for achieving such improvement is the thinking tool called Mind Mapping.

---

[1] Mind Mapping was originated by this author, Tony Buzan.

MIND MAPPING

In traditional note taking, whether it is for memory, for the preparation of communication, for the organization of thought, for problem analysis, for planning, or for creative thinking, the standard mode is linear: sentences, short phrase lists, or numerically and alphabetically ordered lists. These methods, because of their lack of color, visual rhythm, image, and spatial relationships, cauterize the brain's thinking capacities and are literally counterproductive to each of the aforementioned processes.

Mind Mapping uses the full range of the brain's abilities, placing an image in the center of the page in order to facilitate memorization and the creative generation of ideas, and subsequently branches out in associative networks that mirror externally the brain's internal structures. By using this approach, the preparation of speeches can be reduced in time from days to minutes; problems can be solved both more comprehensively and more rapidly; memory can be improved from absent to perfect; and creative thinkers can generate a limitless number of ideas rather than a truncated list.

Benefits of Mind Maps for Management

1. They improve communication between members of staff.
2. They make learning more efficient and effective.
3. They can make marketing and promotion more focused, leading to improved sales.
4. The clearer thinking that Mind Maps fosters results in better management and organization, leading to a happier, more motivated workforce. (This in turn means fewer working days lost through illness and a better public image for the company.)
5. Complex issues may be seen on one page, therefore improving decision making.

SUPER-SPEED READING/INTELLECTUAL POWER PACKS

By combining Mind Mapping with new, super-speed reading techniques that allow speeds well over 1,000 words a minute in conjunction with excellent comprehension (and eventual effective reading speeds of about 10,000 words a minute), one can form intellectual power packs.

Reading at these advanced speeds, Mind Mapping in detail the outline of a book and its chapters, and exchanging information gathered by using advanced Mind Mapping and presentation skills, it is possible for six individuals to acquire, integrate, memorize, and begin to apply, in their professional situation, six full books' worth of new information in one day.

MNEMONIC TECHNIQUES

Mnemonic techniques were invented by the Greeks and were, until even recently, dismissed as tricks. We now realize that these devices are soundly based on the brain's functioning and that when applied appropriately they can dramatically improve any memory performance.

When using mnemonic techniques, one uses the principles of association and imagination, making dramatic, colorful, sensual, and, consequently, unforgettable images in one's mind. The Mind Map, being based upon the natural functioning of the brain, is in itself a powerful multidimensional mnemonic.

Using mnemonics, business people have been trained to remember 40 newly introduced people and to similarly memorize lists of over 100 products, facts, and data. These techniques are now being applied at the IBM Training Center in Stockholm and have been a major reason for the success of its 17-week introductory training program.

MEMORY LOSS AFTER LEARNING

Memory loss after learning is dramatic. After a 1-hour learning period, there is a short rise in the recall of information as the brain integrates the new data, which is followed by a dramatic decline in which, by the end of 24 hours, as much as 80 percent of the detail is lost. The scale remains roughly the same, regardless of the length of input time; thus, a 3-day course is fundamentally forgotten within 1 or 2 weeks of completion.

The implications for business are disturbing. If a multinational firm spends $50 million a year on traditional training, it can be shown that within a few days of that training's completion, if there is not appropriate reviewing programmed into the educational structure, $40 million has been lost with incredible efficiency.

With a simple understanding of the memory's rhythms, it is possible not only to avert this decline, but also to develop personnel in such a way as to increase the amount learned by using associative techniques.

DECLINE OF MENTAL ABILITIES WITH AGE

The usual chorus from business executives in response to the question, "What happens to your brain cells as they get older?" is, "They die!" It is usually voiced with extraordinary and surprising enthusiasm.

Dr. Marion Diamond of the University of California has recently confirmed that there is no brain cell loss with age in normal, active, and healthy brains. On the contrary, research is now indicating that if the brain is used and trained, there is a biological increase in the brain's interconnective complexity; that is, intelligence is raised.

People in their 60s, 70s, 80s, and 90s have shown that in every area of mental performance, statistically significant and permanent increases can be made with adequate training.

THE BRAIN CELL

In the last 5 years, the brain cell has become the new frontier in the human search for knowledge. We have discovered that not only do we each have 1 trillion brain cells, but that the interconnections between them can form patterns and memory traces that permutate to a number so staggeringly large as to be functionally equivalent to infinite. The number, calculated by the Russian neuroanatomist, Professor Anokhin, is one followed by 10 million kilometers of standard 11-point typewritten noughts!

With this inherent capacity to integrate and juggle with the multiple billions of bits of data that each of us possess, it has become increasingly apparent to those in brain research that adequate training of our phenomenal bio-computer, which in 1 second can calculate what it would take a super computer, at 400 million calculations per second, 100 years to accomplish, will enormously accelerate and increase our ability to problem-solve, to analyze, to prioritize, to create, and to communicate.

One of the most amazing events in the 1990s was the first filming, by the Max Plank Laboratory in Switzerland, of a living brain cell. This moving (in all senses of the word) image has been shown to business executives worldwide. On a large screen, they see an independent intelligence, which looks much like the hand of a thousand-fingered baby reaching out to touch the infinitely fascinating universe around it. The film is mesmerizing, and what is even more significant than the extraordinary scientific event itself, are the words used to describe the reaction of individuals to the experience of seeing a brain cell live.

Ability	Energetic	Potential
Active	Fascinating	Power
Alive	Happiness	Searching
Awesome	Hopeful	Self-assured
Beautiful	Incredible	Serenity
Bold	Independent	Splendid
Challenge	Intelligent	Thankful
Communication	Knowledge	Unique
Curious	Life	Unstoppable
Dynamic	Persistent	Wow

These are words that describe the inherent nature of humankind and each individual within humankind, words that describe the proper functioning of that super-computer you invented at the beginning of this article. These words describe the necessary qualities of all management and information systems, and they are the qualities that will bring planet earth and its cargo of intelligence successfully into the next century and millennium.

ORGANIZATIONAL RENEWAL: OVERCOMING MENTAL BLIND SPOTS

Paul J. H. Schoemaker, Ph.D.

L et's make a bet. Write down the ten largest industrial U.S. companies in 1910 (in terms of assets) and see if you can get at least three right. Most people fail this test miserably. (Answers are listed in Table 2.1 in order of total assets.) Companies come and go when viewed in historical terms. Their temporary success, and the arrogance that it breeds, set them up for failure. At first, success actually increases a firm's survival chances, lasting for about 30 to 50 years or so, according to the organization ecologists. Then, the survival curve flattens out, and the tendency to fail in the face of long-term change appears to become the rule rather than the exception.[1]

---

[1] Hannan, M., and J. Freeman. (1989). *Organizational Ecology.* Boston: Harvard University. Press. Foster, R. N. (1986). *Innovation: The Attacker's Advantage.* New York: Summit Books.

Foster, R.N. and S. Kaplan. (2001). *Creative Destruction,* Currency Doubleday.

TABLE 2.1 Ten Largest U.S. Companies in 1910

1. U.S. Steel
2. Standard Oil of New Jersey
3. American Tobacco
4. Mercantile Maine
5. Anaconda
6. International Harvester
7. Pullman & Co.
8. Central Leather
9. Armour & Co.
10. American Sugar

This failure to adapt is still with us today. For example, many leading firms of the disk drive industry surrendered their lead when a new drive (in terms of size and/or technology used) was introduced.[2] Why is it so hard for large, established organizations to adapt to change? External factors play a large part: Legal, fiscal, and national barriers may restrict a firm's growth opportunities; and antitrust laws, state monopolies, price controls, and other forms of regulation constitute barriers to optimal adaptation. However, since organizations have limited influence over these external forces, it is the internal factors that offer the most promising routes to change.

A useful way to understand the barriers to internal change is as a conflict between the learning organization and the performance organization.[3] Firms begin as learning organizations.[4] They are experimental and innovative; employees share information and work together; risk-taking is rewarded. However, once the firm discovers how to earn profits, it transforms into a performance or harvesting culture, striving for reliable performance (see Table 2.2).

---

[2] Christensen, C. M. (1997). *The Innovator's Dilemma: When New Technologies Cause Great Firms to Fail.* Boston: Harvard Business School Press.

[3] Hurst, D. K. (1995). *Crisis & Renewal.* Boston: Harvard Business School Press.

[4] Senge, P. M. (1990, Fall). "The Leader's New Work: Building Learning Organizations," *Sloan Management Review,* 7–23.

TABLE 2.2 Two Prototypical Cultures

THE PERFORMANCE ORGANIZATION	THE LEARNING ORGANIZATION
■ Internally oriented	■ Inquisitive and externally focused
■ Focused on making the numbers	■ Experimental and innovative
■ Rewards consistency	■ Shares information; fluid
■ Dislike of ambiguity and deviations	■ Rewards risk taking
■ Rule and procedure oriented	■ Relies on cross-functional teams

Rules and procedures are developed; employees focus on "making the numbers"; consistency is most rewarded. Those very characteristics that enabled the firm to find a profitable niche in the first place—creativity, flexibility, informality, and experimentation—must largely be suppressed to deliver reliable earnings. In short, the firm's short-term performance may be optimized at the expense of its long-term survival.

Other factors may inhibit the firm's capacity to change as well. For instance, building a large organization with all of its constituencies—shareholders, unions, regulators, licensing partners, other firms, and so forth—requires high organizational legitimacy. Actions must be documented and justified; they must conform to established norms.[5] In addition, decision processes become more complex as the organization grows, straining the abilities of employees to make strategic choices in a timely manner. This organizational sclerosis is compounded, at the individual level, by a human bias toward maintaining the status quo.

For these reasons and more, companies become inert, unable to respond quickly and change sufficiently. To counter these factors, firms must take specific, proactive steps to reinvigorate themselves. It is not enough to know that inertia is a problem—

---

[5] Weber, M. (1947). *The Theory of Social and Economic Organization.* (Trans.: A. M. Henderson and T. Parsons), Oxford University Press.

Weick, K. E. (1969). *The Social Psychology of Organizing.* Reading, MA: Addison-Wesley.

Stinchcombe, A. L. (1968). *Constructing Social Theories.* Harcourt, Brace and World.

managers must recognize the specific barriers that inhibit change and then develop plans to work around them.

One important leverage point for change lies in the company's decision-making process. The procedures used to identify and evaluate alternatives can be fraught with mental blind spots that lead to distorted estimates and judgments, which keep a company from moving in profitable new directions. In this chapter, we discuss mental blind spots and offer guidelines for overcoming common biases and errors in decision making.

MENTAL BLIND SPOTS

At every step of the decision process, our minds filter out relevant information, rely on flawed rules of thumb, and direct us toward the known and away from the unknown. The challenge is that these human psychological biases are not always visible and not so easily corrected. They are like illusions or *blind spots* that persist even after explicit warning or instruction. One of the most powerful of these psychological biases is the very human tendency to prefer the status quo.

MAINTAINING THE STATUS QUO

Imagine a training program for new managers. At the end of the training, half the managers receive company mugs at random and the other half receive company hats of comparable value. The trainer asks if anyone would like to trade for the other gift. Most of the managers choose to keep the gift they received by chance. Is this rational? A priori, there is a 50 percent chance that each person will get the item he or she wants. Therefore, economists expect that half the participants will trade for the other item. Yet, in experiments like this, the majority of participants choose to keep the original gift, preferring the status quo not change.[6]

---

[6] Kahneman, D., J. Knetsch, and R. Thaler. (1990, Dec.). "Experimental Tests of the Endowment Effect and the Coase Theorem," *Journal of Political Economy,* 98(61), 1325–1348.

The status-quo bias affects all types of decisions. For instance, a manager may subconsciously reject a strategy change because he or she is afraid of the mental turmoil it might engender. A manager who has invested significant time in a project may be loath to drop it before it is finished. In yet another case, a team of employees may fail to consider alternatives, believing that the current situation must be superior or it wouldn't be the status quo.

Researchers have identified a series of factors that underlie the status-quo bias. Building on their work, we advance the following list of factors as especially plaguing innovative decision making in established firms.[7]

- **Implied Superiority:** The status quo must be superior simply because it is the status quo. Presumably, things are done the present way for some good reason, even if we don't know what that reason is. The aphorism "if it ain't broke, don't fix it" captures this logic.
- *Transition Costs:* Change can be costly in terms of observable costs, such as time and inconvenience, and in terms of nonobservable, emotional costs, such as fear and mental unrest. Rational transition costs can be a legitimate reason for preferring the status quo, but often they become a rationalization for the irrational factors that tie us to the present.
- *Sunk Costs/Benefits:* If we've made significant investments in the status quo, it may be difficult or painful to abandon it. Sunk costs are irrecoverable and rationally should not be included in the equation, but they create mental ties that are difficult to break. Likewise, there may be sunk benefits—such as reputation or past glory—that should be irrelevant to the decision to change.
- *Omission Bias:* We are more likely to be comfortable with inaction (omission) than action (commission). This

---

[7] Samuelson, W., and R. Zeckhauser. "Status Quo Bias in Decision Making," *Journal of Risk and Uncertainty,* 1998. Reprinted by permission of Kluwer Academic Publishers.

Schoemaker, P. J. H., and J. Casey. (1994). "Status Quo and Change Biases: A Critical Examination," Working paper, The Wharton School.

may be rational from the individual's viewpoint, since most companies require a rationale for action and often accept inaction without further justification. In general, the more alternatives there are and the less we consider them to be viable options, the less regret we feel about not taking action.

Additional factors, of course, can affect the strength of these biases. For instance, greater complexity of the decision and increased importance to the decision maker may exacerbate the status quo bias. However, there are also some factors that may lessen its force and indeed reverse it. Sometimes we overvalue the things that we don't have, because the other side seems "greener." An alternative that has elements of competition or social comparison associated with it, such as someone else's car or job, often seems more desirable than the status quo. Ironically, once we obtain the snappy car or that super job, it may seem less valuable to us. However, the psychological factors tilt toward the side of inertia. They create an atmosphere in which it is difficult for people and their organizations to envision and implement change.

THE DECISION-MAKING ENVIRONMENT

Even before a firm begins to make decisions about a specific investment and new directions, its culture and environment may inhibit or promote good decision making. Some organizations, for example, are more attuned than others to the promise of emerging technologies.[8] They are sensitive to the weak external signals that foreshadow shifts in competition or consumer preferences. They possess mechanisms (such as scenario planning) that amplify key information and interpret lessons from other companies and industries about when and how to innovate. In other firms, especially those that have been successful and are well established, new ideas are shunned or viewed askance as disturbing the existing order.

---

[8] Day, George S., and Paul J. H. Schoemaker (Eds.). (2000). *Wharton on Managing Emerging Technologies*, New York, Wiley.

When a company spends time addressing the larger issues that govern decisions, it is involved in the *meta-phase* of decision making.[9] The meta-phase transcends the cognitive biases of individuals; it also entails questions of organizational design, responsibility, interdepartmental cooperation, trust, and openness to new ideas. Essentially, the meta-phase is a periodic assessment of the optimal balance between the learning organization and the performing organization, which are typically in deep conflict.

FOUR PHASES OF DECISION PROCESS

For specific decisions, organizations typically go through four phases: decision framing, intelligence gathering, coming to conclusions, and learning from experience.[10]

Decision Framing. Decision frames are the mental boxes we put around information that we perceive as relevant or irrelevant to a decision. As we start the decision-making process, we make assumptions about the timeframe, scope, reference points (such as required rates of returns, performance benchmarks, and relevant competitors), and yardsticks (such as return on investment, market share, and measures of product quality). If these assumptions go unquestioned, we are likely to make poor or inconsistent decisions.[11]

For example, many firms use their past performance, or that of close competitors, as the reference point for judging success. Such myopic framing plagued the automobile industry in Detroit throughout the 1970s and Sears in the 1980s.

---

[9] Russo, J. E., and P. J. H. Schoemaker. (1990). *Decision Traps: Ten Barriers to Brilliant Decision Making*. New York: Simon and Schuster.

[10] Russo, J. E., and P. J. H. Schoemaker. (2002). *Winning Decisions: Getting It Right the First Time*. New York: Random House. This section also draws on P. J. H. Schoemaker and L. Marais, (1996), "Technological Innovation and Large Firm Inertia," in G. Dosi and F. Malerba (Eds.), *Organization and Strategy in the Evolution of the Enterprise*, London: MacMillan.

[11] Tversky, Amos, and Daniel Kahneman. (1981). "The Framing of Decisions and the Psychology of Choice," *Science*, 211, 453–458.

More subtly, a firm may look at several investment options and use the status quo as its reference point rather than view it as an additional option that must also stand up to scrutiny. This static view ignores the actions of competitors. At Ford Motor Company, the status-quo option now requires the same scrutiny and justification as other options. It directly competes with them in terms of return on investment.

Common accounting procedures tend to amplify certain framing traps.[12] For example, sunk costs are irrelevant to future investment decisions, as noted above. Costs that are irrecoverable should not rationally influence decisions. But when we include sunk costs on the balance sheet as assets, at historical cost, and as write-offs on the income statement, we reinforce our tendency to factor them into decisions. Likewise, the absence of opportunity costs on the income statement and balance sheet reinforces our tendency to underweigh them.

The essence of the framing phase, however, is to think outside the box. Consider one notable example from the world of insurance. In 1986, insurance companies faced a serious liability crisis and decided to add an "absolute pollution exclusion" to their general commercial liability coverage. This left many firms without any coverage for asbestos removal activities, underground storage tanks, hidden chemical problems, and so on. One small company, however, decided to enter the very market from which everyone was retreating, because it felt that the issues were being framed erroneously. The asbestos nightmare had made insurers blind to the fact that some environmental risks were highly manageable whereas others would not be, even within a given class of hazards such as asbestos.

ERIC (Environmental Risk Insurance Corporation), a private company, had gotten its start in the asbestos abatement and removal business. When, in 1986, its business came to an abrupt halt because no asbestos liability protection was available anymore, it decided to enter the insurance field. ERIC believed that one could safely insure a building or warehouse if (1) an in-

---

[12] Kaplan, R. S. (1989, August). "Management Accounting for Advanced Technological Environments," *Science*, Vol. 25.

depth site analysis identified all major asbestos problems, (2) an insurance policy was tailored to the specific circumstance faced, and (3) subcontractors were trained and hired to perform any removal or abatement according to exacting standards. By combining engineering and actuarial analyses, plus having oversight control of subcontractors, an environmental insurance product was launched in segments that traditional insurers shunned. Reinsurers (such as Swiss Re.) bought the concept, and ERIC has since sold millions of dollars of coverage.

Intelligence Gathering. During the information-gathering phase, managers tend to succumb to three main biases: (1) overconfidence, (2) reliance on flawed estimation rules, and (3) a preference for confirming over disconfirming evidence. Overconfidence is a symptom of not knowing what we don't know. Managers from a range of businesses have been asked questions about their industries and found to be almost uniformly overconfident. For example, 1,290 computer industry managers were asked a series of questions about their industry. They were confident that they had correctly estimated ranges for 95 percent of the questions, but in fact were correct only about 20 percent of the time.[13] Overconfidence is especially likely to plague new technology decisions for which little data exists and in which judgment plays a necessary role. The key is to know when to distrust one's intuitions and how to bring implicit assumptions to the surface.[14]

Estimation rules, short cuts that simplify complex judgments, are unavoidable in most cases. For instance, future market share or interest rates may be predicted from current values. However, these estimates often drag down the judgment and result in underestimation.[15] During periods of

[13] Russo, J. E., and P. J. H. Schoemaker. (1992, Winter). "Managing Overconfidence," *Sloan Management Review, 33* (2), 7–17.

[14] Mason, R. O., and I. I. Mitroff. (1981). *Challenging Strategic Planning Assumptions.* New York: Wiley-Interscience.

Morecroft, J., and J. Sterman. (1994). *Modeling for Learning Organizations.* Portland, OR: Productivity Press.

[15] Tversky, A., and D. Kahneman. (1974). "Judgment Under Uncertainty: Heuristics and Biases," *Science, 185,* 1124–1131.

extreme environmental change, these rules of thumb become quickly outdated and dangerous. Yet, they may stay around long beyond their usefulness. Kantrow[16] recounts a telling example from the infantry. When a cannon was fired, two soldiers would stand at attention, one on the left and the other on the right, with one arm held up to chest height. No one knew the origin or purpose of this ritual. Upon investigation, they found that it traced back to the time that canons were pulled on wagons by horses. The skittish horses need to be held firm when firing the loud canon. Although the horses vanished, the ritual remained. We wonder how many phantom horses still roam the corridors of large established organizations.

Out-of-date rules may persist because of the third bias, a failure to search for disconfirming evidence. Managers seldom approach tasks by looking for evidence that will disprove received wisdom, and organizational filtering reinforces this habit. Often a new generation of managers or start-up companies is needed to make change happen and prove that the impossible is achievable after all. Again, the performance organization, which needs to shield its core activities from disruption, is in conflict with the learning organization, which seeks to question, doubt, and experiment. As George Santyana observed, we only want to believe what we see, "but we are much better at believing than at seeing."

Coming to Conclusions. Numerous informal choices are made along the convoluted path of project idea to formal evaluation, both individually and in groups. The bias against innovation is one factor that influences these choices. In rational models of choice, the ambiguity or uncertainty surrounding a probability estimate should not matter per se. However, people prefer a known probability to an unknown one, even if the plans have the same prospects for success.[17] Thus, projects entailing high ambiguity, such as technological or market uncertainties, are

---

[16] Kantrow, A. M. (1987). *The Constraints of Corporate Tradition*. New York: Harper & Row.

[17] Einhorn, H., and R. Hogarth. (1986). "Decision Making Under Ambiguity," *Journal of Business,* 59(4, 2), S225–S255.

likely to be undervalued as people informally screen projects. In addition, most large firms insist on formal, numerical project justification. The risks of high-ambiguity investments are hard to estimate objectively, which means they may not be seriously considered at all.

Biases creep into other aspects of the choice phase as well. "Groupthink" and other team dysfunctions are well-documented problems of team decisions.[18] These issues must be addressed as organizations and their challenges grow more complex. For instance, in one organization, decision making had degenerated into a guessing game as to what senior management wanted. People abandoned their better judgment in favor of what was politically "correct" or expedient. To counter this, senior managers must encourage diversity of views and the public challenging of accepted wisdom. To be credible, they must reward those who speak out.

One can argue that the choice phase is least marred by biases and errors. Financial analysis imposes strong discipline in the form of net present value (NPV) calculations that would otherwise overwhelm human intuition. Nonetheless, NPV analysis requires unbiased inputs, and finance theory offers little guidance on estimating cash flows and valuing downstream options.

Learning from Experience. Learning from past decisions is an important part of the process, but formidable obstacles get in the way. Ego defenses, such as our tendency to rationalize bad outcomes, make feedback incomplete and inaccurate. Since organizations may make only a small number of truly strategic decisions within any management generation, infrequent feedback is a factor as well. This suggests that process feedback may be more practical than outcome feedback; that is, we need to reexamine how the decision was made, not just whether the outcome was good or bad.

Learning by doing is another kind of organizational adaptation, but it may require a separate organizational unit. IBM

---

[18] Janis, I. (1982). *Groupthink*. New York: Houghton Mifflin.

Kets de Vries, M. F. R., and D. Miller. (1987). *Unstable At the Top*. New York: NAL Books.

adopted this path when developing its personal computer, as did General Motors for its Saturn project. The conflict between the learning and performance organizations is at work here. To optimize efficient performance over the next few periods, the firm should focus on what it knows best; however, to maximize its long-term survival chances, the firm must extend its capabilities through experimentation. The main part of the organization can focus on short-term performance, and a separate unit can look toward the long term. Ideally, however, the two cultures interact. Otherwise, the risk is run that the learning organization fails to leverage the competencies resident in the performing organization. Is it not ironic that IBM produced a highly clone-able personal computer, while being world-class in semiconductor research and development?

OVERCOMING MENTAL BLIND SPOTS

There are a few simple techniques to correct for mental blind spots. In addition to creating general awareness, managers should vigilantly try to do the following.

1. Surface the implicit assumptions underlying an investment proposal.
2. Require the same burden of proof for maintaining the status quo as for other options, while emphasizing that the status quo may erode.
3. Look at each investment through the eyes of customers and competitors.
4. Realize that estimates may be overconfident or anchored on readily available numbers. Ask "What don't we know?"
5. Look at confirming, but especially at disconfirming, evidence.
6. Don't shoot from the hip: make an explicit tradeoff of pros and cons.
7. Test key assumptions by running a few experiments that challenge them.

8. Accept some degree of failure as a necessary price for learning.

Above all, however, senior executives must preach that cannibalism is a virtue in business. Practice it as religiously as Tandem does, with the courage to slash prices on new improved models even though the old product could still be milked at the higher price. Encourage this seemingly destructive, yet fundamentally renewing, frame of mind. The motto is "Eat your young before others do."

CONCLUSION

Continual self-renewal requires a careful balancing act between the harvesting mode of the performance organization and the quest for experimentation in the learning organization.[19] Each company has to strike its own balance, depending on the competitive circumstances it faces and the stage of its industry's evolution. However, as external change increases, the learning organization clearly deserves more attention.

Too often, when confronted with stiff competition or changing markets, companies just reduce cost. This can take the form of layoffs, outsourcing, downsizing, rationalizing, and so on. Consider the reactions of AT&T, General Motors, Sears, or IBM when confronted with upheaval—they laid off thousands of people. Although useful to a point, these measures at best stop the bleeding. You cannot shrink yourself to greatness. Companies must treat the symptoms as well the deeper causes. Bolder companies, while under attack, will actually try to improve their operations. Not only do they seek greater efficiency, but also greater speed and better service through process reengineering. But even that may not be enough. In many cases, doing the same things cheaper or faster will not cut it. The organization may have to fundamentally rethink its

---

[19] March, J. G. (1991). Exploration and exploitation in organizational learning. *Organization Science, 2*(1), 71-87.

business model and organizational form. This is the hardest task of all, since it requires a change in the mental model and culture that made the firm successful in the first place.

In sum, successful reinvention is the exception rather than the rule. IBM was successful in its reinvention, thanks to bold new leadership and a willingness to embark on a profound transformation lasting well over a decade. Most companies, however, are overly specialized to the particular environment they happen to operate in—especially if they are successful—and then start to lose the ability to change. This limited ability to adapt to external change remains one of the most important unresolved puzzles in business management. Many factors are at play, including the blind spots and complacency caused by mental models that were correct in years past. Awareness of these insidious biases is the first step in mounting a good defense.

THE CREATIVITY AND COMMITMENT CONNECTION

Amarjit Chopra

UNBLOCKING INNOVATION

Some people are good at implementing new ways of doing things, regardless of whether or not they work in a place where the culture is "innovation friendly." The ones I've worked with are different from each other in many ways, but they all have one thing in common: the ability to create the right kind of buy-in for new ideas. By "right kind" I mean buy-in that transcends turf issues and that motivates people to put in the extra effort almost always needed to implement a new or better way of doing something.

Why do they all share this ability? Because in any organization with more than a few dozen people—with the possible exception of startups—it's a lack of this kind of buy-in that usually blocks innovation, not a lack of good ideas.

THE THREE STRATEGIES
FOR CREATING BUY-IN

It takes more work to launch a new product, service, or process than it does to keep doing things the old way. And the launch usually requires ancillary changes—in policies, or work habits, or mindsets. These also consume time and energy. No wonder people resist new ideas. Who needs more work, especially in today's lean organizations?

A lot of people will, of course, do almost anything if you pay them enough to do it. But if you can't or don't want to play the money card, you're left with three strategies:

A. **Order them to do it.** If you have the power, you can simply say, "You will do this" (and convey, without saying it, "or else").

B. **Persuade them.** Try to sell them the benefits (to the organization, to them, to the world) of doing it; appeal to their reason or emotions in other ways ("We're counting on you." "You're the only one who can pull this off." "You owe me one.").

C. **Make them co-inventors.** Make them your partners in the thinking that produces the new idea or the action plan for implementing it.

Which of these strategies do you find yourself using most of the time, and why? I've asked a wide range of managers and executives these questions. I can't recall anyone saying Strategy A, except as a back up. You can get compliance this way, they say, but not wholehearted commitment.

I also can't remember anyone not agreeing that, done right, Strategy C is the one that's most likely of the three to succeed in getting people behind a new idea, mind and heart. *In theory.*

In practice, people say, the strategy they use most often is B. And by this they mean that they try to sell people the idea *after the fact*—after the thinking that produced it is largely done. And if this doesn't work, they fall back on strategy A (usually by getting someone higher up to do the ordering).

Why do people rely primarily on strategy B when they know that C could be more effective? Two reasons mentioned often are

■ A lot of the ideas you get are not usable, and it's better to not ask for them than to ask for and then have to reject the ideas.

■ It's hard to do creative thinking in groups, in a way that's productive.

Though most people run into these difficulties, there are some—perhaps 1 in 20—who avoid them. Not always, but enough of the time to make strategy C their first choice. I think of these people as "naturals," because most of them make the strategy work without being clear about exactly how they do it. If you work with enough of them, you see that the key is their intuitive understanding of how the mind makes good ideas. By "good" I mean ones that are both practical *and* better in some way than your current ideas.

THE POWER OF BAD IDEAS

Most good ideas are born bad. They are the end product of a process of evolution that usually starts with ideas that are impractical, half-baked, or even absurd. I see this again and again in my work with teams looking for innovative ideas for a wide range of problems (including technical, marketing, strategic, and people issues). You can also see it in many stories about well-known inventions. Edwin Land, the inventor of the Polaroid instant camera, says the thought process that led to it started with an idea that was a joke.

He was explaining to a child why she couldn't see right away the pictures he was taking with a conventional camera. When he was done, he found himself saying "And that's that, unless I could put the dark room in the camera for you." This playful aside set off a train of thought that eventually led to a practical way to develop film inside a camera.

I'm convinced good ideas are born "bad" because the creative side of the mind produces raw material, not finished product—ore, if you will, and not the metal in a useable form. What's usually missing from the "ore" is practicality.

We all have our share of good ideas, so at some level we all know how to process the ore. But if you aren't aware of how you do it, then, unless you are a natural, it's easy to pick up thinking habits that interfere with this process and make it hard to tap both your own and other people's creativity.

So how do you convert this raw material into something more useable? The process itself is simple, almost obvious once you stop to think about it. But it's not always easy to use, because it requires a change in the way we habitually respond to ideas.

A QUICK OVERVIEW OF THE PROCESS

You evolve or "grow" a bad idea by focusing first on its *nonobvious* side—on what's good about it. You assure the part of your mind that goes instantly to the idea's negatives that you aren't going to forget about them, you aren't going to implement the idea as it stands. But, if you did, what might be the advantages of that way of trying to solve the problem? You focus on these plusses first, because without them, you don't have a foundation for building on the idea.

One or two positives usually come to mind easily. It's important to push yourself to find at least one that feels like an "aha." The most valuable part of the ore is seldom obvious.

You then focus on what the idea lacks—on why you wouldn't or couldn't implement it. You don't use these negatives as counterweights to the plusses, because you are not trying to decide whether or not to say yes to the idea as it stands. You already know the answer is no. Instead, you use the negatives to tell you how to grow the idea. You do this by changing the idea so you keep the plusses but not the negatives.

Here's an example that illustrates and elaborates on this process.

THE PROBLEM

Ed, the COO of a division of a large financial services company, is meeting with some of his direct reports: Roger, Sally, and Bill, who head the division's three business units, and Joan, who is in charge of new product development. They are talking about a team they formed a few months ago to promote cross-selling. Ed believes there is a significant chunk of additional business to be had from their existing customers if people in the business units did more cross-selling, Joan agrees with him. The others aren't sure there's enough of that business to justify giving the activity a higher priority than they give it.

The team's task is to identify cross-selling opportunities and to coordinate efforts to go after them. It hasn't had any trouble spotting opportunities. Where it has run into problems is in getting others to put in the time and effort needed to pursue them. Say the team finds that a customer of unit A is a good candidate for unit B's products. To make any sales, the team has to get the "owners" of the customer—the sales, marketing, and customer-service folks in unit A—to give more than a token amount of time and energy to the undertaking. But few people are willing to give it. They have their regular jobs to do, and those come first.

"We can't really blame them," says Bill. "The way we're set up encourages parochial thinking. What's in it for people in one unit to make a big effort to get business that's going to show up on another unit's bottom line? It doesn't do much for them, given the way we measure their performance—and ours."

"We've talked about changing performance measures," says Roger, "but we said it would take a lot of work and be disruptive. That wouldn't stop us, though, if we were convinced that cross-selling would get us a lot more business."

"The only thing that's going to convince me," says Sally, "is not more debate but some hard data."

"That's what I thought this team was going to get for us," says Joan. "But it seems we've put it in a double bind. They can't convince us there's more business out there than we think there is if we don't give them the resources they need to really go after it. But we don't give them the resources because we aren't convinced the business is there."

"Well put," says Ed. "So how could we give them a fair shot at it? I think we could use some fresh ideas. Anyone have any, including wild ones?"

"A little brainstorming. Okay," says Bill, "so here's a crazy idea."

THE IDEA AND ITS EVOLUTION

"Why don't we," Bill says, "make the three people on the team VP's, same level as us, with the right to draw on any resources they want. But only for six months. If they don't surprise us by then, they go back to where they were. And we quit arguing about the priority we should give to cross-selling."

"Yeah, sure," says Sally. "You guys are VP's, and I don't give you a free shot at my people. Why would I give it to them? And I can't think of a better way to *de*-motivate people than to first promote and then demote them."

(We're trained to go straight for what's wrong with ideas, so our first reaction to "ore" is negative. Ed knows it's critical, in invention, to get past this initial reaction and focus on the idea's other side. Note how he does this, and does it without slapping Sally's hand for being negative. Instead, he acknowledges the validity of her concerns, here and again later.)

"You're right, of course," says Ed, "but that's only part of the story. Let's see what else there is to it, and what other ideas it can lead us to."

He gets up and goes to the coffee table by the wall and pours himself a refill. "Here's what it made me think of," he says as he returns to his chair.

"I thought, all right, we're not going to do this, but if we did, what would it do for us? One plus is that we'd be setting up an experiment that has a chance to show us the full potential of this business. A second is that it may help the team to spot more opportunities, because from a business head level, they would think about cross-selling more strategically—they'd take a longer term and I would hope a less parochial look at it.

"But also—and this was a bit of sideways thinking—they would get access to our customers at a higher level. The higher that level, the more those customers will look beyond their own functions to see if there's a need in their organizations for products of ours they are not now using.

"How might we keep these aspects of the idea, I wondered, in a practical way that would get around the issues Sally raised?"

What came to mind, Ed says, was the thought of treating cross-selling like a new product.

"Joan's testing some financial planning products, a business we're not in now," he continues. "If we decide to get into it, we would set up another business unit with its own people and books and VP. What if we created a mini-business unit for cross-selling and gave it six months to demonstrate potential? The idea isn't all there yet; it needs some more work."

"Okay, it's not as crazy as the idea you started with," says Sally, "but how would you staff this unit, where would the people come from? I'd say it would need, at a minimum, one full-time person plus three half-time. That's a core. They would also need another person's worth of time from each of our three units."

"Sounds about right," says Roger, "assuming the people in the core are competent and experienced. The very kind of people I'd be hard put to let go, even for six months. And I think if we do it, we should give it more time than that."

"Good points," says Ed to Sally and Roger. "Those are the holes in the idea that need to be filled."

"What about retirees?" asks Joan. "They've got the experience. There are several in the area, and I think some of them would be interested in this project. We don't have to hire them, just bring them in as consultants."

"I like that," says Roger. "If we can get them, it would give us flexibility. We could use more or less of their time as needed. But I think the full-time person should be internal. Someone who would see this as an opportunity to show some leadership potential."

"I've got someone like that," Bill says. "She's got the drive and I think the ability. I'd be willing to lend her to this experiment if I can get some of that retiree time to fill the gap. The only problem is that she's a bit young and may have trouble butting heads with us, as the leader of this mini-unit is going to have to do from time to time"

"That may not be a problem if she reports directly to me for the duration," say Ed. "But keeping in mind what Sally said earlier, we need to set this up so it's a positive experience for the people involved, no matter how it turns out."

They agree the idea should be pursued further.

"Our first step should be to see whether we can get the kind of retiree time we would need," says Sally.

Joan volunteers to look into retiree availability. Ed will think more about how to set up the experiment. Bill, Roger, and Sally will think about who of their people they'd be willing to assign to the effort. They'll meet again in 2 weeks to make a final go or no-go decision about it.

THE MORALS OF THE STORY

DID IT WORK?

Whenever I tell a story like the one above, someone will ask, "So, did they do it? And was the idea a winner?"

It's appropriate, of course, to ask how effective the idea was in dealing with the problem it was designed to address. But that is only one way to judge the value of the idea-growing process that produced it. If you focus too much on this one criterion, you can lose sight of the fact that the idea is only one thing you get from the process, *and it's often not the most important thing.*

Okay, but before we talk about the other thing, was the idea itself a winner? The answer is yes and no. Yes, it was implemented—they formed a mini-unit, and set it up right. No, it didn't uncover enough cross-sell business to justify its existence beyond the 9 months they gave it. But yes, it did uncover enough to convince Bill, Sally, and Roger to give the activity a higher priority than they gave to it before.

On to the other thing that you get from the process: It enables you to tap some powerful sources of motivation, not just to help you implement a specific idea, but to help you get things done *in general*.

OWNERSHIP

Bill gave the initial idea. Ed transformed this ore into metal the group could work with. Sally contributed mostly concerns, but without these the final idea would not have taken the shape it took. Joan, Bill, and Roger helped to fill the holes in the transformed idea and to put flesh on it. So at the end, whose idea was it?

The idea-growing process creates room for ownership of an idea by more than one person. Each of the people in the discussion could rightly feel he or she owned a piece of it. Some may have felt a greater sense of ownership in it than others, but all of them felt enough of it to want to move the idea further.

Action plans for most problems include not just one but a cluster of ideas, some having to do with what you are going to do, others with how. In such cases it isn't necessary for each team member to own a piece of every idea. All you need is for all of them to feel they have enough ownership in the cluster as a whole.

FEELING VALUED

When someone gives you a flawed idea, you can respond to it in one of two ways. You can reject it, which is the usual response (ignoring it is a way of rejecting it). Or you can grow it. We've just seen that if you grow it, you get an idea you can use and the other person gets a piece of ownership in any action plan in which the idea is included. But creating this sense of ownership is not the only way you increase that person's motivation to help you implement that plan.

The idea-growing process is essentially one in which you look for and build on the value hidden in another's idea. But when you say to that person, in effect, "I see some value in your idea," you send a second message as well, whether or not that is your intention. Because people identify strongly with their ideas, that message is: "I find *you* valuable."

If you make growing team members' ideas your normal response, you send this message to them again and again. The effect is cumulative. Over time you increase their motivation to help you get things done *in general,* not only those things that include their ideas. This doesn't mean that you have to grow every idea you get. People will understand that you don't have time to process all the ore they give you.

The "I value you" message is most powerful when it's most credible. It's most credible when your purpose in growing ideas is selfish: to get good ideas *you* can use.

AFFIRMATION OF SELF-WORTH

You make people feel valued when you grow their ideas, regardless of whether the ideas are "far out" ones, as Bill's was, or ones that are more down to earth but still flawed enough to be unacceptable as they stand. But there is an additional source of motivation you tap more deeply when you work with ones that are more far out.

Asking for and working with far out ideas is a way of engaging the other person's creative side. The creative side, if you recall, produces raw material that lacks practicality. When you ask for "wild" ideas you are saying, in effect, "Don't worry about practicality at this point." This gives the other person's creative side a green light.

But it isn't enough to just solicit wild ideas. You have to go beyond brainstorming and convert some of the ore you get into more usable ideas. When you do this, you release a lot of goodwill, not just towards those ideas, but toward you. Exercising their creativity in a productive way enhances people's sense of self-worth, and makes them feel good about themselves. If you enable them to have this experience, they will want to be on your team.

THE REAL WINNER

The real winner in this story is Ed, not the idea. There are more innovative ideas where that one came from, and Ed knows how to get them—And to do this in a way that motivates people to help him get things done.

For a more in-depth discussion of how to make people your "partners in thinking," see Amarjit Chopra's book *Managing the People Side of Innovation* (ISBN 1-56549-098-3).

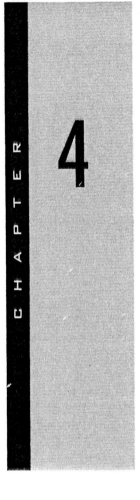

THE NEGOTIATION REVOLUTION

William Ury

E ach profession sees the world through its own prism. Wherever they look, business executives see financial opportunities. Politicians see unconverted voters. Carpenters see houses in need of repair. As a negotiation specialist, I may be guilty of the same distortion, but wherever I look, I see an unheralded revolution happening in business, indeed in every domain of human life. Call it the Negotiation Revolution.

I have spent a fair part of the past 20 years giving seminars on negotiation skills, including many for the Institute for Management Studies. In this brief chapter, I would like to step back and offer a few reflections on the bigger picture that has made negotiation such a popular and necessary subject of study for today's managers.

NEGOTIATION IS A GROWTH INDUSTRY

During the talks I give on negotiation, I usually ask members of the audience how much time they spend *negotiating*— broadly defined as engaging in back-and-forth communication to reach agreement. Whether the audience is managers or schoolteachers, governmental officials or engineers, Brazilians or Americans, the response is invariably the same: The majority of people say that they spend over half their waking hours negotiating. Asked if the amount is increasing or decreasing, almost everyone agrees it is going up.

Nowadays, people seem to be negotiating everywhere and with everyone. It starts first thing in the morning with the family. Who will do the household chores? Who is in charge of the family finances? "We've gone from marriages where very little needed to be negotiated," reports family psychologist Howard Markham, "to ones where nearly everything needs to be negotiated." The process continues at work with coworkers, bosses, and employees. People negotiate with customers and suppliers, with banks, accountants, and lawyers, not to speak of government authorities. We find ourselves negotiating from the moment we get up until the moment we go to bed.

In the corporate world, work is increasingly accomplished in teams and task forces, business is carried out through joint ventures and strategic alliances, and growth is achieved through mergers and acquisitions. Each of these organizational forms requires continuous negotiation—and renegotiation as the business environment changes. Negotiation has become a growth industry.

In the 1970s, the subject of negotiation was hardly a defined field of study and training. Almost no courses were offered in universities. Two decades later, negotiation courses are ubiquitous, taught in many schools of business, government, and law, in most large corporations and many government agencies, and even in elementary schools. The hunger for knowledge about this subject has been overwhelming.

But why? The answer appears to lie in the Knowledge Revolution and its effects on our forms of organization and on the very logic of conflict.

FROM VERTICAL TO HORIZONTAL DECISION MAKING

To survive and thrive in the knowledge economy, organizations of all kinds, from companies to countries, have come to recognize the urgency of breaking down walls of all kinds—communication barriers, tariff barriers, and barriers of rank and status—anything that interferes with the information-sharing process through which new knowledge and wealth are generated. Whereas pyramidal organizations create and reinforce boundaries, network organizations erase boundaries by making connections across them. The tearing down of the Berlin Wall has become a metaphor for what is happening around the globe. As pyramidal organizations everywhere flatten themselves into networks, the primary form of decision making changes from vertical—the people on top giving orders—to horizontal—everyone negotiating.

In order to get their jobs done nowadays, people depend on dozens of individuals and organizations over which they exercise no direct control. They cannot impose a decision; they are compelled to negotiate. Even in the military, the epitome of a pyramidal organization, where people are accustomed to give orders and receive instant obedience, the new reality applies. On a lecture tour in Colombia, I was puzzled to receive a request from General Zuniga, the chief of the armed forces, to give a talk to his generals and admirals. They required negotiating skills, he explained, in order to obtain the budget they sought from politicians, the cease-fires they wanted from guerrilla leaders, and the cooperation they needed from their peers. Even with direct subordinates, he added, they could not get the kind of performance they wanted by simple orders; they needed to negotiate for it.

I often ask audiences of managers to think of the 10 most important decisions they have had to make in the previous year. "How many of those decisions could you make solely by yourself—you decide, that's it—and how many of them did you have to reach with someone else through some process of shared decision making—in other words, through negotiation?" The answers I receive are typically 8 or nine out of 10, or indeed all of them. Negotiation has thus become the preeminent process for making decisions in business. The bottom line of any organization is increasingly determined by the success or failure of a host of negotiations during the course of the year—with customers, suppliers, banks, employees, and strategic partners. Our ability to improve the bottom line depends critically on our ability to negotiate.

FROM A FIXED PIE
TO AN EXPANDABLE ONE

With the Knowledge Revolution, a shift is taking place in the very logic of conflict. Whereas the traditional basic resource of human society, land, is a fixed pie lending itself to destructive fights over its division, the new basic resource, knowledge, is an expandable pie. More knowledge for you need not mean less knowledge for me; we can all partake of it. If I give you land, I have less land, but if I give you knowledge, I do not thereby have less knowledge. Indeed, we can both benefit from the same knowledge. There are limits to land and material resources, but there are no known limits to learning.

In contrast to land, which is typically improved through the act of possession, knowledge is improved through the act of sharing. The core enterprise of the Knowledge Revolution, science, relies on the exchange of theories and information. Scientists compete with one another, as when different teams race to be the first to invent a vaccine, but the competition is mostly in the timing. The fundamental mode is cooperation; no scientist can work effectively without cooperating with colleagues past and present. It is through such cooperation and sharing that knowledge as a resource grows more abundant for everyone.

Even in the profit-making world, where the competition is fierce and companies often guard their knowledge, the best strategy is often to share one's knowledge, sometimes even for free. Consider the first major software program used for navigating the Internet, Netscape. It consisted almost entirely of knowledge, ones and zeros of computer code. It cost the company next to nothing in the form of labor, machinery, or transport to create an almost infinite number of copies. Indeed, the company succeeded by *giving away* most of its product for nothing on the Internet, thereby allowing it to command 85 percent of the market for a period. By positioning itself to sell a host of other products and services to its customers, the company generated enormous value for its investors and was eventually purchased for more than $4 billion.

FROM WIN-LOSE TO BOTH-GAIN

The Knowledge Revolution thus makes it easier for both sides of a negotiation to gain. "Both-gain" does not mean that both parties get everything they want, but rather that they each benefit more than they otherwise would. Companies are finding it to their advantage to pool their resources for research and development, to share production facilities, and to learn from each other. They are forging strategic alliances and joint ventures, sometimes with their most ardent competitors. The largest company in the world, General Motors, created an alliance with its competitor Toyota; IBM did the same with Fujitsu. Benetton's success comes from its cooperative relationships with its more than 700 small, entrepreneurial subcontractors. Benetton concentrates on what it does best—buying raw materials, creating colors, and marketing the clothes—while the suppliers do what they do best—make clothes; as Benetton grows, everyone benefits. Increasingly in today's marketplace, a business's ability to compete depends on its ability to cooperate.

Traditionally, negotiation had a "win-lose" quality to it; it was seen as another form of warfare. Increasingly, however, people and organizations are searching for methods to arrive at solutions for mutual gain. In my work as a third-party consultant, I have had many opportunities to witness hard-bitten union leaders and skeptical managers gradually come to see that "mutual gains bargaining" can lead to tangibly better results than shouting at each other and seeking to defeat the other. "I remember the heartburn, the headaches, the sleepless nights," says teacher union negotiator Arnie Klayman. "This way [mutual gains bargaining] is much less threatening."

Instead of trying to divide up an economic pie that is often shrinking with intensified global competition, management and labor seek to expand the pie through innovative ways to increase productivity and share the profits. "Getting along— that's our competitive advantage," one formerly skeptical union leader, Denny Morris of the Paperworkers Union, told me.

BACK TO THE FUTURE

In one sense, all this is very new, but in another sense, it represents a return to an ancient organizational pattern of humanity.

Working with modern corporations, I have often found myself reminded of the Bushmen and other simple societies whom I once studied as an anthropologist. Many of the most modern management ideas are reinventions of common practices I had seen among hunter-gatherers. Hunter-gatherers, for instance, have long used "flexible self-organizing work teams." With their early morning chatter, I have watched the Bushmen spontaneously organize themselves to do the day's work of hunting, gathering, and making simple tools. Eons before it became a corporate fashion, simple societies practiced "facilitative leadership." The elders led by persuasion, not coercion. And "collaborative decision making" was used to resolve their differences around the campfire.

I have come to appreciate how these similar practices emerged from somewhat similar working conditions. Modern-day managers and hunter-gatherers both live in a constantly shifting environment, pursuing scattered and mobile resources. For hunter-gatherers, the resources are wild plants and animals; for managers, they are bits of knowledge. Both groups rely on the constant exchange of information. Hunter-gatherers trade tips about weather, the whereabouts of food, and threats from predators; modern-day managers trade data about shifting markets and competitors' products. Both groups are also nomadic by necessity: hunter-gatherers are always on the move in search of food, while the new knowledge managers are constantly traveling, whether in person or by telecommunication.

The differences between hunter-gatherer communities and the emerging global knowledge society are admittedly enormous in scale and population, in sophistication of technology, in organizational complexity, and in independence from the natural environment. Yet it is the resemblances that, as an anthropologist, I find striking.

It may be imprudent to describe large historical patterns while in the midst of them, since such patterns usually appear clear only in retrospect. It is hard to distinguish between temporary fluctuations and long-term trends. Nevertheless, let me offer my educated hunch. Humanity is returning to dependence on a basic resource that is, as in hunter-gatherer times, an expandable pie. We are returning to the horizontal relationships that existed among human beings for most of human evolution. The network is once again becoming the defining social organization for the human community. Societies and organizations obsessed with boundaries are slowly becoming more open and inclusive. Just as before, the logic of conflict is less one of win-lose and more one of a choice between all-lose and both-gain. Just as before, decision making is increasingly taking the form of negotiation.

NEGOTIATION: A CORE COMPETENCY

The Knowledge Revolution brings with it a revolution in decision making and dispute resolution in business, as in other domains. The pyramids of power are collapsing, and taking their place are networks—networks of negotiation. To succeed in these new forms of social organization, there is no competency more critical than that of learning how to negotiate cooperatively.

5

THE ROLE OF CHAOS IN THE CREATION OF CHANGE

John J. Scherer

I t has been said, "Success has many parents, but failure is an orphan." When it comes to successful change, however, it seems to me that the same two partners get things going every time, namely *pain* and *possibility*. It is my belief that no significant change can take place in individuals, groups, or larger organizations, regardless of the pain and possibility present, without a passage through *chaos,* the world's birthing center, where fundamental change and innovation come into being.

When I say chaos, I am referring to that space where none of the old rules work and where there is a partial or complete breakdown of the basic concepts and principles that define things. Tom Peters has written at length about the need for innovation and the openness managers need to have to the chaos that accompanies it. It may well be a necessary thing to be in chaos, but how does it contribute to fundamental change?

PAIN: THE FATHER OF CHANGE

Pain is the only motivator that I trust. Too many times I have seen well-meaning managers and their people get scared at the moment of truth and revert back to the old way. The people and systems that are able to create and sustain fundamental change are usually in the grip of some kind of organizational, financial, and/or emotional pain.

By *pain,* I mean the awareness of an unacceptable disequilibrium or a significant discrepancy between the way things are and the way they could be. This pain manifests itself in various ways. In one client system, it showed up as a consequence of an impending failure of a major part of the enterprise. In another, it showed up as a severe drop in both productivity and quality. In another, pain meant increased customer dissatisfaction in service and lost sales. In one situation, it was the strain of unresolved conflict with a colleague, and in another, a breakdown in communication with a spouse and a teenage son.

But pain by itself is seldom enough. The pain of being overweight, for instance, may or may not lead to a new body shape. The pain that comes from the realization that a marriage is not working may or may not result in positive change. The pain experienced by a work team or organization in the face of a failure may or may not lead to a breakthrough.

WHEN PAIN IS NOT ENOUGH

A professional services firm with whom I worked had been teetering on the brink of financial disaster for several weeks. The situation seemed clear to me as an external consultant: Major unresolved conflict between the two senior partners was sapping the business of its strength. Employees were polarized, and prospective clients could sense the firm's trouble. The owners, however, would not—they said they could not—move to make the changes needed, and they had a raft of sensible reasons why nothing fundamentally new or different could be done. The senior partner could not get beyond his fear, retribution, failure, or community embarrassment to do what was needed.

The result was that the two split in an acrimonious series of scenes, and the senior partner eventually filed for bankruptcy. This man likely experienced severe emotional and psychic pain before the firm broke apart. Yet, he was not sufficiently moved early enough to act decisively to fundamentally change the situation. What was missing?

POSSIBILITY: THE MOTHER OF CHANGE

There is another ingredient. The pain must be accompanied by an awareness of an existing gap between the way things are and the way they could be. With pain must come possibility; something not believed to be achievable before. The overweight person must actually see himself or herself as leaner and healthier. The work team or organization must see the possibility of the situation resolved, productivity at peak levels, or the crisis yielding to breakthrough. Without this directional vector, there is no change—only pain.

Possibility not only provides the direction for change, it also defines the space within which change occurs. The greater the possibility, the more fundamental change is likely. People at a seminar, who are there as if their life or job depends on what happens, are more likely to leave changed than people who are there because the boss sent them. The size of the possibility defines the space within which the change occurs: small possibility, small change; big possibility, big change.

WHAT BLOCKS POSSIBILITY?

There are conscious and unconscious forces at work in all human systems, from the individual to the largest corporation, which function to maintain *homeostasis*—keeping things as they are. When we think and perceive the world within a closed system, we are doing "inside-the-box thinking." Standing inside the box, there is no real possibility for fundamental change. There might be change, but inside-the-box change is really only more of the same.

Many clients who ask for help in creating positive change have this kind of superficial work in mind. They may say they want real change, but they want it to happen without having to change anything they are attached to! They want to stay inside the box and still have things change. Fundamental change, or breakthrough, takes place only when the client is outside the box, which is usually preceded by a breakdown.

Both pain and possibility need to be present and acknowledged fully for breakthrough to take place. I call this convergence point in time a breakdown. Jesse Watson, creative change consultant and colleague, talks about a flat tire as a fitting metaphor for breakdown. "Just having a flat tire on your car doesn't necessarily mean that you're having a breakdown," he says. "You have to be going somewhere!" If your car is sitting in the garage and hasn't been used for ages, all the tires can be flat and you won't experience the situation as a breakdown.

Breakdown consists of at least two essential components: going somewhere (possibility) and not getting there (pain). For fundamental change to take place, the people involved must feel some pain, want a new possibility, be willing to admit that they do not really know what to do, and be committed to discovering a new way of thinking about it all, opening up to the possibility of transformation.

Transformation is a complete and fundamental change in the basic form of something. It is not a modification of anything that already is. It is bringing into existence something that was not a moment before. It is an act of pure creation, *ex nihilo*—"out of nothing." This place of nothingness, from which creation comes, is called *chaos*.

CHAOS: THE BIRTH PASSAGE FOR CREATIVE CHANGE

First, order, or superficial change, can occur in any situation with relatively little pain, since it represents a moving around or modification of what is already present. Second, order, or what I am calling creative change, is by definition impossible.

It represents a bringing forth of something totally new that was not there before and that could not have been predicted on the basis of what was already there.

For transformation to occur, the existing mental box must fall away like the discarded skin on a molting snake. The operating pattern must be broken down. We must find ourselves released from the grip of the old context. This leaves us not with a new pattern immediately, but with an empty space within which a new pattern (creation) can occur. In other words, we must find ourselves in a chaotic void, without any life jacket, props, or ideas about how to proceed, with nothing to hold onto and no way to save ourselves. In that instant, we are open to what could show up, which could not have shown up as long as we were holding onto anything that we thought would "work" to save us from the experience of being in an empty space.

In the creation myths of the world's oldest religions, the ancients knew the same basic truth about creation: Some kind of emptiness preceded the birth of the world. Several of these myths actually speak of chaos, but in every case there is the absence of anything familiar or known. The world came out of the unknown. Chaos was not only the birthing context for the origin of the world; it was also seen by the ancient sages to play a central role in bringing about the kind of fundamental change, conversion, salvation, *sartori,* or enlightenment sought by individual believers themselves. For personal transformation to take place, there must be that space of nothingness or emptiness, that "dying to be alive," that "emptying of the mind, so that new life can be poured in."

A SCIENTIST'S VIEW OF DISEQUILIBRIUM

Several years ago, Nobel laureate Ilya Prigogine startled the scientific world with his theories on the thermodynamics of nonequilibrium systems. While traditionalist colleagues in chemistry were still being influenced by thinking from the Industrial Age, which emphasized order, predictability, stability, and equilibrium in a world that was essentially a closed system operating with linear cause and effect relationships, Prigogine and his students in Brussels School were focusing their attention on the disorder, apparent randomness, instability, and disequilibrium of nonlinear relationships they found in chemical reactions. A central idea he put forth was that new order and organization can arise spontaneously out of chaos in systems that are "far from equilibrium" through a process called self-organization:

> When a molecule's implicate (existing) order starts to fall apart, the entity faces a moment of choice, the "bifurcation point." It can either go out of existence, or reorganize itself at a higher level to accommodate the new variables.[1]

If Prigogine is correct, the potential for innovation or radical change is directly proportional to the lack of order present in the structures holding or defining the situation.

Social scientists have taken Prigogine's work to heart and applied his principles to human systems. The potential for deep change in any social system, from the individual to the latest organization or society, is directly related to the breaking down of those basic concepts that have held things together in the past *(homeostasis)* and are now, usually inadvertently, holding back the movement to a higher level of organization. When things look darkest, that's the moment when the system is most open to a new configuration. New order comes out of braving and moving through the emptiness and chaos.

But what a frightening prospect! Does this mean that we have to be driven into a world of chaos where all our treasured operating principles crumble in front of us before any kind of fundamental change can take place? If Prigogine and the ancients are right, the answer may be yes. Every transformational human being, from Jesus and the Buddha to Ghandi and Martin Luther King, Jr., has operated from this position: that the current basic concepts must be let go, especially those that have kept us from seeing what was really there, before creative change, innovation, or transformation has a chance.

---

[1] *Order Out of Chaos.*(1988). Ilya Prigogine and Isabelle Stengers. New York: Bantam.

There is some apparent relief, however. What breaks down is not reality, but our concept of reality. It is our illusions that we need to let go of so that we might see reality uncovered. It's our current map of the way things are that we have to drop, not life itself. We must end up essentially lost and not knowing what to do. The instant we let go of the one piece we "know" we can count on, and act as if we do not know, we are open to the breakthrough.

CHAOS AND CONSULTING: FACILITATING CHANGE IN THE REAL WORLD

We have now identified the antecedents to fundamental change: pain and possibility converging in a moment of breakdown, held in the context of chaos or confused emptiness, where the past and present offer no useful guidance and an act of pure creation is required.

But, even all that may not be enough. Many, maybe most, people and organizations, finding themselves in this situation, simply become resigned to the way things are or settle for superficial change that doesn't make any real difference. Managers and their organizations are rewarded for not being lost and for knowing what to do, or at least for acting as if they do. When they become lost and confused and, like the atom under pressure, face annihilation or breakthrough, they frequently go out of existence—that is, out of business or out of a job.

6

FUNDAMENTALISM AND PANACEAS

Russell L. Ackoff

The hijacking of commercial airliners by members of the terrorist al Queda group, and the willingness for self-sacrifice by those hijackers to make a point while killing thousands of Americans when they smashed the planes into the World Trade Towers and the Pentagon, gives dramatic and emotional emphasis to the wide gulf between fundamental thinking and what our high-tech world has come to represent to some people.

Bear with me, because I am about to make the big leap of faith here by comparing some of today's executives and their styles with those terrorists because of their fundamental approach to management.

Fundamentalism, a fixed set of beliefs about acceptable ends and means, is a response to an environment that is undergoing an accelerating rate of change and rapidly increasing complexity, conditions that combine to produce a turbulent or chaotic environment. Consider the white noise of stock market crashes, downsizing, increased competition, emails coming 24/7 at executives like snow flakes at a windshield instead of the old once-a-day mail, markets shifting, technology constantly changing, media analyzing, overanalyzing, everything faster and more global. Such an environment is characterized by discontinuities and uncertainty, hence unpredictability. It is one in which it is easy for individuals and organizations to become disoriented.

Change is everywhere and happening at a faster and more complex state every day. It is not possible to achieve a static equilibrium in a turbulent environment; the only kind possible is dynamic, like the stability achieved by an airplane flying through a storm. A dynamic equilibrium requires changes that are discontinuous as well as continuous and qualitative as well as quantitative. Coping with such rapid change requires vision, clarity, and above all flexibility.

Those who do not want to change try either to prevent it (*conservatives*) or unmake it and return to a previous relatively stable state (*reactionaries*). In contrast, there are those who are willing to make disjointed incremental changes in relatively limited aspects of the real world (*liberals*). However, incremental improvements or reforms are neither adequate nor effective in dealing with the "messy real world." A radical transformation is required.

Conservatives are willing to settle for the way things are. Their attitude toward change is expressed in such aphorisms as "Let well enough alone," "Don't rock the boat," and "If it ain't broke, don't fix it." They believe that liberal efforts to improve the current state of society are the major cause of its deterioration. Therefore, they prefer inactivity to change, or activity that does not change anything: make-work. Because people find it difficult to "do nothing" when engaged in make-work, they tend to concoct unproductive work for those who have productive work to do: for example, red tape.

The type of organization that best meets the conservative's needs is a bureaucratic monopoly. These are subsidized in one way or another. For example, government service agencies and corporate service departments are usually subsidized by budgets authorized from above. Such organizations can ignore the need to change, because they need not be responsive to their consumers, who have no alternative source of the service, and the monopolies do not depend on them for their income.

Liberals fail to produce the kind of change needed because of their lack of understanding of the nature of the systems they try to change. The performance of any system depends on how its parts interact, not on how they act, taken separately. Therefore, it is possible to improve the performance of every part of a system taken separately and reduce the performance of the system taken as a whole. For example, suppose that for every part required for an automobile, you determine which is the best available by examining every one of the more than 400 automobiles available. Then, you remove the parts identified as best from the automobiles of which they are part, and try to assemble them into one automobile. You would not even get an automobile, let alone the best one, because the parts would not fit together. A collection of parts considered best when considered separately do not the best systems make. This is why conservatives and reactionaries currently see the liberals as often harming the systems they try to improve.

Reactionaries try to undo change and resolve problems by identifying their sources and removing or suppressing them. In this way, they try to return to a previous state that they prefer to the current one. For example, they try to eliminate alcoholism and drug addiction by making alcohol and addictive drugs illegal. They try to reduce crime by apprehending and incarcerating criminals. These efforts have failed, but their failure has not discouraged the reactionary. They argue that we have not tried hard enough or did not do it right.

Some reactionaries seek generalized forms of retraction or suppression of change, real or imagined, and its agents, real or imagined. Such reactionaries become fundamentalists.

FUNDAMENTALISM

Fundamentalism consists of a fixed set of beliefs about acceptable ends and means. These beliefs are taken to be absolutely true. The principles derived from them define the one and only "good." Their good requires strict adherence to basic principles and doctrines by disciples. No exceptions are allowed; no transgression is tolerated. Fundamentalism ends the need for thought and therefore gives emotion free reign.

Truth and goodness are revealed to fundamentalists either by a God directly, through a religious leader with whom their God is alleged to be in direct contact (e.g., Ayatollah Khomeini), or through a secular leader (e.g., Saddam Hussein or Hitler).

Since fundamentalists consider truth to be an act of faith, critical thinking is irrelevant: Faith alone provides them with a complete basis for belief and action. Therefore, there is no discussing the validity of their principles. Fundamentalists dismiss any opposing point of view. They see no point in listening to their opponents, let alone in trying to understand them.

TYPES OF FUNDAMENTALISTS

Fundamentalists fall into one of two major categories: *introverted* or *extroverted*. Introverted fundamentalists seek isolation from the rest of society and want only to be. They prefer to restrict their communication to the source of their beliefs and carry this out privately and silently. They, or their representatives, interact with others in commerce and other ways required to obtain necessities, but these contacts have no effect on their beliefs or behavior. Most introverted fundamentalists do not try to proselytize or otherwise affect "outsiders," but they do invite inquiries and conversions. They are nonviolent.

Extroverted fundamentalists are exactly the opposite. They consider those who do not accept their doctrine to be enemies who obstruct their pursuit of the ultimate good. Therefore, such fundamentalists (we, us) take the elimination of enemies (they, them) to be necessary for pursuit of the ultimate good.

This end justifies the means. Such fundamentalism is exemplified by the Shiite Muslims, Hitler's Nazis, and the Ku Klux Klan in the United States.

TREATMENT OF FUNDAMENTALISTS

Today, introverted fundamentalists are not considered a threat to society. They are occasionally an inconvenience at most. However, in the past, they were often persecuted or annihilated. When possible, they escaped and emigrated to other lands. The United States was settled by many such groups. Puritans, Quakers, Shakers, and Amish are examples. Some remain intact today, though without the buckles and odd hats we associate with Thanksgiving.

Extroverted fundamentalists are another matter: They are a threat to those with whom they seek to come in contact. How can such fundamentalism be dealt with effectively? In the past it has been dealt with in the following ways: (1) capitulate, (2) ignore, (3) ridicule, (4) contain and isolate, (5) retaliate, and (6) suppress or eliminate.

Ignoring extroverted fundamentalists has no effect on them and is not feasible when they engage in physical attacks on those who try to ignore them. Ridicule fares no better; it only strengthens their belief and resolve to conquer nonbelievers. Containment and isolation (e.g., sanctions) is difficult at best and therefore has had only limited success. Witness the current treatment of Cuba, Iraq, and Libya. Their isolation is not very effective because, first, rather than weaken the beliefs of those so treated, it has strengthened their resolve. Such treatment confirms their perception of themselves as victims rather than victimizers. Second, it is relatively easy for them to continue proselytizing outside the walls that are intended to contain them; it certainly has not limited their terrorist activities. Terrorists are fundamentalists who are willing to use violence to accomplish their objectives. Not all fundamentalists are terrorists, but most terrorists are fundamentalists.

Retaliation for terrorist attacks has also only strengthened terrorists' resolve; they often believe that dying in their aggressive efforts assures them of better life after death. Therefore, even the threat of death is not a deterrent for many of them. Peace-seeking societies or publics have yet to find an effective way of coping with terrorism. Witness the continuing difficulty the Israelis have had with Palestinian terrorists and the continuing conflict in Northern Ireland. Israel has also had difficulty with Israeli fundamentalists—for example, the recent assassination of Rabin.

Efforts to eliminate fundamentalists have usually resulted in large-scale loss of life and atrocities, such as have recently occurred in Bosnia, Chechnya, and East Timor. Unfortunately, those who rely on terrorism to further their cause appear to leave no short-term alternative but retaliatory violence with even a remote chance of reducing their threat to the freedom of others. There is, however, a long-term alternative.

To eliminate or significantly reduce terrorism, it is necessary to eliminate or significantly reduce extroverted fundamentalism. To do this, it is necessary to significantly reduce or eliminate the uneven distribution of quality of life, standard of living, and opportunity between and within nations. This cannot be done by existing international agencies, as has been convincingly demonstrated by International Monetary Fund (IMF) and the World Bank. It requires an intervention strategy resembling the one used in Mantua, a so-called urban ghetto in Philadelphia, which had the following components:[1]

- Make available to a nation or community an amount of money to be used only for development of its members; that is, for increasing their ability to satisfy their needs and legitimate desires and those of others. A *legitimate desire* is one the fulfillment of which does not decrease the ability of any other to satisfy their needs and legitimate desires.
- The funds may only be used in ways determined democratically; that is, by decisions made by either those affected by it, their elected representatives, or elected guardians or advocates of those who are incapable of

---

[1] Ackoff, Russell L. (1974). *Redesigning the Future.*, New York:, John Wiley & Sons.

such participation (e.g., children, the mentally ill, and future generations).

■ Corruption must be excluded from the handling of the funds.

■ Experts are available to assist the decision makers in any way they desire. In addition, they are responsible for seeing to it that these conditions are met.

PANACEAS

Panacea proneness—the desire for a quick fix, a template that can be applied and can fix everything—is a diluted form of fundamentalism commonly adopted by corporations, schools, hospitals, government agencies, and other types of organizations. In general, organizations that do not deal effectively in turbulent environments turn to panaceas for help—for example, total quality management, process reengineering, benchmarking, outsourcing, downsizing, SAP, continuous improvement, scenario planning, value chain analysis, core competencies, cognitive therapy, and organizational learning. When executives are confronted with rates of change and increasing complexity, the effects of which they do not understand and with which they cannot cope, they look for simple and simpleminded solutions to their problems: *panaceas.* Incapable of solving business challenges rationally, panacea-prone executives turn to offerings, usually made by managerial evangelists and/or gurus, which they accept on faith.

Panacea-prone executives differ from fundamentalists in that they do not confine their faith to one set of beliefs; they have a large array of offerings to choose from. They normally buy into a number of them sequentially, but may try a number of offerings simultaneously.

Unlike the fundamentalists who are willing to die for their beliefs, executives are unwilling to sacrifice even a small amount of their security to bring about fundamental change. They seek to reform their organizations, not transform them, and to change the way they do what they do, not what they are doing it for. Adopting a panacea involves no personal risk for the executive; its failure can always be attributed to either its author or its implementer.

Panaceas are about doing things right, not doing the right things. They do not bring objectives and goals into question. As a result, they are used more frequently to do the wrong things right than to do the right thing. Therefore, the more right managers do the wrong thing, the more wrong they become. A headline from the July 6, 1993, issue of *The Wall Street Journal* read "Many Companies Try Management Fads, Only to See Them Flop." Little wonder! Here is a sample of the relevant press.

> Companies have spent big dollars on programs to train employees in the latest quality practices, yet few organizations have gained substantial benefits in return. In fact, two out of three companies that grab for the quality brass ring fail to see much improvement in performance or customer satisfaction.... *Fortune* reports that TQM disasters have spawned a new niche for consultants who specialize in cleaning up the mess.[2]

> Without question, many American companies entered this decade in need of serious organizational change. But the typical response—cost reduction through layoffs—has proven to be a short-term fix at best... Kim Cameron, a University of Michigan business school professor, conducted a study of 150 companies that had downsized. His findings: 75 percent of them ended up worse off than before.[3]

> Three out of four companies slimmed down their staffs in the past five years, but the majority saw little improvement in either business or productivity, according to a study of 1,204 companies nationwide...[4]

---

[2] Thomas Kiely. (1993, Dec. 15/Jan.1, 1994). "Total Quality Management," *CIO*, 36–37.

[3] Robert W. Keidel (1994, March 12). "Laying off workers can backfire," *The Philadelphia Inquirer*, p. A17.

[4] Andrea Knox. (1992, Mar. 9). "Most cuts in jobs don't help firms, survey indicates." *The Philadelphia Inquirer*, p. D1.

...A survey last summer by Arthur D. Little Inc....found only 16 percent of executives "fully satisfied" with their reengineering programs. No surprise: about 68 percent were experiencing unanticipated problems... Michael Hammer, the father of corporate reengineering asserted that 70 percent of reengineering projects fall short of their stated goals.[5]

In the end, even the re-engineers are re-engineered. At a recent conference...representatives from 20 of America's most successful companies all agree that re-engineering...needs a little re-engineering of its own.[6]

It is little wonder then that

A new generation of better-informed managers is more skeptical of the sometimes simpleminded solutions proposed by management consultants.[7]

TREATMENTS OF PANACEA PRONENESS

Panacea-prone executives are more open to learning than are fundamentalists. If they can be led to understanding the nature of the changes that occur in their environment and why they occur, they can generally be induced to try more profound and fundamental approaches to their problems than are offered by panaceas. Education of executives is the key.

But, here is the rub: The higher the status of executives, the less susceptible they think they are to useful learning. Pretense of already knowing it all comes with reaching the pinnacle of status.

We have yet to develop a generation of executives who take pride in their ability to learn and adapt, rather than in what they already know. Until we do, the market for fundamentalism and its weak sister, panacea proneness, will be very large.

---

[5] Stephen Barr. (1995, Jan.). "Grinding It Out," *CEO*, 27.

[6] "Re-engineering, with Love." (1995, Sept. 9). *The Economist*, 69.

[7] "Solution-peddlers Lose Their Charm," (1991, Feb. 9). *The Economist*, p. 67.

II

FACILITATING
CHANGE:
THE LEADER'S
ROLE

7

LEADERSHIP
IN THE
NETWORKED
ECONOMY

Albert A. Vicere

G lobalization and the information technology explosion have combined to create a "networked economy," which in turn challenges traditional approaches to management and leadership. Globalization has brought us flatter, faster-paced organizations with global reach. Information technology has enabled us to work in partnerships linked by powerful information networks. Together these forces are triggering the reconfiguration and restructuring of virtually every major industry worldwide, and they are redefining the essence of leadership. Here, we have an opportunity to explore the nature of leadership in the networked economy and discuss suggestions for enhancing approaches to leadership development.

THE CHANGING LEADERSHIP LANDSCAPE

Traditional or "old economy" views of leadership and management were built on notions of control. People were controlled through structure and hierarchy, and resources were controlled through vertical and horizontal integration. Companies like General Motors, U.S. Steel, IBM, Xerox, and Eastman Kodak are prime examples. These companies ruled their industries for decades. They were the poster children for traditional old-economy management philosophies.

However, these companies grew up in a world in which markets were primarily domestic. To be sure, they sold products outside the United States and likely even manufactured products overseas, but the soul of their businesses was a robust and growing domestic marketplace where, as dominant players, they set the standards and effectively controlled the pace of development in their respective industries. Globalization changed all of that.

Take the steel industry, for example. When competitors from Japan entered the North American steel market in the 1960s and 1970s, U.S. Steel's dominance of the domestic marketplace was irrelevant to them. They had their own sources of materials and capital, and they were able to develop new channels of distribution. Whether they were subsidized or not is irrelevant. What was most important was that they forever changed the rules of the business game.

Unencumbered and unafraid of dominant U.S. market leaders, these "foreign" competitors attacked industry after industry, including steel, machine tools, consumer electronics, and automobiles, until finally the big U.S. companies had no choice but to respond.

During the 1980s and 1990s, U.S. companies aggressively pursued a new organizational model, one that was faster, more efficient, closer to the customer, and above all, flatter. The delayered, downsized organization was a natural response to global competition. After all, speed, efficiency, and customer focus were the very competitive advantages that offshore competitors were using to defeat established U.S. market leaders, and it was difficult to argue against the logic that by flattening an organization these benefits were more likely to be accrued.

Yet, downsizing alone did not prove to be the answer. A recently downsized company might see short-term improvements in business conditions only to find itself back in trouble a few quarters down the road. This led many companies to engage in a cycle of continuous downsizing that not only failed to pay off in business performance improvement, but also often fueled a challenge to traditional views of employee loyalty and commitment in the workplace.

THE NEXT WAVE

The logic behind downsizing is simple: Organizations must be faster, more efficient, and more customer-focused in the global economy. Yet, reducing headcount alone does not produce sustainable performance improvements for an organization. When an organization simply has fewer people doing the same things that were done in their pre-downsized incarnation, the end result is likely to be confusion and burnout, not performance improvement.

In order to reap the benefits of downsizing, organizations must adapt to what might loosely be termed the principle of *focus*—to focus on core competencies or the things the organization does or needs to do better than anyone.[1] We learned in the 1990s that downsizing, coupled with a focus on core competencies, could enable an organization to flatten, focus, and move ahead with exceptional intensity.

There is a catch, however. The flat, focused organization does a few things exceptionally well, but it needs help. That help comes in the form of tactical partnerships, such as outsourcing arrangements, which enable an organization to efficiently handle operational tasks that are not core competencies. It also comes in the form of strategic partnerships that

---

[1] Core competencies and organizational focus were brought to attention by G. Hamel and C. K. Prahalad in their landmark book, *Competing for the Future*, Boston: HBS Press, 1994.

help an organization grow revenue through joint ventures or alliances. We learned in the late 1990s that flat, focused organizations operating in webs of partnerships were far more likely to succeed than those who stayed committed to tall, monolithic bureaucracies.

No organization typifies this model better than Cisco Systems. In less than two decades, even accounting for the recent market downturn, Cisco has become a world leader in its industry with a relatively small base of regular employees. How does Cisco do it? Surrounding Cisco is an armada of partnerships and relationships that have helped fuel its phenomenal success.

Cisco has the advantage of having been born in the networked economy environment, but what about the many long-established companies out there? What about organizations that for the most part are accustomed to control, hierarchy, and going it alone? Organizational effectiveness in the networked economy is based not on control, but on relationships. Without question, there is a fundamental difference between management processes based on control and those based on relationships.

That is not to say that control is foregone in the networked economy—in fact, just the opposite. The information technology revolution has spawned the development of computer and telecommunications networks, e-commerce systems, enterprise software, and other forms of connectivity. These systems align networks of business partners together in a new business infrastructure, one built upon webs of information linkages. The interconnected webs enable organizations to control their businesses in ways never before imagined. As a result, they are redefining the nature of doing business in the networked economy.

The dominance of the information superhighway as the foundation for a new wave of economic development is nearly undisputed. The e-explosion is changing the face of nearly everything around us, especially processes for managing organizations, and the demise of the dotcom sector is only helping us to get it right. It isn't just buying and selling via the Internet that is the soul of the e-revolution; it is the fundamental reconfiguration of business infrastructure. From massive gains in productivity, to operational flexibility, to the gathering of insightful customer intelligence, to the opening of new markets and the creation of new channels of distribution, to real-time learning platforms, "e" is impacting all aspects of the value chain, including processes for leadership development.

THE LEADERSHIP CHALLENGE

Just what does this shift in the essence of organizational effectiveness suggest for leadership development? Core competencies, by definition, are knowledge sets and technical skill sets. It seems, then, that until companies master the science of creating knowledge-management systems, core competencies will continue to reside in the minds of the people inside an organization. Relationships, by definition, are owned by people within companies and not by the companies themselves. That means that the new focus on core competencies and relationships brings people issues, and therefore leadership development, to the forefront of business strategy.

The explosive growth of the search-firm business is just one indicator of this shift. As companies compete for the best talent, raiding other organizations for talent has become a commonplace event. Yet, assembling a group of highly competent but uncommitted knowledge workers is unlikely to lead to the formation of a highly productive, healthy organizational culture.

These individuals need to feel involved, committed, and inspired to achieve and to help the organization to achieve. They need access to the latest thinking and the tools that will enable them to put that thinking to the test. They need to be assigned to visible projects where they can demonstrate their mettle. They need to be acknowledged and rewarded for their contributions. Above all, they need to feel that they are part of an organization that respects them for the knowledge and ideas they bring to the business: They need effective leadership.

NEW LEADERSHIP MINDSETS

Throughout my 23 years as a professor, I have had the great fortune to work with scores of organizations and to spend time with their leaders. There is no question that the most effective leaders realize that the essence of their job is to get results and at the same time to build commitment to the organization's culture and values. But, there is little doubt that today's leaders must carry out those responsibilities in an incredibly complex environment.

They not only are charged with ensuring the performance of the organization and building on its cultural legacy, they are also charged with helping the organization transition to the new economic order. Based on discussions with dozens of leaders, as well as in firsthand observation of their leadership challenges, I have identified four key roles for effective leadership in the networked economy:

1. Boundary-less thinker
2. Network builder
3. Diplomat
4. Interpreter

The framework is not intended to serve as a competency model, but rather as a delineation of the perspectives essential for effective leadership in today's transitioning economic environment.

BOUNDARY-LESS THINKER

Leaders in the networked economy need to think beyond current orthodoxies and to help their organization to do the same. That means they can't be bogged down in traditional ways of thinking. They must be open to new ideas. They must help their organization and the people within it to know themselves—their strengths, competencies, and limitations. Also, they must help those same people to recognize both the value of new ideas and the strengths and capabilities of potential partners, both internal and external to the firm, who can be sources of unique synergies and differentiated competitive advantage. Three skill sets are essential to developing this broad-based mindset:

■ *Big Picture Perspective:* The ability to rise above details and activities to see a situation in terms of correlations, patterns, and potential.
■ *Openness to Ideas:* The ability to appreciate and integrate new ideas and different ways of thinking into the leadership process.
■ *Willingness to Look Beyond Oneself for Capabilities and Resources:* The understanding that no one individual or organization can possess all the capabilities and resources necessary for success in today's environment and that partnerships and linkages, both internal and external to the firm, are essential to the future.

NETWORK BUILDER

Leaders who think in a boundary-less manner are more likely to have a relationship mindset, one focused on helping the people around them to share ideas, information, knowledge, and capabilities. Organizational effectiveness in the networked economy is rooted in relationships and networking. Complementary partners must be identified and linked together in focused pursuit of mutual success. That a degree of comfort with the new information-based infrastructure is essential to this mindset goes beyond question. But, more than that, four additional skill sets are essential to developing a network-oriented perspective:

■ *Relationship Mindset:* Openness to finding and linking with complementary partners.
■ *Knowledge of Personal Uniqueness:* Ability to identify and articulate the core competencies, capabilities, and capacities of oneself and one's organization.
■ *Ability to Recognize Others' Uniqueness:* Ability to recognize, identify, and appreciate the core competencies, capabilities, and capacities of potential partners.

■ *Searching for Synergies*: Ability to recognize and articulate how one's own competencies, capabilities, and
capacities, when combined with those of a potential
partner, can create potential well beyond what exists for
the standalone entities.

DIPLOMAT

To develop and maintain the effectiveness of networks, today's
leaders must have the capacity to bring constituencies together, the ability to help them work together, and the insight to
help them see that by working together they can achieve more
than they ever could on their own. Three critical skill sets
comprise this dimension:

■ *Ability to Relate*: Ability to identify and connect with
others.
■ *Ability to Communicate*: Ability to effectively communicate and interact with others, both on an interpersonal
basis and via information networks.
■ *Ability To Negotiate:* Ability to create connections and
commitments among potential partners.

This particular dimension requires some pause and reflection.
It seems that in the traditional "tall pyramid" organization of the
Industrial Age, senior leaders had the luxury of "outsourcing" the
above requirements to professional functionaries (the public relations department, the human resource management department,
the legal department, the IT department, etc.). Often, the specialists did all the heavy lifting around these skill sets with the leader
as the advisor. In the networked economy, these requirements
have emerged as hands-on, roll-up-the-sleeves, and get-in-there-
and-do-it imperatives for leaders. They are absolutely essential
leadership skills in the networked economy.

INTERPRETER

To complement their skills of diplomacy, leaders must have the
ability to interpret the nature of business opportunities to the
network; the insight to help partners understand each other;

and the ability to coach, facilitate, and provide feedback to an organization that is no longer a collection of lines and boxes, but a living, growing, expanding ecosystem. Three skill sets are essential to this role:

- *Solid Knowledge of the Organization:* Ability to explain and articulate the value and uniqueness of the business and to delineate its capabilities and cultural characteristics.
- *Broad Knowledge of Marketplace:* Awareness of market trends and developments as well as competitor's capabilities and those of potential partners.
- *Ability to Influence Others:* Ability to convince others with regard to recognized challenges and opportunities.

MEETING THE CHALLENGE

The roles and challenges described here help frame the task of adjusting to the demands of the networked economy. Given the changing nature of leadership and organizational effectiveness during this period of economic transition, and the implications of this transition on leadership development processes, what can an organization do to meet the challenge of leadership development in the networked economy? The following are some suggestions:

- *Expand the Definition of Diversity.* In the networked economy, diversity takes on a whole new meaning and a whole new sense of criticality. Diversity is no longer an individual or personal issue. It is a strategic issue that requires a new view of people, structures, and strategies. Organizations and their leaders must seek out and work with people and partners who possess different skill sets and ideals. They must not only respect these differences, but also have the capacity to align them with their own unique capabilities to create competitive synergy. Understanding and embracing diversity in this broader context is a critical strategic imperative.

■ *Teach Leaders to Lead.* In the old economy, leaders were often auditors. They watched over things, approved things, and kept things running smoothly. Today, that's not enough. Today's leaders must facilitate, interpret, coach, teach, mentor, and develop both people and relationships. However, they can't do these things unless they have the right skills and mindsets. They won't develop these capabilities until they are educated in them and held accountable for demonstrating them. Leadership development, in this sense, may be the biggest challenge facing organizations over the next few years. Organizations must aggressively move forward to enable leaders to master the shift from the old, control-oriented management philosophies of the Industrial Age to the new relationship philosophies of the Information Age. No company will continue to grow and succeed until it addresses this challenge, until it ensures not only that its leaders can generate short-term results, but that they can do so while demonstrating the ability to be boundary-less thinkers, network builders, diplomats, and interpreters.

■ *Hold Leaders Accountable for Leadership.* McKinsey and Company found in its "War for Talent" study not only that knowledge workers seek out effective leadership, but also that companies that excel at leadership actually perform significantly better than their peers. Today's organizations must view people as a resource. They must see leadership as a source of inspiration and challenge, and they must make the organization itself a cause that commands attention and commitment. This means that they must hold leaders accountable for attracting, teaching, engaging, and inspiring the talented people who will drive the organization forward.

■ *Facilitate Networks.* A networked-economy organization is made of talented people who work together, share resources and information, and are committed to both personal and organizational success. The best-performing companies today have a secret weapon. They have learned that if they seek out the best minds in the organization, regardless of where they reside, put those collective minds to work on challenging opportunities, and create mechanisms to share the knowledge across the organization, they are far more likely to drive performance and generate growth. Leaders in networked-economy organizations must keep people challenged and connected, help them to learn from and with each other, and support their continued growth and development.

■ *Facilitate Learning.* Critical to an organization's ability to make the transition to the networked economy is its ability to continuously seek out and learn from information and ideas. Knowledge management is not a fad, but an essential capability. Those organizations that lead the way in the effort to unlock the secrets of effective knowledge management systems development will be the leaders in the early 21st century business environment. This means companies must develop and leaders must harness the power of real-time, information technology-based enterprise learning platforms through which organizations can catalog and disseminate the organizational wisdom gained through experience and research. Similarly, on-going opportunities for education and development are essential in the networked economy. However, due to the pace of change and the nature of today's knowledge workers, these experiences should be less classroom-oriented and more linked to real-time learning from hands-on experiences among groups of people. These experiences should be designed to facilitate not only learning and skill development, but also personal networking. That's why action learning, leader-led development, and just-in-time education are the watchwords of the day for strategic leadership development in the networked economy.

CONCLUSION

The networked economy requires that companies redefine requirements for leadership effectiveness, refine practices and policies for leadership development, and hold leaders accountable for real leadership in the networked economy. In many ways, these observations and recommendations are responses to obvious changes that have been taking place in the workplace over the past decade. Why, then, do so many organizations seem to be struggling to accommodate them? Perhaps too few organizations have engaged their leaders in discussions that help them assess and understand the transition to the networked economy and its implications for leadership and organizational effectiveness. Moreover, perhaps too few companies have taken the time to both redefine the essence of effective leadership in the networked economy and to hold leaders at all levels accountable for developing the mindsets and capabilities essential for success in a changing world. Navigating the economic change that surrounds us requires that every organization and every leader take a hard look at how effectively it is addressing the evolving demands of leadership for the networked economy.

8

THE ORGANIZATIONAL CHANGE LEADER[1]

W. Warner Burke

At the outset let us be clear about four important points. First, change for an organization can begin anywhere in the system, from a bench scientist in research and development who discovers a new chemical compound, to some computer whiz who develops a new piece of software, to a middle manager responsible for sales who demonstrates that customers want an entirely different version of products instead of what the company has been producing for decades, to the CEO who knows that the competition is slowly but surely encroaching on the business he or she leads and that something different must be

---

[1] This article is based on a more expansive version from a chapter in a forthcoming book: Burke, W. W. (2002) *Theory and dynamics of organization change*. Thousand Oaks, CA: Sage Publications. (In press.)

done—now! Second, for organizational change to occur successfully, leadership is required. This leadership can come from anywhere in the organization and from any level in the hierarchy—not just from the top, but leadership must be exercised from somewhere in the organization. Third, if we are considering planned organizational change, and if the organization has any semblance of a hierarchy, which is highly likely even in today's "virtual" times, then leadership for change must start at the top. This third point, then, sets the stage and context for what follows: our discussion of *planned organizational change*. Finally, and perhaps most importantly, even though we typically plan organizational change in a step-by-step, linear fashion, the implementation thereof is anything but linear. But if it is planned organizational change, then plan we must. It is useful, therefore, to think in terms of phases, since they blend with one another and concrete, discrete steps do not bind us. The final point is this: One can plan but cannot anticipate everything that will happen as change unfolds. Providing leadership that is adaptive is the key.

What follows is a phased way of considering organizational change and the leader's roles within each phase.

FOUR PHASES OF ORGANIZATIONAL CHANGE AND THE LEADER'S ROLES

THE PRELAUNCH PHASE

Management is more personal than leadership. Leadership is about influence and how a person in the role uses himself or herself. Knowing oneself—strengths and limitations, how feelings affect behavior, and how one is perceived by others—is critical to being an effective leader, especially a *change leader*.

Self-Awareness. Prior to leading a significant organizational change, it is wise for the leader to spend some time in self-reflection: The leader should be as clear as possible about how he or she "comes across" to others, particularly to those who are or will be followers. There is now evidence that self-awareness is related to performance. High performers in organizations view themselves more closely with how others see them than moderate or low performers do. In other words, with respect to the latter group, their self-ratings are less congruent with others' ratings of them than is true for high performers.[2] With respect to leading change, the prudent leader spends time reflecting on, if not obtaining, feedback about such personal dispositions as one's (a) tolerance for ambiguity (needs to be high rather than low); (b) need for control (needs to be at least moderate, but not to the stage of being a "control freak"); (c) approach to decision making (decisive about direction, highly participative regarding execution); (d) understanding of self in times of conflict and crisis (knowing how feelings affect one's behavior and having self-control); and (e) extraversion versus introversion (more of the former is better) and sensing versus intuition (more of the latter is usually beneficial).

Motives. Being knowledgeable about one's motives in general is a part of self-awareness; however, two motives in particular are significant regarding the change leader. The first is ambition. James O'Toole, no stranger to the key ingredients of leadership, claims that ambition is the "only inherent character trait [that] is essential for effective leadership."[3] A leader needs drive to perform well and to make things better. The second important motive is one's need for power—not mutually exclusive from ambition, of course, but in this case power coupled with high inhibition and moderate to low affiliative needs. The McClelland and Burnham study clearly demonstrated that high-performing managers were those who had a high need for

---

[2] Atwater, L., & F. Yammarino. (1992). Does Self-Other Agreement on Leadership Perceptions Moderate the Validity of Leadership and Performance Predictions? *Personnel Psychology, 45,* 141–164.

Church, A. H. (1997). Managerial Self-Awareness in High-Performing Individuals in Organizations. *Journal of Applied Psychology, 82,* 281–292.

[3] O'Toole, J. (1999). *Leadership A toZ: A Guide for the Appropriately Ambitious.* San Francisco: Jossey-Bass.

power (it is difficult to lead if one has little need to influence others); a low need for affiliation (wanting to be liked does not bode well for effective leadership, particularly during tough situations); and were high in inhibition (that is, their need for power, while high, was characterized as socialized, that is, not self-serving nor abusive toward others.)[4]

Values. This is a matter of the change leader's personal values being aligned with the desired organizational values that form a part of the future state. It is critical that the change leader embodies and lives the values espoused by the organization, since organizational members constantly scrutinize his or her behavior. Discrepancies between the personal leadership and organization values the leader espouses and the actions that he or she takes will immediately be seen as "not walking the talk" and change motivation will suffer. In addition to focusing on self-awareness, motives, and values during the prelaunch phase, the change leader needs to gather information about the organization's external environment, establish a need for change, and provide clarity of vision and direction.

The Organization's External Environment. As part of the prelaunch phase, the change leader must monitor and gather as much information as possible about the organization's external environment—what competitors are doing (or not doing), changing technology, customers' needs, how the general economy is affecting the business, and so on. From the standpoint of organizational change, the primary purpose for this data gathering is to build the case for how and why the organization needs to change.

Establishing the Need for Change. People in the organization need to be convinced that the proposed changes are necessary. Therefore, the change leader must prepare (or have prepared) the argument for and the documentation to support the change. The case for change should be tied to the long-term survival of the organization. (It should include a plan not only for survival, but also for success.) It should include analyses of

---

[4] McClelland, D. C., & D. H. Burnham. (1976). Power is the Great Motivator. *Harvard Business Review*, 54(2), 100–110.

the following: (a) who the customers of the future will be and how their needs will differ from today; (b) who the competitors will be;—they may not be the same as today; (c) the changing nature of the technology on which the organization depends; and (d) other factors, such as the changing nature of the economy and global concerns, demographic changes, government regulations, and so on.

Providing Clarity of Vision and Direction. The final aspect of the prelaunch requires that the change leader develop a vision statement that will establish a clear direction for the organizational change effort. James O'Toole has written about vision statements, and he provides one of the best descriptions:[5]

> A robust vision mobilizes appropriate behavior. It uses memorable, simple concepts that make clear what needs to be different about tomorrow. It describes the distinctive competencies needed to deliver on the desired end state (for example, "Here's what we have to do differently in order to succeed"). Leaders don't even have to create visions themselves (although many do). But, at a minimum, they must initiate a process for developing a vision and then engage themselves fully in generating buy-in. Shared commitment to a vision can be built either through wide-scale participation in the act of its creation or through involvement immediately thereafter in its dissemination

> ...We're not talking quantum mechanics here. This is simple stuff—so simple that many leaders gloss over the basics. For example, by definition, vision has to do with "seeing, sight, and sensing with the eyes." Recognizing that simple fact, effective leaders make their visions, well, *visual*. Remember Ronald Reagan's budget message when he explained that a trillion bucks amounts to a stack of dough as high as the Empire State building? By using that visual reference, he got Americans to *see* that federal spending amounts to real money! In doing so, he changed the terms of the national debate and, for the first time, created a majority in support of lower taxes. It was his most effective moment as a leader.

---

[5] O'Toole, J. (1999). *Leadership A to Z: A Guide for the Appropriately Ambitious*. San Francisco: Jossey-Bass.

THE LAUNCH PHASE

For the change leader, the launch phase of planned organizational change involves (a) communicating the need, (b) an initial activity or set of activities, and (c) dealing with resistance.

Communicating the Need. Having worked on the case for change in the prelaunch phase, it must now be communicated. If the CEO doesn't personally communicate the message—more often than not, this is the person to do it—he or she must see that the job is done. Sometimes another senior executive can communicate the case for change as well as, if not better than, the CEO. The critical criterion of the communicator is credibility. At British Aerospace (BA), the CEO arranged for his number-two executive to deliver the message, because as an engineer this executive had a background thought process similar to that of most of the executives and managers in the organization and so could more easily speak the primary audience's language.[6]

Initial Activities. Imperative for a successful launch is to conduct an event that will create the reality of the coming change by providing focus and capturing the attention of everyone. A quote from Lord Colin Marshall, at the time CEO of British Airways, provides the rationale and a brief description of such an event:[7]

> But to get people to work in new ways, we needed a major change in the company's culture. That meant refocusing everyone on the customer, on the marketplace, and away from the exclusively engineering and operations focus we'd had. That had to be done, of course, without sacrificing safety, technical, or maintenance standards. And that proved tricky. People had difficulty understanding why I kept hammering away at the need to focus on customers while also saying,

[6] Evans, R., & Price, C. (1999), *Vertical Take-off: The Inside Story of British Aerospace's Comeback from Crisis to World Class.* London: Nicholas Brealey Publishing.

[7] Burke, W. W., & Trahant, W. (2000). *Business Climate Shifts: Profiles of Change Makers.* Boston: Butterworth Heineman.

"We've got to fly these aircraft at a very high technical standard, too." The focus before had always been on the technical side alone, but I made the point repeatedly that we had to do both. It was at this point that we saw the explicit need for a culture-change program...The first thing we did was to launch a program called "Putting People First"...a two-day seminar. We took roughly 150 employees at a time and drew people from various departments within BA and from various geographical areas. The program focused on how one creates better relationships with people, with one's fellow employees, with customers, even with members of one's own family.

Dealing with Resistance. To understand resistance to change, it is helpful for the change leader to discern from among its various forms and across organizational levels. There are at least three forms of resistance, according to Hambrick and Cannella.[8] First, there is *blind resistance*. Fortunately, there are not many people who simply resist change, but there are some. Any change is at first frightening for this handful of people. It is best to give them time and space to get used to the idea. It may be that a few will have to be moved into different jobs or let go. Second, there is *ideological resistance*. People may disagree with the change because of different values and beliefs or because of different ideas about what is best. In this case, the change leader needs to be rational, using data, experience from others, and documentation to persuade. Finally, there is *political resistance*. The person believes that because of the change, he or she has something of value to lose—position, status, power, size of budget, access to other resources, and so on. In this case, the change leader must negotiate, bargain, and trade, especially with those whom the organization does not want to lose.

Resistance can also be considered according to organizational levels—*individual, group* (e.g., department, business unit, team, etc.), and the *larger system*. At the individual level, the change leader should be sensitive to the possibility that

---

[8] Hambrick, D. C., & A. A. Cannella Jr. (1989). "Strategy Implementation as Substance and Selling." *Academy of Management Executive, 3*(4), 278–285.

people may feel as if the change is being imposed on them. The change leader should find ways for individuals to have choice and to be as involved in the process, especially the implementation details, as possible.

At the group level, resistance takes the forms of closing ranks, protecting one's turf, and demanding a new structure, if not new leadership. Helping groups achieve closure about the past so that they can more readily embrace the future is a change leader's responsibility. Having a symbolic funeral can help in dealing with resistance.[9] In addition, reconstituting a group with new members can help, as can almost any activity that involves individuals in important decision making.

At the larger system level, resistance can take the form of many organizational members getting on the cynical bandwagon. Common statements might be, "This too shall pass" and "It's just another fad." Diversionary tactics can be common as well. In the face of resistance, the change leader must persevere, stay the course, and state again and again the case for change.

POST-LAUNCH: FURTHER IMPLEMENTATION

After the flurry of initial activities has been launched and the change process is underway, the change leader will deal with a myriad of consequences. Some organizational members will run with the change, others will complain about the lack of structure and clarity. Still others will ask, "Who's in charge?" With the change unleashed, the change leader will likely feel that things are out of control. At this stage, he or she needs to understand that these phenomena are not abnormal. Theory from the life sciences suggests that when disturbance (seeming chaos) occurs during this change phase, "the components of living systems self-organize and new forms and repertoires

---

[9] For an example, see Burke, W. W. (1994). *Organization Development: A Process of Learning and Changing*, 2nd ed. Reading, MA: Addison-Wesley. (pp. 147-148).

emerge from the turmoil."[10] It behooves the change leader to resist the natural temptation to seize control. The prudent behavioral choice is to be patient and allow self-organizing to occur—that is, to let creativity, innovation, and new forms emerge. These new forms might be developing new business strategies and tactics, inventing new business processes and information systems, or even establishing a whole new line of business.

More specifically, the change leader should consider the following five key actions during this implementation phase:

1. *Multiple leverage*: Organizational change is too complicated for one intervention to do the job. Many managers believe that structural change is sufficient—a new organizational chart with different accountabilities, decision making, and authority is produced. A study by Burke, Clark, and Koopman[11] showed that organizational change failure was most often associated with a structural change when that was the only intervention made. In a more recent description of seven case studies of successful organizational change, two characteristics stood out: the need for strong leadership and the success of multiple interventions—all seven cases were examples of multiple interventions.[12]

2. *Taking the heat*: When change is underway (unleashed is perhaps a more apt descriptor), not everyone gets on board. Some continue to question the need for change, revisit the case that was made at the beginning, and now in the midst of chaos, complain. The

---

[10] Pascale, R. T., M. Millemann, & L. Gioja. (2000). *Surfing the Edge of Chaos: The Laws of Nature and the New Laws of Business*. New York: Crown Business.

[11] Burke, W. W., L. P. Clark, & C. Koopman. (1984). "Improve Your OD Project's Chances for Success." *Training and Development Journal*, 38(8), 62–68.

[12] Burke, W. W. (2001). The broad band of organization development and change: An introduction. In L. Carter, D. Giver, & M. Goldsmith (Eds.), Best practice in organization development and change (pp 3-9). San Francisco: Jossey-Bass/Pfeiffer.

change leader must be capable of listening without responding defensively. Sir Richard Evans, then CEO of British Aerospace and now the company's chairman, described his experience as follows:[13]

> ...but I got a lot of pushback from people. People asked, "Why do we need to do this? We're operating perfectly well. We all have big change programs to deal with in our own businesses. Why the hell do we need to do all this other stuff?" Many seriously thought and believed that I had some sort of hidden agenda and simply wanted to be told what to do so they could go away and do it (Burke & Trahant, 2000: 146).

> The folks questioning Evans were a minority, but vocal nevertheless, and he was wise to listen to and be patient with them. Evans worked to get everyone on board, but even without having unanimity, he pressed on with the change effort.

1. *Consistency:* The change leader's behavior is constantly scrutinized by organizational members, but especially so during this phase when plans can go awry. During this phase, those resistant to the process can have more influence than at other times. Does the change leader really mean it? Will he or she see this change effort through and stay the course? Behaviorally, what is most important for the change leader is that his or her actions match his or her words. Any discrepancy will not only be noticed, but will perhaps be blown out of proportion. The core of consistency here is that behavior is congruent with the words used to describe vision, values, and mission.

2. *Perseverance:* During this implementation phase, the change effort can get bogged down. The excitement of the launch is over, and now the hard work of making the organization move to a new place becomes critical. One of the best examples of a change leader's "staying

---

[13] Burke, W. W., & W. Trahant. (2000). *Business Climate Shifts: Profiles of Change Makers.* Boston: Butterworth Heineman.

the course" was Lord Colin Marshall of British Airways. His words clearly demonstrate perseverance:

> I made a particular point of attending every one of these "Managing People First" sessions (one of the change interventions). I spent two to three hours with each group. I talked with people about our goals, our thoughts for the future. I got people's input about what we needed to do to improve our services and operations. The whole thing proved to be a very useful and productive dialogue. We found it so valuable, in fact, that in cases when I was away, we offered people the opportunity to come back and have a follow-up session with me. So I really did talk to all 110 groups in that five-year period.[14]

3. *Repeating the message*: This action is another form of perseverance. The message to be repeated is, of course, the vision, mission, values, and why the change is necessary. The more the change leader can put the message into story form, the better. Again and again, the change leader tells the story of where the organization is going, and preferably face-to-face rather than via video, so that dialogue can occur. Howard Gardner's thinking and suggestions in this regard are quite useful. By story he means[15]

> ...to call attention to the fact that leaders present a *dynamic* perspective to their followers: not just a headline or snapshot, but a drama that unfolds over time, in which they—leaders and followers—are the principal characters or heroes. Together they embarked on a journey in pursuit of certain goals, and along the way and into the future, they can expect to encounter certain obstacles or resistances that must be overcome...the most basic story has to do with issues of *identity*. And so it is the leader who succeeds in conveying a new version

---

[14] Burke, W. W. & Trahant, W. (2000) *Business Climate Shifts: Profiles of Change Makers*. Boston: Butterworth Heineman.

[15] Gardner, H. (1995). *Leading Minds: An Anatomy of Leadership*. New York: Basic Books.

of a given group's story who is likely to be effective. Effectiveness here involves fit—the story needs to make sense to audience members at this particular historical moment, in terms of where they have been and where they would like to go.

In summary, to help make the post-launch/implementation phase effective, the change leader (1) should employ multiple interventions to leverage the transformation of the organization; (2) be willing to take the heat from time to time—to listen and be patient; (3) be as consistent as possible regarding words and deeds; (4) stay the course even at the risk of being labeled "stubborn"; and (5) tell the change story over and over again, preferably in person.

SUSTAINING THE CHANGE

While the implementation phase of organizational change is not exactly easy for the change leader, sustaining the process is the most difficult of all. For this fourth phase, let us consider three ways of thinking about sustaining change and suggestions for action—dealing with unanticipated consequences, momentum, and launching new initiatives.

Unanticipated Consequences. As noted at the outset of this article, organizational change is *not* a linear process. The change leader cannot think of or predict everything. When the change is launched and underway, the equilibrium of the organization is disturbed. Many different reactions to this disturbance (or *perturbation,* as scientists refer to it) occur at the same time. In the language of Pascale and his colleagues,[16] the system moves to the "edge of chaos." Some examples of unanticipated reactions include (a) some people who were expected to be resistant turn out to be supportive and enthusiastic—and vice versa; (b) different organizational units behave quite different-

---

[16] Pascale, R. T., M. Millemann, & L. Gioja.eee (2000). *Surfing the Edge of Chaos: The Laws of Nature and the New Laws of Business.* New York: Crown Business.

ly regarding the change effort, either interpreting the new vision and future direction to fit their own desires or interpreting the future entirely contrary to what the desired future may be; and (c) expected support for the change from certain groups, like younger organizational members or the union, does not occur.

The change leader must anticipate these unanticipated outcomes, for as Pascale and his colleagues point out, disturbed living systems, including for sure organizations, seek equilibrium—as defined by those affected—and will behave accordingly. The change leader, however, must seek disequilibrium or discomfort with the status quo (since equilibrium eventually leads to death) and proceed with the change by following paths that will most likely be "disturbing," as well as facilitate movement toward the change objectives.

Momentum. At the conclusion of a description of the successful change of British Airways, Goodstein and Burke stated:[17]

> It may be that BA's biggest problem now is not so much to manage further change as it is to manage the change that has already occurred. In other words, the people of BA have achieved significant change and success; now they must maintain what has been achieved while concentrating on continuing to be adaptable to changes in their external environment—the further deregulation of Europe, for example. Managing momentum may be more difficult than managing change.

Finding ways to celebrate milestones reached, recognizing and rewarding those who have championed and facilitated the change, and finding "new blood"—different people assigned to key positions for supporting and continuing the change—are examples of ways to maintain the change momentum.

Launching, Yet Again, New Initiatives. With time and energy having been spent on the change effort, perhaps over a period of two or three years, it becomes critical to identify and implement

---

[17] Goodstein, L. D., & W. W. Burke. (1991). "Creating Successful Organizational Change." *Organizational Dynamics, 19*(4), 16.

new initiatives in order to renew organizational members' enthusiasm and vigor. New initiatives should not be activities only in the service of renewal, but clearly aligned with the original change goals and the new mission, vision, values, and culture. Examples of new initiatives to help sustain the larger goal of organizational change might be

- Acquiring another business or organization;
- Building a strategic alliance, joint venture, or partnership with another organization;
- Starting a new business or creating a new product line;
- Initiating a new program that will improve efforts that are already underway, such as new technology, new ways to enhance quality and service to customers (e.g., six sigma), or establishing a broader version of determining organizational performance, such as the balanced scorecard; and
- Finding new markets for current products and services as a function of, say, changing demographics.

Again, the point is to find ways to "disturb" the equilibrium of the system, and the change leader must press on with such initiatives in the face of resistance.

SUMMARY

Much has been written about leadership. Some of this literature is based on sound theory and research, but much of it is merely opinion, if not hype. In this chapter, we have attempted to provide greater clarity about leadership during times of organizational change. The basis for this attempt was twofold: (1) the theory and research literature and (2) experience via a few selected case examples of successful change leaders. This base culminated in the four-phase model of organizational change and the leader's role. For each phase, certain roles and functions for the change leader were specified, namely

1. Prelaunch phase requiring
   - Self-examination including self-awareness, motives, and values; and
   - Gathering information about the organization's external environment in order to (a) establish the need for change and (b) provide clarity of vision and direction.

2. Launch phase requiring
   - Communication of the need for change;
   - Initiating key launch activities; and
   - Dealing with resistance.

3. Post-launch phase/implementation requiring
   - Multiple leverage;
   - Taking the heat;
   - Consistency;
   - Perseverance; and
   - Repetition of the message (story).

4. Sustaining the change requiring
   - Dealing with unanticipated consequences;
   - Momentum; and
   - Launching, yet again, new initiatives.

Organizations change all of the time with or without leadership, but planned organizational change cannot occur with any degree of success without leadership. The change leader is a necessary and critical ingredient to the process. Since change is now considered a constant, knowing more about the leadership role is therefore essential.

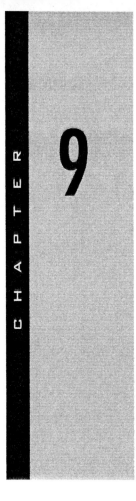

9

ENTREPRENEURIAL LEADERSHIP: BUILDING CAPACITY FOR SPEED, RISK, AND CONTINUOUS INNOVATION

Joel R. DeLuca

This chapter proposes a working model[1] as a guiding approach and framework for placing significant issues related to the subject together and in perspective. The model was carefully crafted to be simple and powerful. It attempts to provide enough background to pinpoint a key emerging pattern of behavior common among those seen as successful entrepreneurial leaders. The purpose of this chapter is to stimulate thinking so that others can frame their own sense of entrepreneurial leadership.

---

[1] This working model has now been used with success as the framework for over 1,500 business graduates at the nation's top rated MBA program *(Business Week Magazine)*: the Wharton School, in its core leadership course; over 1,000 high potential leaders at Ford Motor Co.; the engineering graduate program at the University of Pennsylvania; as well as in several corporate universities.

HISTORICAL BACKGROUND

The ancient Greeks had a word, *pou sto,* meaning a place to stand, a base, or a set of principles from which to operate. This chapter proposes one such *pou sto* for an area barely named, yet that is expanding wildly. It can act as a place to stand, reach out, capture, consolidate, and integrate the myriad of quickly converging trends related to entrepreneurial leadership. First, though, here is a bit of context.

If stages of civilization could be put in four words, those words might be *seek, grow, make, know.* Hunter-gatherers sought out their food, while farmers grew theirs; manufacturing made the machinery to grow food faster and make new products; now knowledge workers dominate the workplace. With the development of science, knowledge moved from incrementally additive to explosively exponential. Business is rising up this exponential slope with knowledge doubling at ever-faster rates, thus fueling the pace of change. Riding these waves of change has fundamentally altered the nature of business and leadership requirements.

Tribal leaders became kings of agricultural economies, who became captains of industrial economies, who are now becoming new breeds of leaders in information economies. Single-leader, chain-of-command pyramids operating 9 to 5 are transforming into multiple-leader, value-chain, virtual networks operating 24/7. Interaction between leaders, which for most of history was limited by the speed of a horse, has now moved to the speed of a photon (i.e., light). This is quickly shrinking the business planet to the anywhere, anytime global operation.

There have always been entrepreneurs and leaders. Previously, these roles have been examined as separate disciplines. However, the percentage of each needed in business populations of modern economies is shifting from minute to the majority, and skill convergence appears to be occurring. Sample evidence on each role contains surprises and similarities.

ENTREPRENEURSHIP

The emergence of the entrepreneurial society may be a major turning point in history.

—PETER DRUCKER

What characterizes those at the forefront of this turning point? Mounting evidence indicates conventional wisdom contains many misconceptions:

- ■ *Learned trait*: Entrepreneurs vary widely and do not seem to have an "inborn" trait guiding to success. Success seems more related to discipline and learned behaviors.
- ■ *Opportunity-focused*: Successful entrepreneurs are not risk junkies or even risk-focused. Most are opportunity-focused people who have learned to manage risk well.
- ■ *Innovation*: Core to most entrepreneurs is a drive for innovation that allows them to take advantage of the opportunities. Thus, entrepreneurs tend to embrace change rather than fear it, because they know change often creates the breeding grounds for opportunities.
- ■ *Continuous learning*: Entrepreneurs make plenty of mistakes. What differentiates successful entrepreneurs is that they make mistakes based on calculated risks, so their batting average is high. They also learn quickly from mistakes. They avoid blame games and learn enough to turn mistakes into learning for future gain.
- ■ *Speed*: Entrepreneurs move quickly to take advantage of opportunities before competitors do. There is enormous emphasis on speed of operation. Entrepreneurs have little patience for bureaucracy and low tolerance for cultural "sacred cows" that impede action. They are open to new ways of operating and quick to question past ways of doing things.

The skill set of entrepreneurs often includes other traits, such as the ability to mobilize capital, financial expertise, a quantitative mindset, and an improvisational spirit. Their boss is generally the environment rather than the hierarchy, and often they are profit-driven.

LEADERSHIP

Whenever the world changes so dramatically, what characterizes appropriate leadership also changes.
—JOHN NAISBITT, CO-AUTHOR OF *MEGATRENDS*

...As markets evolve, so does the definition of leadership.
—*FORTUNE MAGAZINE*

While initiative and inspiration remain, leadership too is an evolving concept. Next-generation leadership will likely include characteristics in tune with entrepreneurial needs of organizations. These include:

■ *Distributed leadership*: Classical bosses are a dying breed. This trend may grate against the "too many chiefs, not enough Indians" belief, but in the future it is likely that everyone will be expected to contribute leadership.

The biggest change in leadership is our perception of who can be a leader. The response we heard over and over again is that everyone can be a leader.
—RIEVA LESONSKY, *ENTREPRENEUR MAGAZINE*

The development of leadership in everyone is probably the single most important activity that any organization can be involved in. For the global business world, leadership is the competitive advantage.
—STEPHEN COVEY,
AUTHOR OF *SEVEN HABITS OF HIGHLY SUCCESSFUL PEOPLE*

■ *Vision*: Setting the goals, direction, and strategic intent becomes even more important as it establishes the arena to seek opportunity.

Vision makes a true leader.
—WARREN BENNIS

■ *Change mastery*: Like entrepreneurs, leaders will need to embrace change rather than resist it.

A final theme in the new leadership definition is mastery over change.
— 21ST CENTURY LEADERSHIP

■ *Continuous learning*: Arguing against the notion "leaders are born, not made" is the evidence that future leadership depends upon the willingness to change behavior based upon learning.

Our research has shown that leadership skills are developed and replicated by people on the basis of experience— trial and error, doing it, getting the feedback, making mistakes, and doing it again. The first and most important way to be educated is trial and error, particularly in the most difficult situations.
—JAMES KOUZES, PRESIDENT OF TOM PETERS GROUP/LEARNING SYSTEMS

[In a 20-year study of Harvard Business School graduates' success as leaders] I found that two elements stood out: competitive drive and lifelong learning.
—JOHN KOTTER, PH.D., LEADERSHIP RESEARCHER.

■ *Speed*: A recent addition to leadership is valuing speed, as in first to market or faster cycle times.

The big won't beat the small, the fast will beat the slow.
—JOHN CHAMBERS, CEO, CISCO, INC.

THE EMERGING CONVERGENCE OF TWO SHIPS

As dynamic markets begin to dominate, these two roles are becoming more similar. The hulls of the two ships—entrepreneurship and leadership—are rapidly evolving into a catamaran-like vessel of entrepreneurial leadership. A catamaran uses two hulls, connected by overlapping structures, to move much faster with the winds of change than either hull alone can move. Some of the classical stereotypes of each skill and areas of potential overlaps are illustrated in Figure 9.1.

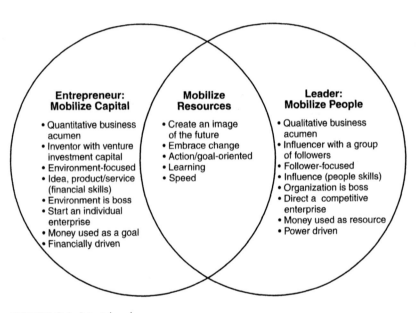

Entrepreneur: Mobilize Capital

- Quantitative business acumen
- Inventor with venture investment capital
- Environment-focused
- Idea, product/service (financial skills)
- Environment is boss
- Start an individual enterprise
- Money used as a goal
- Financially driven

Mobilize Resources

- Create an image of the future
- Embrace change
- Action/goal-oriented
- Learning
- Speed

Leader: Mobilize People

- Qualitative business acumen
- Influencer with a group of followers
- Follower-focused
- Influence (people skills)
- Organization is boss
- Direct a competitive enterprise
- Money used as resource
- Power driven

FIGURE 9.1 Potential overlaps.

There is not widespread agreement on definitions of either leadership or entrepreneurship, which makes defining entrepreneurial leadership doubly difficult. However, there is a commonality. Both entrepreneurs and leaders have behaviors that mobilize resources. From this, we propose a working definition of *entrepreneurial leadership*: mobilizing resources to create and capture opportunities. This definition requires leaders who can build capacity for speed, risk, and continuous innovation.

DYNAMIC STABILITY: A BASIS FOR ENTREPRENEURIAL LEADERSHIP

Dictionary definitions of *stability* include phrases such as "not changing or fluctuating; permanent; resisting forces tending to cause motion; develop forces to restore equilibrium of original condition." On the other hand, dictionary definitions of *dynamic* contain phrases such as "deals with forces and their relation primarily to motion; pattern of change; forces sometimes associated with equilibrium." While in many ways the definitions seem opposite, they overlap around the concept of equilibrium. Entrepreneurial leadership requires a model that generates a special form of equilibrium, based not on stability of content or structure, but on stability of process. Dynamic stability is based upon equilibrium produced by continuous, often relentless movement. An example is the gyroscope that guides terrain following aircraft moving at supersonic speeds. Another example is the bicycle. On a bicycle, the faster you go the more stable the bike is. When you slow down, you wobble. *Dynamic stability* represents a "next-generation" basis for a leadership model. It is a basis that seems to contain the countervailing forces appropriate to entrepreneurial leadership.

A WORKING MODEL OF ENTREPRENEURIAL LEADERSHIP

The carefully developed working model pictured in Figure 9.2 resulted from a historical review of the evolution of leadership and entrepreneurship models of researchers and practitioners and after many interviews with those seen as successful leaders in entrepreneurial environments.

The words in the model serve as mere placeholders for entire leadership domains, each with its own complexities. By design the model is applicable to individual, team, and organizational levels. It is compatible with more cumbersome leadership, educational, change, entrepreneurial, and cybernetic

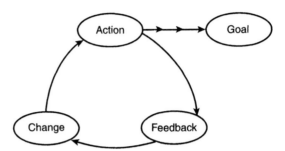

FIGURE 9.2 A working model of entrepreneurial leadership.

models. It can be shown to fit with the scientific method. The model depicted might result from taking many existing models, stripping them down to their common core, souping up that core into a dynamic engine, and streamlining that engine by using basic business concepts.

THE POTENTIAL VALUE OF THE MODEL AS A WORKING GUIDE

The model is simple, *deceptively* so. While it appears simple, embedded in the model is much of the complexity intrinsic to entrepreneurial leadership. The model was crafted to attain a form of elegant simplicity that would bring some order to the wild diversity of entrepreneurial leadership. The overall result is a model easy to learn but difficult to master. Like the martial arts, the elements are already built into our brains and bodies. However, achieving black-belt level requires deeper understanding, discipline, and conscious practice.

The continuous-motion aspect of dynamic stability is represented by using a continuous learning cycle as the core engine that powers the model. In this sense, the model is as old as humanity and as modern as the 21st century. The model is old because the basic elements of trial-and-error learning are embedded (action = trial; error = negative feedback). It is modern because key leadership issues are shown in dynamic relation to one another. The model also connects the elements *goal, action, feedback,* and *change* in a step-by-step fashion, like a dance routine laid out in steps on the floor. Put in continuous motion, the sequence of steps become the jazz dance of entrepreneurial leadership, requiring spin, grace, agility, rhythm, and discipline. It is in the relationships that issues such as speed, risk, continuous innovation, and performance-building capacity become more apparent. Businesspeople already use various forms of goal, action, feedback, and change as well as trial-and-error learning everyday. A model that integrates these often disparate processes, along with other issues of entrepreneurial leadership (such as systems thinking, cycle time, innovation as part of change management, speed, distributed leadership), can make the complex set of links between them more understandable. It can also help leaders zero in on key leverage points to increase overall business success.

KEY COUNTERINTUITIVE BEHAVIORS OF ENTREPRENEURIAL LEADERS

As markets become more dynamic, leadership evolves from building upon past practice, to envisioning the future, to developing a present discipline for rapidly evolving responses to opportunities. As a consequence, much of conventional wisdom is reversed in entrepreneurial leadership. Using the model as a guiding framework, a few such examples include

Goal: Instead of goals as endpoints, use goals as starting points. Conventional wisdom would set the goal as the endpoint or destination. Yet, entrepreneurial leaders in dynamic environments often use goals as the starting point for the cycle of the model. The goal acts as a stake in the ground around which things move.

Action-Goals: Instead of action following goal clarification, action precedes goal clarification. Conventional wisdom assumes that goals precede action. However, in dynamic environments, it is difficult to fully clarify goals. This situation produces ambiguity. In ambiguous situations people get stuck and don't act until they receive further clarity. Entrepreneurial leaders put the issue in a different frame and ask, "In an ambiguous situation, which comes first, clarity or action?" When framed this way, most people break out of the "waiting-for-clarity" deadlock that paralyzes many organizations. It is sometimes useful to act first in order to develop and clarify goals; thus the conventional wisdom of action following goals is reversed in this "chicken and egg" dilemma.

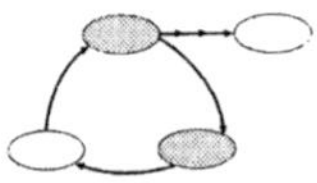

Action-Feedback: Instead of action generating feedback, feedback generates action. Normally, feedback follows action in order to determine how well the action leads to the goal. However, in dynamic situations, the feedback structure actually affects both risk taking and speed of action. Figure 9.3 illustrates how the feedback structure affects action. The structure that works best is lots of feedback and low repercussions for hidden mistakes. This dynamic is a key skill of successful entrepreneurial leaders. They lower risk and accelerate initiative by finding ways to increase feedback and reduce the price of mistakes.

	Environment is Feedback:	
Price of a Mistake is:	*Poor*	*Rich*
High	**PLAN** completely	**Act** or **Plan** first, Your choice
Low	**PLAN** next step—**Act**, **PLAN,** etc.	**Act** Then Adjust

FIGURE 9.3 Plan-act matrix.

Feedback: Instead of passively receiving feedback, actively solicit feedback. This is probably the fastest growing area in leadership and business. Stakeholder reviews, competitive benchmarking, 360° appraisal, and Internet search are just a few examples of actively soliciting feedback. Conventionally, feedback was simply information received regarding the results of an action. Entrepreneurial leaders see feedback as the fuel for innovation and speed of response. They build feedback into consumers and suppliers' systems. Realizing that feedback comes from the task, others, and oneself, entrepreneurial leaders are much more assertive and systematic in seeking out feedback.

Feedback-Change: Instead of feedback to keep action on track, feedback is used to raise fundamental assumptions. Conventionally, feedback initiated change that modified action to keep it focused on the set goal. In entrepreneurial leadership, feedback is also used to raise fundamental assumptions. Questioning basic assumptions often leads to new ways of seeing markets, thus stimulating innovative responses. Leveraging this dynamic is critical to continuous innovation.

Change: Instead of change focused on action, allow change to focus on goal, feedback, and change process. Traditional change focused on the action component, ensuring behavior was modified as needed to achieve the goal. In entrepreneurial leadership, change also focuses on the goal itself, in which a new vision and related goals may arise that could possibly change the business the organization is in. This would be a type of double-loop learning. Change might also focus on modifying the feedback component by adding customer and competitive feedback to historical benchmarks. This enriched feedback can fundamentally alter the meaning of success. The change process itself can be changed: for example, using the entire top team and/or adding succession-planning individuals into the change process. Action is just one aspect for change to address. Entrepreneurial leaders are more likely to use the full range of options.

Change-Action: Instead of implementers involved after change decision, implementers involved before change decision. Historically, change decisions have been enacted by implementation through the hierarchy. Implementers enter the process after key decisions are made, and often at a slow, inefficient pace. Entrepreneurial leaders are more likely to value commitment than obedience. They often reverse the process and involve implementers prior to the decision, which can speed up change and help beat competitors to market.

SMART MOVES

Entrepreneurial leaders integrate both conventional and unconventional wisdom. "Smart moves" demonstrate this integration in practice and embody the essence of the entrepreneurial leadership model. A smart move is more than a smart risk. A smart risk focuses on whether the action is worth taking. If costs outweigh benefits, action stops. Since a smart move is opportunity-focused rather than risk-focused, movement continues despite risk, but it is based on whether the opportunity is worth seeking. A smart move aggressively manages risk within the situation by integrating various leverage points in the model, such as breaking the action into (1) smaller, (2) faster, (3) low-cost, and (4) feedback-rich steps. Such steps can lower risks and speed learning. Faster learning leads to faster assumption raising, thus facilitating innovation and faster change to improve actions as well as faster discovery of new opportunity goals.

Smart moves are either successful or a good investment for future success or both. These moves integrate parts of the model and their relationships into the agile jazz dance of entrepreneurial leadership. When spun to full speed, continuous smart moves power up the model to the point of dynamic stability where the process can have a "buzz-saw" effect, taking on obstacles bit by bit but at such speeds that it can cut through them extremely rapidly. Entrepreneurial leaders grow their business by building this capacity for continuous smart moves. They set up their organizations to take quick, small, low-cost, feedback-rich steps by helping workers become experts in probing, prototyping, and piloting; using multiple trials with fast turnarounds; and creating highly enriched feedback environments involving multiple stakeholders, especially customers. They create climates of learning versus punishment. (See Figure 9.4.)

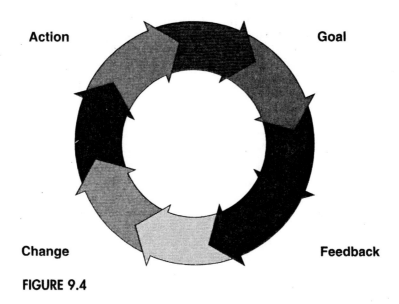

Action   **Goal**

Change   **Feedback**

FIGURE 9.4

HOW THE BUSINESS PLAYING FIELD IS SHIFTING

Entrepreneurial leadership, with its emphasis on smart moves, fundamentally alters the success landscape, as illustrated in figures 9.5 and 9.6. Historically, mistakes have equaled failure. Pressure for immediate performance overshadowed actions that built capacity by learning from mistakes. As a result, Figure 9.5 was more the norm. Entrepreneurial leaders recognize that if a mistake generates data and learning that rapidly increases performance capacity, then it could be seen as a "positive failure," something hard to imagine from a traditional performance mindset. Also in this new landscape there can be "negative successes." How can a success be negative? An example might be meeting performance targets by selling off the research and development function responsible for future innovations and profits. Getting the job done in ways that burn out top talent who then leave the company is another example. Mistakes from "smart moves" that generate valuable feedback are now a part of good entrepreneurial leadership behavior. In new, fast-changing markets, mistakes fuel the learning essential to building capacity to continually grow the business. Figure 9.6 is a better depiction of the shifting success landscape.

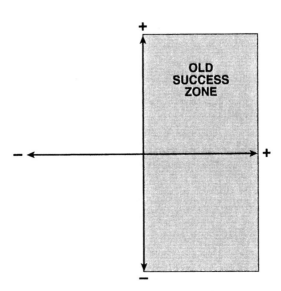

FIGURE 9.5 Performance capacity: old success zone.

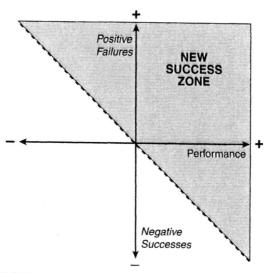

FIGURE 9.6 Performance Capacity: new success zone.

SUMMARY

Both leadership and entrepreneurship are evolving and rapidly converging. Organizational size matters little, as both the big and the small need these skills. In the past, a leader's confidence often came from knowing the answer, and thus avoiding mistakes. A major shift for future success in entrepreneurial leadership will not be from knowing the answer, for today's answer may last just until tomorrow's newspaper headline or Internet flash. The confidence of entrepreneurial leaders will come from knowing a *dynamic,* yet *stable* process for rapidly evolving an effective response to an opportunity even if the response will be of value for only a short while. They will then use their *capacity* to quickly *mobilize resources* into *smart moves* to evolve a new response. Powering this continuous learning process in a disciplined way can excite and ground organizations to more confidently act with the *speed, risk,* and *continuous innovation* that can *create and capture new opportunities.* Hopefully, such an approach can be a *pou sto* from which people have the confidence to dare.

CHAPTER 10

LEADERSHIP: REFLECTIONS AND LEARNINGS

Robert Terry

For over 35 years, I have been a leadership educator and trainer. As I look back, I realize that I have concentrated more on in-depth inquiry, insight, and understanding than on skill building. In the last few years, a new commitment has emerged; I have become a leadership architect as well as educator. My latest book, *Seven Zones for Leadership: Acting Authentically in Stability and Chaos,* reflects my new identity. I have finally linked personal, professional, and organizational authenticity, setting the context for leadership inquiry, action, and development.

Once I had the breakthrough of the three dimensions and their intimate linkage, I realized how seldom they are connected. Most leadership books and programs concentrate on one or two. Few leadership programs ask, *What does it take to build a robust, enduring organization for the long term?* Most focus on who you are—leading from within—and what your role and function require—leading from positional responsibility and accountability.

A popular phrase in leadership studies is "walk the talk." Of course this is important. In order to lead effectively, you must know yourself and live your values. What do you think of this reflection? I know many people who walk the talk every day—*off a cliff!* They may embody integrity, yet they have little or no worldly savvy.

As I ponder my past, it has become clear that two things, a question and a concept, have driven my life: The question is, what is really going on? The concept is authenticity. I differ from most advocates of authenticity. While increasingly popular in leadership studies, it is often couched in such words as *genuine, honest, transparent, real, true,* and so on, which focus on the individual and/or role. This brings us to my cliff image. It is not enough to be true to yourself if you are naïve or if you lie about the world.

At leadership seminars, I am often asked the "Hitler" questions: Was Hitler a leader? Did Hitler exhibit leadership? And, I frequently hear the conclusion: Hitler was authentic; he lived his beliefs. My view is contrary. Yes, Hitler was a "leader" in that he was elected and supported by followers. However, he rarely exhibited leadership: He was a tyrant, oppressor, exploiter, and despot.

This conclusion brings us to the role of ethics in leadership. Is leadership intrinsically ethical, or can it be both ethical and unethical? Regarding authenticity, Hitler did live his beliefs, but he lied about the world. He claimed Jews and others were inferior. To declare anyone else inferior, he had to claim to be superior. Thus, as he lied about the world, he lied about himself and destroyed both.

The other aspect of the authenticity quest that rarely gets surfaced is the responsibility of the followers. Was Hitler the real problem, or was it the willing followers who supported and killed for him? Leadership is not reducible to one person. *It is a set of relationships that unfold over time.* It is one thing to attend to the character of the leader; it is quite another to attend to the character of the relationships. Bosses hire employees; bosses fire employees. Followers pick their leaders; it is hard, if not impossible, to fire a follower. Work in a volunteer organization and this reality at times is overwhelming.

Authenticity is not reducible to an inside focus. The quest for truth takes one inside and outside. In fact, there is no inside or outside. They are linked as in the Mobius Loop, always connected and impacting each other, hence the linkage of personal, professional, and organizational. To be true and real, inside and outside, is a life long process.

What follows from this insight is that leadership development is a life-long process. The learning never ends. Sadly, I have seen too many executives who cease to learn. They become fixers and problem-solvers, surrounding themselves with valued clones. To cease learning avoids authenticity and thereby engages in denial, escape, derailment, and, at the deepest level, frustration and fear. The quest for deeper truth leaves the table and reality is temporally sidestepped. However, I have learned over the years that reality—that abiding sense of what is true and real inside and outside—never goes away.

For years, I was an existentialist. I thought human beings shaped reality, created meaning, and were in charge of their existence. I have now come to embrace the paradox: We both shape and are shaped by life. Do not just tell life what is real and what to do. Listen, discern, and attend to the stirrings in yourself, your role, and your organization. We are not just definers of truth; truth defines us as well. Attend to the voices within and without. Assess them and act thoughtfully. Without this commitment to listen as well as direct, leaders fail to exhibit leadership and trap themselves in their own ego and position.

Given this context, I will now share a series of reflections and learnings that have challenged my own understanding and practice of leadership as an educator and architect. I hope these insights will stimulate your inquiry and deepen your wisdom so that you make thoughtful, adept choices. These reflections are not just for executives. I am a great believer that leadership, while often linked to positions, is not reducible to position. Leadership is possible for all of us. The question is, Are we prepared for it and courageous enough to make it happen?

A CONSCIOUSNESS-COMPETENCE FRAME

A colleague, Warren Hoffman, shared the following framework (Figure 10.1) with me. I found it intriguing and engaging, because it challenged me to look inside and outside myself in worldly contexts. In some ways, it parallels the Johari Window from the 1960s.

	Conscious	Unconscious
Competent	"I know." Self-aware	Things come easily. I don't know why I get along well with people or why I am good at that.
Incompetent	I know that I'm not good at doing _____ .	I know what I don't know.

FIGURE 10.1 Conscious-competence frame.

Of course, the goal is to become conscious and competent. None of us are conscious and competent in everything. Many leaders live in the upper right box: "I do what I do and do not know why. I'm good at some things, yet I'm stunned when asked how I learned to do it." Some people call this humility and want to take no credit for their actions. In this model, that is action grounded in competent unconsciousness.

Many people live in the lower left box: "I am not good at a lot of things and I know it. I hate details, follow-through, and deadlines. I hate concepts, creativity, and uncertainty."

Much awareness of the two boxes—upper right and lower left—comes from Myers-Briggs and feedback instruments like the Kilman Conflict Inventory. It also comes from friends, colleagues, peers, even opponents and enemies. When I ask people from whom they learned a lot about life and leadership, guess who often is identified? Terrible bosses, bad parents, crummy employees, and dreadful peers. Positive role models are not the only effective teachers.

The lower right box requires interpersonal feedback. Even the advice to take an instrument must come from a friend or colleague. The person does not know what he or she does not know and thus will not inquire. Think about a time when you received that you did not expect. It made no sense initially; yet eventually you embraced it as profound insight. Leadership is not learned solo. Wisdom about our roles, our organizations, and ourselves is often the gift of others and is often not invited. The challenge is to listen and weigh the feedback, without avoidance, and learn. Say "thank you" to yourself: Receive the gift, even though it may be unwanted.

CORE VERSUS SHARED VALUES

Values are hot today in organizational life. The lists are on the wall, in performance reviews, and on a card in your wallet or purse. Back in the 1960s, I worked for Detroit Industrial Mission, an ecumenical organization that connected faith-based values to business realities. No one was doing that very much. As a matter of fact, values were not on the radar screen of many corporations or unions at the time. Today, they are everywhere. I have helped many organizations through the value maze, and I have learned a distinction that I find very helpful: the difference between core and shared values.

Core values tie to the business you are in; *shared values* are values we have in common that are not directly tied to the business. I learned the core value concept from Collins and Porras's book *Built to Last: Successful Habits of Visionary Companies.*[1] For example, if you work for a tobacco company, freedom of choice constitutes a core value. If a bank employs

---

[1] Collins and Porras. (1994). *Built to Last: Successful Habits of Visionary Companies.* New York: Harper Collins.

you, you will hear the values of honesty and integrity if the core values are specified.

Most organizations with which I work do not make the distinction. A fire chief held up a list of 25 values. They were labeled core; yet they were shared. Here's a clue: If there are more than five or six values, they are shared. There are usually just two or three core values, and they are easily remembered. The clearest way I know to illustrate the difference is with Clinton's near-impeachment. The Republicans argued that the scandal was not about sex; it was about lying in court. That violated a core value and significantly damaged the government. The Democrats argued that it was about sex, and that Clinton had violated a shared value of family trust and fidelity. That violation is not impeachable. Of course, I am not dealing with the politics of the debate, just with the substance of the arguments.

If you want to build a great organization for the long term, ground it in core values, not shared values. As Collins and Porras argue persuasively, the more securely the foundation is grounded in core values, the more wild the BHAG—Big Hairy Audacious Goals. However, the values must be lived every day by everyone, especially by those at the top. They are watched by the middle and the bottom for authenticity, and not just personally and professionally, but also organizationally, as the values are built into the everyday life at work for everyone.

CHANGE

It is not location, location, location; it is change, change, change. The popularity of the book *Who Moved My Cheese?*[2] and the preoccupation with people who resist change dominates the workplace. Joseph Rost defines leadership as follows: "Leadership is an influence relationship among leaders and followers who intend real change that reflect their mutual purposes."[3] He reflects the popular view that leadership is about change.

---

[2] Spencer Johnson. (1998). *Who Moved My Cheese?* New York: Putnam and Sons.

[3] Joseph Rost. (1991). *Leadership for the Twenty-First Century* New York: Praeger, p. 102.

What about stability? Are some things worth preserving? Does leadership ever involve resisting change? What about this for the opening speech of a new CEO? "Ladies and gentlemen, I am excited about my new role, and I want you to know I am absolutely committed to no change." I suggest that is half the speech. Preserve the core values and also advocate BHAGs.

Stability and change are a polarity. One defines the other, as both exist at the same time. Both require attention and cannot be avoided without danger. One cannot even identify a change without contrasting it with something that is not changing.

I was sitting in a restaurant recently, and a friend, who is a judge, introduced me to a state Supreme Court Justice. He asked me a leadership question: "Is leadership from the top down or the bottom up?" I said, "Yes." He thanked me and sat down. I decided it was my turn, so I asked him, "Is leadership ever committed to absolutely no change?" He looked surprised. "Leadership is all about change. That is why we are here as leaders." I replied, "So, it's okay to lie in court now?" He got the point. Part of his leadership responsibility is to preserve the best of the court and constitutional system.

MISSION STATEMENTS

I have helped more than 100 companies figure out their mission and, at times, advised reducing it to a seven-word statement. No longer. I do not believe in mission statements anymore. I believe in identity clarity. All mission statements have a word in them that reduces impact. That word is "to." We are here "to...." What about replacing the word "to" with "we are..."? Mission is future-oriented; identity is present-oriented. Because the future is unknown, it is not the way to define the essence of an organization. To avoid accomplishing the mission is not the end of the world; to violate the identity of the organization is betrayal and worthy of serious reflection, review, and action.

Consider this map image. I love moose, so I want to go to Maine to see some. Which direction should I travel? In Minnesota, everyone says northeast. Then I say, "I will be in

London, England, when I leave for Maine." You can't know which way to go unless you know where you are. Likewise, we cannot know where we are going unless we know who we are.

What goes into identity? Based on what I learned from another colleague, Bruce Gibb, a renowned consultant in Ann Arbor, Michigan, identity consists of three aspects: what business you are in, who you serve, and your level of service. Our leadership firm is a guild of seasoned leadership architects and educators. Partners with for-profit and not-for-profit organizations, we co-create and deliver a full array of leadership programs. These comprise mostly long-term programs inside organizations and include coaching and mentoring, organizational assessment, and follow-through that link personal, professional, and organizational realities that are grounded in research, professional experience, tested success, and authentic significance. This is who we are, and when we do not practice this every day, we are inauthentic and we betray the creditability and trust that is the basis of our long-term customer commitment and depth.

CORE COMPETENCIES

Have you seen the list of core competencies of your organization? I no longer believe in them. Many of the organizations with which I work have them and do not use them. If they do, a standard of perfection is implied and imposed. I have learned that leadership is not reducible to an ideal type. It is contextual, requires different skills by level and function, is grounded in personal gifts and talents, and involves long-term learning and development. Jay Conger and Beth Benjamin question core competencies in their provocative 1999 book— *Building Leaders: How Successful Companies Develop the Next Generation.*[4] Other colleagues are moving in the same direction. It is better to teach actual and potential leaders to assess themselves, their roles, and their organizations, and then figure out their readiness to lead appropriately. Core

---

[4] J. Conger and B. Benjamin. *Building Leaders: How Successful Companies Develop the Next Generation.* San Francisco: Jossey-Bass, 1999.

competencies, once defined, become constants. They are not core values, and they require continuous updating, which is rarely done. Another mistake.

BEST PRACTICES

I worry too about the popularity of best practice. It is too easily a code for "fad-of-the-month." Six Sigma, a very good practice in some contexts, is not so great in others. Rarely does the context enter the discussion. Practices embody values and frameworks that are implicit and not addressed. Consultants often advocate best practices that are good at delivering: open-space technology, large-scale interventions, humor seminars, and so on. The list is endless. Part of the wisdom of leadership is to know what to do and when it is appropriate. That requires organizational savvy to determine fit. Always ask the upsides and downsides of the practice and how it matches what is needed for long-term organizational vibrancy. The creative challenge of best practices is good. They push boundaries. Go beyond the boundaries and ask the tough questions. Learn from the inquiry and your leadership will be enhanced.

VISION STATEMENTS

If you want to kill a vision, reduce it to a sentence. Instead, build a vision picture that captures the imagination and inspires action. How about this for a vision statement? *Be the Best.* In my view, it is a throwaway. The firm that proposes it is in the midst of a technological upheaval, the character of the work is up for grabs, and the competition is just as confused. Be the Best does not offer a picture of the future that can guide decisions and engage organizational energy.

I took an eating disorder organization through a futuring process in which it created its imaginary future. The organization was stunned. It saw a new building, shaped with new technology, sustainable systems, and new forms of communication.

As people create the picture of their future, the picture is also a very good diagnosis of the current organization. What is built into the picture is not in the present or is dysfunctional as it currently operates.

LANGUAGE

The language that people use frequently opens the door of insight into reality. For example,

- *Don't have enough time.* We all have the same amount. This is a clue about priorities, not time. Listen for what is important to the speaker and this window will reveal a lot.
- *Try.* "I try very hard; I try to work with my peers; I try to get things done on time; I try to listen." The word try, when used often, is a code word for "no commitment." It is a popular cover to avoid responsibility. "Don't try; just do it," is an alternative.
- *Should.* Too often we get "should" on. It is a word of judgment, often judgmental. Replace should with could. It opens up options and choices.
- *But.* "I love you, but your habit of being late drives me crazy. You do a great job of getting people motivated, but you do not always follow through." But disconnects. It is so built into our language that we hardly hear it. Instead of affirming two truths, it negates one for another. Replace "but" with "and," or start the next sentence.
- *Why?* "Why are you late? Why did you forget to give me the outline of the plan?" Why is best used by scientists seeking objective truth. When used with humans, it closes down truth seeking, replacing it with defensiveness. Instead, ask, "What is going on?"

Language reveals a lot about us. It is not just a window into others; it is one into ourselves as well.

COACHING AND MENTORING

I have the privilege of mentoring over a dozen senior executives. On the surface, they are successful. The longer we talk, however, the more apparent the stirrings. "What is worth doing for the rest of my life? What is my function? What is going on in this organization?" The more I mentor, the clearer the distinction between coaching and mentoring becomes. One coaches for success; one mentors for significance. As a hairdresser, if I want to improve my hair-dyeing skills, I hire a coach. If I am contemplating my fit in the business, I hire a mentor. Many executives get it wrong. They want a mentor and hire a coach, or the reverse. Authenticity invites the right match.

TEAM AND GROUP BUILDING

Teambuilding and the use of the term *team* invade the workplace. I have had a breakthrough. Teams differ from groups, and both need to be built.

A team: Clear goals; have to work together to accomplish goals in a specified timeframe.

A group: Vague goals; do not work together on a regular basis; loose timeframe.

The latter, we call "executives." Executives are often sent off for teambuilding, yet bring nothing back. The trip was inauthentic. They are a group. Group building involves members helping each other be better in their own areas. Groups often sponsor teams without being one. We need both; each is crucial in building a vibrant organization long term.

BEYOND SPIRITUALITY IN THE WORKPLACE

In Minnesota, is *spirituality* a code word for Lutheranism? Books and seminars abound on the subject. What I find fascinating is the diversity of meanings for spirituality, especially in the leadership literature. It varies from belonging to the universe, to shared values, to creation of meaning. For all, there seems to be a push for inclusion in contrast to religion, which is often portrayed as an exclusive, separating set of behaviors and beliefs.

What is behind the quest for spirituality? What is really worthy of our trust? What is the basis of our hope? Spending most of my adult life as a secular humanist, I am skeptical of religion and wonder whether the spiritual search is deep enough. Since 1993, I have been a secular theologian, asking the hardest questions I know of about life, death, good, and evil, what is real, and what is disguise. In 2001, a group of colleagues connected to Luther Seminary, St. Thomas University, and by friendship, convened and invited a set of CEOs in the profit, not-for-profit, and governmental worlds to meet regularly to discuss theology and the workplace. I have long believed that some of the best theologians are atheists. They ask the hardest questions, particularly in a society that is intolerant of such inquiry. The goal is not to bring religion to the workplace. It is to explore the deepest questions of fear, hope, courage, and faith every day, personally, professionally, and in the organization. It is to go beyond, under, or around spirituality. Twenty CEOs are involved. I am profoundly excited.

LEADERSHIP EDUCATION

As a leadership educator, I am deeply committed to leader preparation. For years, I have done leadership seminars. The seminars have personal, sometimes professional impact. What

I have learned, however, is that they have little organizational impact. If you want to build leadership into the organization, a different strategy works.

Here is what does not work organizationally: Bring strangers together for short periods of time, with no shared leadership framework, no 360° feedback, no live cases, and no support back at work. There is usually a 90 percent drop-off of what was learned in the seminar. (Conger and Benjamin, mentioned earlier, pioneered in this research.)

What does work? Work inside organizations, long term (a year or two) with peers who know each other. Use real cases; have mentoring and coaching support; engage in personal, professional, and organizational 360° feedback; and use a comprehensive frame for linking the three dimensions (personal, professional, and organizational). This is the fundamental reason I have added leadership architect to my identity and the identity of my leadership firm.

Leadership education is a life-long process. Regardless of the born versus made debate, leadership education is no quick fix. I am often asked how long it takes to become a leader and exhibit leadership. I am now guessing anywhere from 5 to 10 years sets the base. However, as the world gets more complex and chaotic, the old leadership styles and approaches no longer fit. New learning and experimentation are required.

Leadership is contextual. Just think how different it is when the world is orderly, fixable, and predictable in contrast to it being complex, emerging, and self-organizing, and in further contrast, filled with surprises and chaotic. What does leadership look like when life makes no sense, when evil takes over, and devastation surrounds us?

Authenticity is the only aspect of life that profoundly keeps me centered. Be shaped and shape, listen and discern, let go and take hold, and admit our inauthenticity as we embrace our authenticity. Authenticity does not require perfection. It is not a core competency. It invites us to own who and what we are, what we do, and what we understand about life. Welcome to *leadership*: Serving the promise and reality of authenticity.

FOLLOW-UP

If this material intrigues you and you want to connect directly, contact us at our Web site, *www.Zobius.net,* or email us at
zobius@qwest.net. Share what you have learned over the
years and our guild will continue to share our new learnings.
Wisdom is never finished. Join us for the authenticity quest
and discovery.

11

EXPERIENCE IS STILL THE BEST TEACHER

Michael M. Lombardo
and Robert W. Eichinger

M uch is written about the increasing pace of change, the new challenges leaders face, and what old and new skills it takes to cope. Less is said about how managers and executives develop the skills they need for any future—past or future. In this chapter, we deal with the challenges that create the need to grow—what they are and why they work.

We'll do this by asking you to consult an expert on development—yourself.

THE NATURE OF THE EXPERIENCE

Think back through your life, focusing on work and school experiences. Pick four experiences that may have lasted a few minutes or a few years that have had a lasting impact on you.

Regardless of their length, they share a common truth: They have made a lasting impact on you as a person, how you respond to the world, the skills you now use, and how you approach work. You learned more from these experiences than any others.

1. _____

2. _____

3. _____

4. _____

THE EXPERIENCE CATALOG

There continues to be one major finding from all of the research on how people develop the skills they use to be effective: *People learn most of the skills they need on the job.*

There are four kinds of experiences reported by executives, managers, professionals, teachers, principals, coaches, men, women, and high-school students (everyone who has been studied):

1. Key jobs
2. Important other people
3. Hardships
4. Courses (and books, tapes, Internet)

Depending on the study, skill development is reported as 75 percent to 90 percent learned on the job. The events that matter most occur there.

KEY JOBS

Most of the hard job skills that matter for performance (e.g., strategy, planning) people learn on the job when they hit fresh challenges. The jobs most likely to teach are starting something from nothing or almost nothing, fixing something broken, switching from line to staff, big changes in complexity or scale, and various kinds of projects (see the exercise in this chapter for more details).

The jobs that are least likely to teach are straight-upward promotions, doing the same type of job again and again, and job switches aimed at exposure rather than at tough challenges.

IMPORTANT OTHER PEOPLE

As with jobs, the people who develop most have the widest variety of other people from whom to observe and learn. Role models play a critical role throughout life, and learning from others is a large category of learning in organizations. Those most remembered are usually bosses and those higher up.

Bosses matter because of what they model: how their values play out in the workplace. The so-called soft skills come into focus here—how people walk their talk, deal with poor performers, make tradeoffs between results and compassion, form networks and alliances, and deal with diversity or solve ethical dilemmas. They also matter because they are a substitute for direct experience—role models can teach through their actions. A novice can learn how a superb marketing manager thinks through marketing plans or observe how an experienced negotiator reaches agreements.

HARDSHIPS

No one sets out to have a hardship—hardships just happen to people: missed promotions, demotions; getting fired; business blunders; career ruts; intractable, impossible direct reports; and the like. The key is what people learn from the bad bounces of life.

One key difference between the successful and the less so is that successful people are more likely to report blunders they made and had to rally from. They are much more likely to embrace whatever happens to them, whether they created the situation or not. Rather than resorting to blame, successful people are much more likely to see what can be learned from the situation.

COURSES

Curiously, at first, we notice that the content of the course comes in second when people talk about the value of coursework (the Harvard Business School had a similar finding). What we came to understand as we looked further was that timing is everything—it is less what the course is about and more—overwhelmingly more—that the person needs the information badly, right then, to perform on the job. A really developmental course looked more like the other job events above than one would think—it was the first time, different, and difficult. The number one benefit gleaned from courses is self-confidence—belief that a person can grow, change, and improve upon demand.

Now back to you. You probably thought of the four categories of experiences above. You remembered starting a new business or activity or an international assignment or a remarkable boss (2 to 1 odds that you remember the boss fondly), or you recalled something that hit you like a truck—a missed promotion, a truly awful job, a blunder, or having to fire someone. Or you remembered a course that opened a door in your mind just when you needed it most. *You remembered all these experiences for the same reasons:*

> *You knew very little about it going in.* You had little or no experience in the area. Development is the world of the first-time, the tough, and the different. The varied and the adverse create a need to learn, and most learning occurs while we are in difficult transitions.
>
> *You felt you had a significant chance of failure.* One of the truths of the human psyche is that people try hardest when there is a 50 percent to 67 percent chance of success. More, and it's too easy; less than half, and we start to cut our losses. So, although there were some strengths you had to fall back on, you thought you might fail. You learned because you had

to get through the situation. For the job and the boss, your skills weren't quite up to the challenge; for the hardship, you didn't know if or how you could bounce back—the temptation to blame and deny was tremendous; for the course, it was just-in-time training for your job. Something in the course—whether it was personal self-awareness or a job skill—was pivotal to your performance. Having something at stake lubricates the learning.

You had to make a difference. You had to take charge and lead. You didn't have time to check off with everyone or collect all of the data you needed to feel comfortable.

You felt a tremendous amount of pressure. You experienced deadlines, people looking over your shoulder, travel, or an overwhelming workload. When the stakes are highest is when we are also most motivated to learn.

There are many other challenges that create learning, but these are the most common denominators people recall from any key event or experience. *Development is a demand-pull—the experience demands that we learn to do something new or different, or we fear we will fail.*

Development is full of paradoxical conditions: adverse, difficult, first-time, varied, full of new people, bosses, good and poor legacies, strong emotions, lack of significant skills, closely watched and yet lonely. It is usually not that pleasant at the time, but it is exciting—much more so than straight-line promotions or succeeding at jobs we already basically know how to do. Development is discomfort, because comfort is the enemy of growth. Staying in our comfort zone or building our nest encourages repetition. Going against the grain, being forced, or venturing outside the cozy boxes of our lives demands that we learn.

Now think of your current job as it exists for you today. Compared with other jobs you have had, how would you rate each of the following on the five-point scale?

EXERCISE: Developmental Heat

Rate the following statements according to this scale: 1 = Little challenge; 2 = Some challenge; 3 = Like most of my other jobs; 4 = More than other jobs; and 5 = Much more than other jobs.

1.____ Success or failure are both possible and would be obvious to others and myself. I think I could fail or not perform well at this job.

2.____ Requires take charge, aggressive, individual leadership.

3.____ Involves working with new people, lots of people, or people with different skills.

4.____ High personal pressure (deadlines, high stakes, large shift in scope or scale, travel, long hours, work is viewed as critical).

5.____ Requires influencing people, activities, and factors over which I have no control (e.g., supervisors besides boss, lateral relations, partners, peers, outside parties, political situations, customers).

6.____ Involves a high variety of tasks, doing something very different from what I've done in the past (e.g., line/staff switch, promotion to headquarters, changing functions, lines of business/technology).

7.____ Is closely watched and monitored by people whose opinions count.

8.____ Requires building a team or something from scratch or fixing/turning around an operation in trouble (e.g., downsizing, restructuring, new product line, new business, establishing a new operation, poorly performing unit, major staffing issues, inheriting a failing unit).

9.____ Involves a tremendous intellectual/strategic/problem-solving challenge with little or no history for guidance.

10.____ Involves interacting with a significant boss (whether supportive or not, the boss's view is critical to success in this job.)

11.____ Am missing something important (e.g., lack of management support, limited resources, not aligned with strategy or core of the business, poor legacy, missing key skills or technical knowledge, lack of credentials/credibility).

This exercise is adapted from *Eighty-Eight Assignments for Development in Place: Enhancing the Developmental Challenge of Existing Jobs* by Michael M. Lombardo and Robert W. Eichinger. Center for Creative Leadership.

We developed this exercise from the Center for Creative Leadership's studies of developmental assignments. The research team deduced the core elements (reasons why an experience was developmental) of over 2,000 experiences recounted in detail by executives and middle managers. We used this as an exercise in a course for some years. Thousands of people have filled it out and many organizations use it to rate the developmental potential of jobs and other experiences. Following are some interpretive guidelines.

If you scored above 45 (out of 55 possible), this is a very developmental job for you. You are likely in a start-up, a fix-it, or an international assignment. There is very little about this job that you have ever done before. Unfortunately, the job may also be too large a jump for you or anyone else.

If you scored 35 to 45, this is where most developmental jobs fall. Half or more of the challenges are present in a big way.

If you scored 21 to 34, you may have been in this job for three years or more, it may be a straight-line promotion, or you perhaps changed companies (but not basic responsibilities) some time ago. Your performance might not be as good as it once was; you may be getting bored.

If you scored 20 or less, you are comfortable coasting and retired on the job, or you are plotting ways to change your situation or quit. Your résumé may be on the street. You've been in the job too long, it's old hat, it's no longer challenging, and you probably dread going to work in the morning.

TRUE DEVELOPMENT

Traditional career paths generally produce narrow and limited specialists. Experience paths that lead to general management and leadership are in reality a zigzag of challenges that have little to do with job titles. They are by their nature predictable only in the sense that we know the enduring challenges or experiences that create the conditions for growth. This year's dead-end assignment may be tomorrow's golden goose if the answers to the questions below are yes.

1. Am I missing significant skills?
2. Will my performance in this role make an obvious difference in the performance of the unit?
3. Do I get the chance to be a big fish in a small pond?
4. Will the role expose me to different types of people I have not worked with before?
5. Do important people care what happens in this role?
6. Is there something particularly adverse or contentious about this role?
7. Is there a lot of variety in what I will have to do?

The list could go on, but the core of development is always the same—variety, adversity, jobs, people, courses, and hard times that you're not quite ready for.

FOR EXPERIENCE TO MATTER

People need to master something first. Healthy branches spring from sturdy trunks. Interfering with the process of mastery makes people feel like impostors later. Fast-track, quick promotions continue to derail countless people each year. Real development involves finishing something, having your mistakes come around, and having to fix them.

People need to experience optimum variety of job challenges. Starting things and fixing things and forming strategies at an early point eventually lead to skills growth. Just like for fledgling tennis pros, development is about the small wins that become big wins later.

Development involves heat, emotions, and stakes. We endorse the Mark Twain approach: "People say if a cat wants to sit on a hot stove lid, let her. She'll learn. Now that is true, but she'll never sit on a cold one again either." Development is much more than throwing people into nasty situations and seeing who swims. The goal is to learn to perform, not simply to survive.

What you do has to make an obvious, measurable difference. People don't learn much from situations in which they couldn't influence the outcome. To learn to manage and lead, you have to manage and lead—the success or failure of something has to depend unambiguously on what you do.

That is the how and why of development. We learn most directly from the experiences we have. The more variety and the more transitions we pass through, the more the potential for learning the skills we need later to manage and lead.

12

POLARITY MANAGEMENT: ONE TOOL FOR MANAGING COMPLEXITY AND AMBIGUITY

Barry Johnson

EFFECTIVE LEADERS MANAGE COMPLEXITY AND AMBIGUITY

Through a combination of experience, intuition, and hard-earned wisdom, effective leaders have developed the ability to look within complex issues, identify opposites in tension, and capitalize on that tension. These interdependent opposites are sometimes called dilemmas or paradoxes. I call them *polarities*.

We all have a degree of ability in managing polarities. We have an implicit understanding that there are many opposites in our lives. Yet, most leaders do not have an explicit model and set of principles to both enhance their skills with these issues and to collaborate with others to intentionally manage them better.

A MULTIPURPOSE SWISS ARMY KNIFE FOR THE LEADER'S TOOLBOX

The Polarity Management map and set of principles provide a user-friendly resource for effectively addressing organizational complexity and the dilemmas within that complexity. Like a Swiss army knife, they have multiple applications in a variety of situations. For example, they have been used as a core competency in leadership development; in change efforts as a way to convert resistance to change into a resource for change; to build cross-cultural competence, both domestic and international; in mergers and acquisitions as a way to capitalize on the best of two or more cultures; as a key to integrated healthcare; in identifying corporate values, which are best seen as pairs in tension; in strategic planning; and in South Africa to assist in the ending of Apartheid. These situations have a number of things in common:

- They involve complex issues at many levels of the system.
- There are key, underlying polarities (dilemmas, paradoxes) within the difficulties.
- The "problem-solving" mindset alone is not up to the challenge these issues present.
- Identifying and intentionally managing one or more key polarities has made a big difference.

HOW IS THIS TOOL USED? TWO APPLICATION STORIES

STORY ONE: THE EXPANSIVE LEADER

While interviewing executive team members to identify current organizational issues, I was told by one executive, "Barry, if you really want to make a contribution here, I suggest you just leave as soon as possible and don't look back." I inquired as to whether there was an option B. He smiled and said, "It's nothing personal, Barry. It's what you represent. You are the most recent in a long line of people who have been invited in here by Don [the CEO] because he wanted to try out the latest fad. We keep starting one thing after another and never finish any of them. We are overwhelmed and frustrated with unfinished projects all over the place. So, you are a part of the problem.

"If you are serious about helping us out, I can think of one thing that would really help. Get Don to be more focused and provide some clear direction. We need to choose a few projects and make sure they are completed. Then people wouldn't be so overwhelmed and would have a sense of completion and accomplishment. Can you help us get Don to do that?"

Don had asked me to help apply Polarity Management to a few key issues within the company. I used this complaint to explain Polarity Management to the three executive team members who had raised it. On a flip chart, I summarized the issue of Don by drawing a simple model. (See Figure 12.1.) The executives wanted my help moving Don from A, which was seen as the problem, to B, which was their solution. Don would then become a more effective leader.

Looking at Figure 12.1, it is obvious that an organization with the problems illustrated in A would benefit from moving

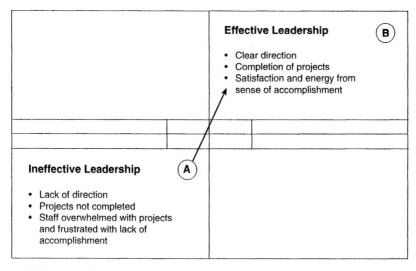

FIGURE 12.1 The expansive leader (problem-solution map).

to the solutions found in B. This is an understandable change strategy, which is based on a problem-solving mindset using *gap analysis*. First, you describe the present state in negative terms and declare it the problem = A. Then, you describe an improved future state in positive terms and call it the solution = B. Finally, you decide on a strategy to bridge the gap between A and B, which is symbolized by the arrow.

Looking at the model on the flip chart, the executives agreed that the model summarized their statement of the issue. I explained that this situation was a good example of a polarity to manage rather than a problem to solve. If the polarity were to be treated like a problem, with B as the solution, Don would resist efforts to move him to area B. Even if they could get Don to agree to go to area B, he wouldn't go there.

They looked surprised. "Who have you been talking to?" they asked. I told them just the three of them. One of the executives said, "You just described exactly what happened two years ago. We had a meeting with Don to tell him our frustrations with the lack of direction, too many uncompleted projects, and our need for direction and completion. He agreed to move to B, but we haven't moved an inch in that direction."

I told them that from a polarity perspective, it was quite predictable. The problem with the model they were using was not that it lacked accuracy. It was accurate. If you have a lack of direction, you need direction. If projects aren't completed, you need to complete them. The limit of the model was that it was incomplete. It was based on the assumption that this was a problem to solve when it is actually a polarity (dilemma, paradox) to manage.

Figure 12.2 is a polarity map. It is the mental model I drew as I heard the executives' previous attempt with Don.

The underlying tension between the poles is described in Figure 12.2 as Being Expansive (E) and Being Focused (F). Don liked being expansive, but his executives wanted him to be focused. Don would not go to the upside of Being Focused (B) because he strongly valued the upside of Being Expansive (C). He liked being flexible and innovative, and he enjoyed exploring new ideas and opportunities. The stronger his value for the upside of Being Expansive (C), the stronger was his fear of the

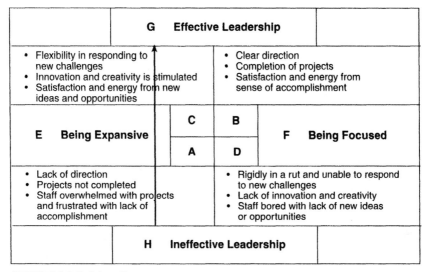

FIGURE 12.2 Polarity Management map.

downside of Being Focused (D). He avoided falling into a rut in which a lack of innovation and creativity lead to boredom for himself and his staff.

Notice that Effective Leadership (G) moved from area B, as in Figure 12.1, to the top of Figure 12.2. The arrow pointing to it separates the two halves of the polarity map. The goal is not to get Don to area B as the solution. The goal is to be at the upside of Being Expansive *and* at the upside of Being Focused, which move in combination toward Effective Leadership. Also, Ineffective Leadership (H) moved from area A, as in Figure 12.1, to the bottom of the polarity map. This indicates that there are two ways, in this example, to become an ineffective leader—overconcentrate either on Being Expansive or on Being Focused.

Once the executives saw the larger picture and began to understand the dynamics of how polarities work, it changed the whole conversation and approach to addressing their concerns with Don. Paradoxically, if you want more focus, you have to embrace the benefits of being expansive and be clear that you are not rejecting expansiveness. The shared challenge is to get the upside of both over time. That is what it means to manage a polarity well.

STORY TWO: THE MULTINATIONAL WITH A SILO PROBLEM

The part/whole polarity is common. I have worked with it often, as have all leaders, though they may not have called it a polarity. For example, a multinational company was very plant-centered and proud of it. In this context, each plant represents a part in the part/whole polarity. Corporate, with its efforts to integrate and coordinate all the parts, represents the whole. Because of the strong organizational value for the uniqueness of each plant and the country and culture in which it was located, they promoted plant-based freedom, initiative, and creativity.

Predictably, the organization's plants were in the downside of "focus" all over the world. The red-flag indicators pointing to the downside of the part pole were too much inventory ($12 million) and the 18-month timeframe to purge outdated products.

Everyone at the company had a basic understanding of polarity management. They brought one person from each of their plants to a one-day meeting. At that meeting, each person filled out a polarity map and wrote out action steps. Then, they took the maps back to their plants.

They did not waste time or increase resistance to needed changes by implying that this was a problem to solve and the solution was to stop acting like silos and start acting like an integrated team. Instead, they regarded it as an out-of-balance polarity to manage. They understood that they needed to figure out (1) how to get the polarity back in balance, and (2) how to sustain the balance over time in order to minimize either downside.

As a result of this effort, inventory went from $12 million to less than $1 million and holding 6 years later. Also, the purge rate went from 18 months to a few weeks and holding 6 years later. This is an example of how a few people and a little time can produce sustainable results when everyone has a basic understanding of polarity management.

If an issue is seen as a problem to solve, it will become a power struggle between the advocates of each pole, and the organization will lose twice in the process: (1) It loses by expending tremendous energy to "win" in the political power struggle between the two groups, and (2) it loses again when one side wins, because the organization is set up to experience, over time, the downside results of the winner's preferred pole. If you have a polarity to manage, it is either win/win or lose, because neither pole is sustainable without the other.

The map in Figure 12.3 shows some of the generic upsides and downsides of the part/whole polarity used by the multinational. It also includes the action steps outline that helps manage a polarity effectively over time.

POLARITY MANAGEMENT—A SUMMARY
INTRODUCTION

As with all other polarities, the generic part and whole polarity is very scalable. The parts could be individuals on a team, and the whole would be the team. The parts could be diverse ethnic and racial groups within the larger community as a whole. Regardless of the size of system or the complexity of the issues, it is helpful to distinguish, within the complexity, which are the key polarities to manage and how we can be intentional about managing them better.

If they are polarities going in, there are a number of things we know:

- They are not going away.
- They will not be solved in any final sense. The best we can do, which is a terrific opportunity, is to capitalize on the inherent tensions between the poles in a way that elevates and sustains the whole system.
- If they are treated as a problem to solve, with the solution being the upside of one pole, either solution will generate its own resistance.
- Both sides will see themselves as attempting to save the company from the other—and they will be half right.
- No matter which side wins in the power struggle between equally valid opposing views, the organization will lose twice.

How to Gain/Maintain Positive Results	Effective, High-Performing System	How to Gain/Maintain Positive Results
1. 2. 3. 4. When, who? By date or frequency 1. 2. 3. 4.	Parts want to maximize their functioning as a part. They want the freedom to celebrate their uniqueness, take initiative, and express their creativity as a part. ←	Those supporting the whole want to maximize the functioning of the whole. They want accountability to the whole, equality of the parts, and to celebrate the connectedness of the parts by promoting integration and synergy among the parts in the name of the whole.
		1. 2. 3. 4. When, who? By date or frequency 1. 2. 3. 4.

	Individual Plants	Global Organization	
Red Flag Indicators	**Parts**	**Whole**	**Red Flag Indicators**
$12-million inventory 18-month purge rate Who will know? What will they do?	Over-focus on the parts undermines the functioning of the whole; freedom leads to excess competition, isolation, inequality, resentment, and a loss of synergy among the parts. This is often called the *silo effect*.	Over-focus on the whole undermines the functioning of the parts; loss of freedom, creativity, and initiative by the parts along with excess conformity and bureaucracy. This is often called *group think*.	Who will know? What will they do?

Ineffective, Low-Performing System

FIGURE 12.3 Part/whole polarity.

■ If both sides can see it as a polarity to manage and intentionally create a map and action steps to manage it well, this organization, over time, will outperform those organizations that treat this as a problem to solve—every time. It's not even a fair contest.

COMPETITIVE ADVANTAGE

Research shows that there is significant competitive advantage for organizations that can both solve problems and manage polarities. Organizations that tap the power of polarities outperform those that don't. Three examples are shared below.

1. In *Managing on the Edge*, Richard Tanner Pascale studied the 43 companies identified in *In Search of Excellence* 5 years after the original research. He discovered that 14 companies retained their "Excellent" rating and 29 did not. The key factor that distinguished the 14 from the 29 was that they managed seven polarities better. He calls it "managing contention."

2. In *Built to Last*, Collins and Porras call it, "The Genius of the 'AND'." This was a central distinction between the 18 "Silver" companies that outperformed the stock market for the period from 1926 to 1990 by a factor of 2 and the 18 "Gold" companies that outperformed the stock market during that same period by a factor of 15! The Gold companies tapped the power of polarities = The Genius of the AND.

3. In *Charting the Corporate Mind*, Charles Hampden-Turner calls it, "re-solution of dilemmas." His research shows that organizations that effectively manage key organizational dilemmas have better bottom-line performance than those not managing the same dilemmas well.

THIS PHENOMENA IS EVERYWHERE

The phenomenon of interdependent opposites (dilemma, paradox, polarity) has been written about in philosophy and religion for over 4,000 years. It is a central reality in all of life and all human systems. However, only within the last 20 years has it been explicitly identified by business and industry as an important dimension that can give a competitive advantage.

It does much more than that. Life itself, both figuratively and literally, emerges out of the synergy between opposites. We are created male and female, and our uniqueness as men and women must be combined through sperm and egg to create new life. Even in cloning there is a cell differentiation between muscle cells, bone cells, and so on. We are made up of unique parts that serve the whole and sustain life.

Atoms and our solar system are sustained by managing the tension between tight and loose. Electrons and planets circle the center with enough speed to keep from being pulled into the center and collapsing the system into itself (too tight). However, they can't go too fast or they will escape the attraction of the core and end the system's existence in its historical state.

In our brains, we have two hemispheres with interdependent functioning.

In our organizations, we are constantly managing the inherent tension between centralization and decentralization, collaboration and competition, local culture and global culture, increasing quality and reducing cost, change and stability, personal life and work priorities, employee interests and company interests, and mission and margin.

As leaders we need to use our heads and our hearts. We need to show all people respect as human beings, regardless of performance, and we need to respect good performance. We need to listen and talk. We need to manage and to lead. This list could go on, but you get the idea.

It is not a question of whether or not there are polarities in your personal and organizational life. Polarities are everywhere: They have existed since the beginning of time. Knowing this, the questions we should ask are, How we can learn to see polarities more clearly? And, how can we tap the wonderful potential within key polarities to enhance our lives rather than allow the inherent tension between the poles to become destructive?

MORE THAN ONE MODEL

There is a host of bright, compassionate people who have been doing some creative thinking about this phenomenon of interdependent opposites. Our experiences have led to different models. However, our common desire is to create more effective organizations. And it goes beyond effective organizations to our quality of life and our relationships as nations and unique groups within nations.

Below are a few of those helping us understand this phenomenon:

- Charles Hampden-Turner has many books on this subject. His most recent, with Fons Trompenaars, looks at cross-cultural issues: *Building Cross-Cultural Competence, How to Create Wealth From Conflicting Values.*
- Prasad Kaipa has created a pyramid, a tetrahedron composed of four equilateral triangles, which combines several polarities. I call it a *multarity* model. Find out more about this rich model through his Web site: *http://www.selfcorp.com.*
- Peter Koestenbaum has created the Leadership Diamond, which is a multarity of four. All combinations of the points of the diamond are polarities. His book is titled *Leadership, The Inner Side of Greatness.*
- Ken Wilber, in *A Brief History of Everything,* has synthesized the scientific and the spiritual, which includes the combining of two polarities: (1) interior and exterior, and (2) individual and collective.

SUMMARY

Polarities are everywhere. You have been dealing and will continue to deal with them. The question is, How well will you deal with them? Polarity Management is one user-friendly model and set of principles to help you

1. Distinguish between problems you can solve with traditional problem-solving skills and polarities (dilemmas, paradoxes) that require an alternative approach.
2. Be intentional about managing these polarities effectively over time, by understanding and applying a model and set of principles that applies to all polarities.

Much time is wasted and tension invoked in power struggles and ineffective problem-solving when appropriate mapping of polarities more clearly presents the issues to be managed. Polarity Management is more than one more passing fad of management gurus; it is a path to perception, understanding, communication, and a more efficient organization.

13 FACING THE PARADOXES OF LEADERSHIP: EIGHT RULES

Peter Koestenbaum

A paradox, or polarity, consists of two conflicting paths of action that do not have a single solution. They both make good sense but are incompatible. These are typical situations of life and business. "I love to play golf, but I need to make a living" is a simple but not uncommon dilemma.

EXPERIENCE LIFE AS PARADOX

When you experience and interpret life as a series of paradoxes, you are in control. You are a manager and your signature project is not progressing with the speed and success you desperately want. How can you reenergize it to "rev up" the passion and expand the creativity for innovative strategies? Best is to see this not as a linear but as a paradoxical assignment. On the one hand, you push hard to increase the energy and spur unremittingly to act smarter. On the other, you are tempted to give up—for to continue the struggle is just too much trouble. Let it be!

Now that you have a paradox to work with, you apply the principles below. The first is to explore in greater depth the truth and the value of both sides of the dilemma. It is not only that you are drawn to succeed; you are also drawn to peace and quiet, to serenity and decompression.

Which will it be?

Do Not Rationalize
but Feel the Pain

Just as there is pain in truth, so there is truth in pain. In Argyris' well-known exercise, the "right-hand column" might say, "I can take it like a 'man,' like an adult. I am always positive, affirming." Here is the rationalization.

The left-hand column might contain, "I am scared to death. I don't know what to do. I feel like crying." Here is the pain.

Only as you probe the depths of the paradox will it reveal its healing power.

Polarities Need Each Other

Polarities require each other to make sense. We know light because of darkness. We know life because of death. And we know we are awake only because we sleep. Reflect on that. In business, the concept of the individual does not make sense if not contrasted with the reality of teams. Conversely, organizations cannot be comprehended but for knowing they are made up of individuals.

Stability is not noticed if there is no change for contrast. Nor can we spot change except for an underlying reality that remains constant.

Forcing a choice in a polarity is to try clapping with one hand.

ALTERNATION BEATS PRIORITIZING

You look for danger signals to detect polarities that are becoming excessive. Too much concern with short term creates problems with investors looking for growth. Then it's time to think long term. When quarterly returns begin to slide, it's time to reassess grand strategy to fix the problem. Catching excesses early is good prophylaxis against polarity pathology. Prioritizing is difficult; alternating, as in recreation, is easy.

THERE IS POWER IN DIALOGUE

Communication is not two bunkers with short-wave radio stations, but a solar system with two suns. Dialogue creates a common field of awareness with an emotional alliance, a sense of community, and a personal bond—all of which can supersede individual differences and alienating confrontations. Dialogue can settle intractable conflicts.

PARADOXES PROVOKE THE MIND TO BREAKTHROUGHS

Forcing the mind to confront an apparently insurmountable dilemma, such as short term versus long term, challenges it to "extrude," or give birth to, a new form, a neonate, that has these polarized antecedents as parents. Often, the breakthrough is no more than to be happily reconciled with the demand to work harder and smarter, ratchet up the level of commitment, and literally stop worrying about the conflicts. It's not unlike learning to play the piano with two hands rather than just one. It requires a decision, a snap in the mind, to accept that your two hands playing different melodies can actually perform at the same time. Learning how to swim, drive, fly, and skydive is, for the uninitiated, absolutely impossible. Yet once you make up your mind that it can be done, voilá, you can actually accomplish it!

You solve a paradox with a dimensional change in attitude and commitment, with a transition from negative to positive evaluation, and lethargy to energy—and not just in prioritizing. That is a decision. And it is a breakthrough!

EACH CHOICE CHANGES YOUR ENVIRONMENT

Each decision changes your world—for the world responds. You must make a decision in order to understand what the next decision is to be. This is the nature of competitive games, from soccer to chess. Each time you make a choice, you enter a new scenario. Your next step is determined by this new scenario—and not by the last scenario. This simple and obvious insight can make it more manageable for you to make difficult decisions.

Given a paradox, such as your daughter's ballet performance as opposed to the decisive negotiation on the hostile takeover with which your company is threatened, you worry about making the wrong decision. But the consequences of decisions are not written in stone, for you keep making new, subsequent, decisions. Each functions as a new entry into a spreadsheet. One choice—and your whole universe changes. You start anew with each decision. This is unsettling as well as reassuring, for whereas you get few definitive answers, you nevertheless are permanently in control. With enough experience and sufficient self-confidence, you can rescue yourself and get value out of virtually any scenario that your prior choices have brought about. Your worries are now under control. Here, indeed, practice makes perfect.

PRACTICE DEMOCRACY

Resolution of paradox lies in the democratic personality structure and the democratic institutions of society. These value diversity and change it to inclusion, from negative to positive.

At the center of our political thinking is the commitment to democracy. We deal with polarity not with a public massacre but with freedom of speech. Democracy is a breakthrough transformation on how people experience contradictions and how they respond to them. Thoreau said it well: "The fate of the country...does not depend on what kind of paper you drop into the ballot box once a year, but on what kind of man you drop from your chamber into the street every morning."

CONCLUSION

These eight rules in themselves can transform employees and managers from dealing with otherwise paralyzing paradoxes and polarities to performing in a way that leads to progress, productivity, and competitive advantage.

How much is that worth to a business and an organization?

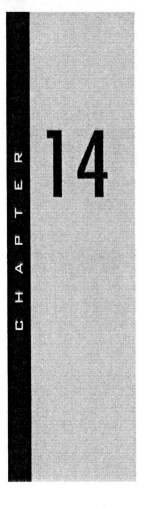

HUMAN INFLUENCE

14

Charles E. Dwyer

G etting people to do what we want them to do is often considered the most important and challenging of management tasks. In this article I attempt to summarize what I believe to be the essential elements in any successful approach to human influence.

VALUES

I believe we each act as we do in an attempt to take care of what is important to each of us, to serve our values. While intrinsic values (those things that we value for their own sake) vary from culture to culture, a list of contemporary intrinsic values for Americans includes security (physical, material, and emotional), autonomy, acceptance and approval by a relevant reference group, recognition, praise, gratitude and thanks, success and achievement, respect, status and esteem in the eyes of others, fun, and self-esteem. While many of these values are shared by other cultures, it is always a good idea to learn the value similarities and differences when dealing with someone from another culture. It is too easy, and often a mistake, to assume that others value what you do. If you are not appealing to a person's values, then you are not influencing that person.

People also act in order to gain *instrumental value*—those things that are valued as a means to the service of an intrinsic value. Money is often regarded as the chief instrumental value, because it is perceived as a means to the satisfaction and protection of so many of one's intrinsic values. But, anything valued intrinsically or instrumentally is a potential source of human influence.

Frequently, people engage in behavior in order to protect against a loss in value satisfaction. Therefore, fear, coercion, intimidation, and threat can also be effective in influencing others. But, there are a number of cautions to be observed when using such negative approaches to human influence. These are dealt with below.

BEHAVIOR

When attempting to influence, it is probably best to focus on the concrete, clear, unambiguous, specific, observable behavior (or measurable performance) that you want from another. We tend to frame what we want from others in terms of attitudes, dispositions, personality, characteristics, and quality of relationships. "He has an attitude," "She has a personality problem," "He has a lousy disposition," and "She is in a bad mood," are all too familiar ways of talking about people. We say that we are looking for respect, recognition, support, cooperation, loyalty, and the like. These are less than optimal ways of thinking and talking about what we want or do not want from others. If you could limit your descriptions of what you want from others in terms of observable behavior or measurable performance, your effectiveness with others would improve markedly. You would know precisely what you wanted and so would the target of your influence.

People often do not do what we want them to because they do not know what we want them to do, and they do not know because we use vague descriptors. I think the reasons we use those attitudinal words and phrases (particularly the negative ones) are, at least in part, because it is easy to label people in this way; it bonds us with our friends (anyone who dislikes him for any reason can identify with the broad, vague, "He has an attitude."), and it confirms our beliefs and justifies our negative feelings about the person and makes us feel superior. For these reasons, it is not easy to give up these automatic, comforting habits of thought, feeling, and action. It is costly to do so, since we are foregoing the value satisfactions that come from drawing such (negative) psychological portraits of others.

CHANGING SELF

What is clearly suggested here is that if you wish to become considerably more effective with others, you will be required to change yourself in ways that will probably make you uncomfortable. All that each of us has available to us in influencing others is our own behavior. This means that changing one's own patterns of behavior is the first task toward increased effectiveness. Likewise, changing one's own behavior requires changing both the way one thinks as well as how one feels, since these three (thoughts, feelings, and behaviors) are inextricably linked. Many people talk of changing the world, few of changing themselves. While I will suggest what some of these changes are and how to go about producing them, the change itself is up to you.

We now know that imaginative rehearsal of new ways of thinking, feeling, and behaving can enable one to override old, automatic responses. One deeply imbedded program that inhibits effectiveness in most people is the socialized practice of rationalizing about issues of human influence. In defense of our egos we have been taught to scapegoat, blame, and externalize when people fail to do what we want them to do or when they do things we do not want them to do. This results in fewer attempts at influence (we rationalize instead), in less persistence in dealing with people, and it creates a psychological barrier between them and us as we attribute negative characteristics to them, such as the familiar "we versus them" phenomenon.

You can override such automatic belief programs by rehearsing an alternative response. The one that I teach people is, *Never expect anyone to engage in a behavior that serves your values, unless you give that person adequate reason to do so.* This moves you away from rationalization, toward 100 percent responsibility for your own effectiveness, and toward action. And, the only adequate reason you can give people for changing their current behavior is their perception that the new behavior is better than their current behavior in the service of their values.

PERCEPTION AND ANTICIPATION

People, while attempting to serve their values, are not necessarily successful. People do not, in fact, do what serves their values. They do what they perceive will serve their values. First, this means that there is always a time gap between the brain's consideration of a behavior and the behavior itself. Second, the processing that takes place in this time period, I refer to as perception. The process is usually subconscious rather than conscious but is nonetheless subject to influence. It is in that perceptual process that all influence takes place. That is what advertising, selling, marketing, merchandising, politics, religion, parenting, spousing, and negotiation and conflict management are all about. Advertisers, if successful do not change your intrinsic values; rather, they change your perception of what behavior on your part is in the best interests of your values, (i.e., they reshape your instrumental values). You have been successfully shaping those perceptions in others since you first cried and managed to get someone to feed you.

Perceptions are personal, subjective, idiosyncratic, fragile, and infinitely malleable states. These characteristics mean that influence can be costly and fragile, but potentially unlimited and permanent. As noted above, it may well be costly and risky, particularly to your ego, to do what is necessary to shape others' perceptions. But on the other hand, because of the malleable nature of perceptions, your power with people is potentially unlimited and permanent.

THE MOSAIC

When approaching someone with the intent of influence, we, of necessity, create a mosaic. By this, I merely mean that there are a great many choices available to us in how we approach the person, including timing, tone, language, mode of communication, gestures, direct or indirect approaches, and so on. It is in the selection of these options that the power of the mosaic is determined. But most of the time we do not make use of the huge set of options available. Instead, we go by "default" to the one with which we are most familiar, or which is easiest, safest, or most comfortable. These are rarely the options that maximize our effectiveness. For example, approaching someone indirectly through others is often the most powerful option, but few Americans use the indirect approach to influence. They have been socialized to prefer the direct approach and to disregard the indirect. Likewise, we have all learned the importance of timing and reading context in attempting to influence someone. But, often overly impressed with the "power" of our own idea, we believe that the idea itself will be sufficient for influence, and thereby ignore timing and context.

FILTERS AND DATA FRAGMENTS

Each of us, including those we wish to influence, is flooded on a daily basis with 2,000 to 3,000 messages trying to influence us. Every ad, every commercial, every piece of mail at home and work, every phone call, email, fax, voicemail, every meeting, every informal encounter, every trip to the mall or the supermarket is jammed with messages trying to influence us. The human consciousness cannot possibly process all of these thousands of messages vying for our attention. And so, we have filters, quick, rough, automatic filters, to keep most of those messages out of our consciousness.

For example, each day when you process your mail, you use a very sophisticated filtration mechanism and toss most of your mail into the trash, unopened. You pick up a few "data-fragments" of information, such as the return address, how it is addressed to you, the postage, and make an instant decision whether or not to give it further consideration. We do this all day long with multiple, complex, and dynamic filtration systems. Those who have succeeded in influencing us have packaged their ideas in ways that gets through our filters.

It is highly likely that you have, on occasion, thrown out the "good" mail with the "bad." Because we must rely on these fragments of information for our decision making, our filters are not perfect. Therefore, independent of the quality of your idea, independent of your altruistic intentions, independent of the actual value you are offering another, if you do not package your idea effectively, you are in effect in the other's mind, junk mail.

LANGUAGE

In the majority of situations, of all of the fragments we use in creating our mosaic, language is by far the most critical. Frequently in our attempts to influence (primarily because of technology), language is the only category of fragments available to us. And words are extremely fragile vessels in the work of constructing appropriate perceptions in the minds of others.

So, what language should we use? While there are many well-researched answers to that question, I will list a few of the more powerful ones. The first is obvious but, in my experience, rarely used. When attempting to influence someone, use a few of their words, their favorite ways of expressing key ideas, their pet expressions. They have an affection for their words. They already have a place neurologically carved out in their brains for their words.

Also, contrary to your English teacher's advice, use synonyms and paraphrases in expressing your key ideas and when describing the behavior or performance you want. Since you do not know in advance which words a person will respond most positively to, it is best to use several, thereby multiplying your chances of success.

Use stories that put flesh and blood on the bones of your ideas. We know that much decision making is done at a subconscious level and involves both emotion and imagination. These can be brought into play by short, relevant stories. Autobiographical stories, relevant to the desired behavior, can build credibility and trust with those you wish to influence. These are just a few of the language-based tools that can increase the likelihood of compliance with a request.

VALUES, PERCEPTIONS, AND BEHAVIOR

I maintain that all behavior, with very minor exceptions, is a function of an individual's perception of the relationship of the behavior to that person's values; that is, we do those things, at any given point in time, that we perceive will best serve our values overall. I use this simple concept to formulate a model of the human information process that leads to decisions about which behavior to engage in. The model has five steps. While I do not argue that this is an invariable sequence of steps, I do believe it represents a reasonable approximation of the decision calculus human beings use in their decision making. You can use it to probe for ways to frame your behavior so as to elicit the behavior or performance you want from others.

1. Capability: Can the person perform the behavior?
   ■ Does the person have *knowledge* of exactly what the behavior is?

- Does the person have the minimum *competence* to engage in the behavior?
- Does the person have the minimum *self-confidence* necessary to engage in the behavior?

How can you increase each of these, if need be?

2. What does the person perceive as the *potential value satisfaction* he or she may receive by engaging in the behavior, and how can you increase that perceived value satisfaction?
3. What does the person perceive as the probability of value satisfaction (to what extent does the person believe that he or she will experience the value satisfaction if he or she engages in the behavior?) How can you increase that perceived probability?
4. What is the person's perception of the costs (e.g., lost time, energy, or lost opportunity) of engaging in the behavior? How can you reduce those perceived costs?
5. What does the person perceive to be the risks to him or her of engaging in the behavior? How can you reduce those perceived risks?

PROBLEMS WITH THE NEGATIVE APPROACH

The above is the positive approach to influence. I noted earlier that a person can also be influenced by the negative approach: having the perception of potential loss of value satisfaction if he or she fails to engage in a particular behavior. The practical problem with the negative approach (leaving possible moral issues aside) is that people do not like it used on them and have developed coping mechanisms when they perceive they are faced with it. These include attempting to escape your influence, giving as little of the desired behavior or performance as possible, and seeking to reinstate their self-esteem and autonomy by threatening the values of the one they perceived threatened theirs (i.e., revenge). In general, you should try to avoid the use of the negative approach if at all possible, even though at times it may appear tempting.

APPLICATION OF THE FIVE-STEP MODEL

There are six situations in which you can apply and practice this model of human information processing:

1. When you fail and, instead of rationalizing, you want to learn from your failure;
2. When you are planning to influence someone (or a group);
3. When you meet resistance but are willing to persist;
4. When you succeed in influencing someone after overcoming objections;
5. When someone succeeds in influencing you; and
6. When you see successful influence of which you are only an observer.

DEALING WITH GROUPS

Often we are required to influence in a group, team, task force, or committee. When doing this, I still look at it as influencing individuals and use the same model but with some adaptations in application. When dealing with a group, try to identify those individuals who are closest to the threshold of the behavior you want. Focus on the informal leaders in the group. As you bring them across, others will follow. Offer multiple value satisfactions and protections against perceived costs and risks, knowing different people will respond to various combinations offered.

In summary, remember that most of what is powerful in influencing people is costly and risky to you, particularly in terms of ego needs. You can have as much power with people as you are willing to pay for!

MAKING THE GRADE: NEW LEADERSHIP SKILLS

15 HELP THEM GROW OR WATCH THEM GO: A DEVELOPMENT EDGE GIVES RETENTION RESULTS

Beverly L. Kaye

Today's business world is characterized by globalization, increasing competition, an ever-accelerating pace of change, an overabundance of information, a never-ending technology revolution, a growing number of mergers and acquisitions, and a declining talent pool. In this chaotic world, a business can only *survive* if it can attract the "best and the brightest" to its workforce. It can only *thrive* if it continues to grow and develop, and thus retain the talents of its workforce. This new business reality demands that managers, not the human resource department, take responsibility for attracting, developing, and retaining the talent in their organizations. Managerial success is now inextricably linked to talent management. So, how do you manage talent?

When studies are conducted to find out what employees look for in a job, or what they want from their work, or what would keep them at their current organizations, something having to do with their *careers* seems to pop out before the expected answers of dollars, perks, or benefits. Still, organizations look primarily at the latter as a motivator or a reason for people to stay. Far too many managers throw up their hands and say that if there are no direct paths to promotions available, with the commensurate dollars, perks, and benefits, there isn't much they can do to support the careers of their people. We think there is another way to look at this.

Our research in career development over the last 20 years has shown us that there is something managers *can do,* and *doing it* can make a huge difference. What employees say they really want, vis à vis their careers, is a relationship with their managers whereby they can have open, honest, two-way conversations about their abilities, interests, and options. They want their managers to listen to their perspectives, offer their points of view, and provide encouragement and support. They don't expect their managers to have all the answers, but they really want to have the dialogue.

A POP QUIZ

As a manager, if you are wondering where to start, here's an idea. Take a few minutes to complete the following short assessment. Think about your current relationship with your direct reports and the degree to which you do the behaviors listed in each box. Give yourself points in the space provided under each box: 1 point if you are not sure, 2 points if you feel you do this but realize you could definitely improve, and 3 points if you feel you do this naturally and think you're pretty good at it.

The points you gave yourself on this assessment provide you with a quick indicator of your use of, and hence your comfort level with, each of five "managerial musts" or skills we have found are fundamental to the process of career develop-

EXCERCISE 15.1 Management Self-Assessment

Scale: 1 = not sure   2 = needs improvement   3 = better than most

1. Help people identify their marketable competencies and skills	2. Assist people in indentifying the types of work they find most interesting	3. Help people discover what they find challenging in their current positions
# of points _____	# of points _____	# of points _____
4. Provide people with regular feedback on their job performance	5. Explain your criteria for evaluating the quality of people's work	6. Discuss with people their reputation in other parts of the organization
# of points _____	# of points _____	# of points _____
7. Show people how to recognize industry trends relevant to their current positions or their career plans	8. Discuss with people how the strategic aims of the organization can affect their career options	9. Identify potential obstacles to people's career paths (e.g., diminishing need for certain skills)
# of points _____	# of points _____	# of points _____
10. Help people identify a range of realistic career options and goals	11. Assist people in exploring ways to make their current jobs more interesting or rewarding	12. Show people how to link their career goals to the organization's strategic aims
# of points _____	# of points _____	# of points _____
13. Assist people as they develop detailed action plans based on their career goals	14. Arrange for people to participate in high visibility activities outside your work unit	15. Provide on-the-job work experiences to help people develop their skills
# of points _____	# of points _____	# of points _____

ment coaching. We have assigned labels, beginning with the letter L, to each of these coaching skills:

- Listen
- Level
- Look ahead
- Leverage
- Link

While each of these skills has its own unique focus and direction, they build on one another to form a comprehensive model for career development conversations and coaching between managers and their employees. Managers who want to effectively and successfully manage their talent will develop and use these coaching skills in regular career conversations with their employees. This can result in increased employee satisfaction, performance, and ultimately retention. Let's take a closer look at each of these skill sets.

LISTEN FOR EMPLOYEE'S SKILLS, INTERESTS, AND VALUES

The first three behaviors in the assessment relate to the skill of listening. To get peak performance from your employees, to help them grow and develop in a meaningful way, to maximize their potential, and to get them to want to stay, you have to really get to know them. You have to know them not just as employees, but also as individuals with unique skills, interests, values, career aspirations, and desires. If you answered "not sure" or "needs improvement," you'll want to pay special attention to the following description and suggestions.

As managers, all too often we assume that we know the skills and abilities of the people who report to us. Unfortunately, this is not always the case; as a result, valuable corporate assets, the talents of our people, are underutilized or misdirected. The more accurately you can deploy the talent on your team, the more you will be able to match a business need with an appropriate and timely response and the more likely you will be to meet or exceed your business objectives.

The concept of matching people (their skills, interests, and values) to positions (duties, responsibilities, competencies, and skill requirements) is known as *career fit*. Career fit suggests that when people "fit" with their positions, the result is increased job satisfaction, quality, productivity, morale, and a greater likelihood that they will continue to grow and develop. As a manager, how do you get the information that you need to assess career fit?

Encourage your employees to talk about themselves: their skills, interests, and values. Ask your employees questions to help them understand, clarify, and articulate their unique attributes and how these qualities contribute to the organization. Probe more deeply into their career aspirations and dreams. Challenge them to think about their potential for growth and development, and help them talk about any concerns they may have about their current position or their future career aspirations.

The toughest part of getting your people to talk is to be quiet and listen, really listen, to what they have to say. Listen without problem solving, judging, or interrupting. Listen and ask questions to make sure that you really understand what makes them "tick." Listen as if you were sitting on a jury in a high-profile case.

If you listen carefully and ask effective, clarifying questions, you will learn about them and their career fit in their current positions relative to their future career aspirations. You will build a new relationship and establish a valuable bond. You may uncover a goldmine of talents not previously recognized. From a retention perspective, your ability to listen is critical. Employees want their managers to know them as individuals, to understand their abilities, and to capitalize on them. Try the following questions:

- Which assignments have most challenged you? Least challenged you? Why?
- When you are having a really good day at work, what values, skills, and interests are present?
- What part of your education or work experience has been the most valuable to you over the years?

LEVEL ABOUT THEIR STRENGTHS AND DEVELOPMENT NEEDS

Behaviors 4, 5, and 6 in the assessment relate to the leveling skill. Leveling means giving employees honest and direct feedback regarding performance and development needs. This isn't the annual performance appraisal feedback session many companies require, in which you critique the employee's performance over the past year. This is constructive, developmental feedback, provided on a regular basis throughout the year that focuses on the employee's strengths and opportunities for growth and development in the future, in line with his or her current position and career aspirations.

As a manager, your job is to have a conversation with each of your employees to determine if they are in the right positions or if there are other positions in the organization in which their talents could be better utilized. You also need to ensure they understand and can perform the duties and responsibilities required by their positions and that you have established clear performance standards and expectations. Once you have had this conversation, you are in a position to monitor their performance and provide them with feedback on both what they are doing well and any opportunities that are available for performance improvement, growth, and development.

This conversation is a two-way street. As manager, you need to be open and honest about how employees are performing in their current positions, how they can improve, and what they need to do to achieve their career goals. Cite specific examples. Employees have a major responsibility too. Employees need to ask for feedback, not just from you as their manager, but from other managers and colleagues as well. When employees solicit feedback from multiple sources, they get a more accurate picture of who they are and how they are perceived. When employees receive feedback, they need to ask questions to ensure their understanding; they need to reflect on what is said and on the areas they know they can improve. Your feedback and the feedback of others will help employees make better career decisions and establish more realistic career goals. It will also help employees grow and develop in a meaningful way that is aligned with both their current position and their future career aspirations.

Constructive developmental feedback will help employees grow faster and smarter, while increasing retention. Our research suggests that employees often leave organizations because they have no idea how they are perceived in terms of strengths or development needs or if they are valued as key contributors. This underscores the importance of the feedback process to both the individual and the organization. Some questions you might ask to begin this conversation include

- If you asked three people in the organization to give you feedback on your greatest strength, what would they say?
- If you were to list your number one strength and number one liability, what would each be? How do you know?
- What would you say are the most critical areas I would select as essential in your current position? How would you rate yourself in these areas?

Look Ahead at Trends, Business Needs, and Company Culture

Behaviors 7, 8, and 9 in the assessment relate to the skill of looking ahead. Looking ahead means that you and your employees have to look into the future to identify emerging trends, business needs, and cultural characteristics. Looking ahead means that you and your employees have to look beyond your departmental borders, beyond your comfort zones, to identify and collect information on the larger organization as well as your industry, profession, and community. You may also need to identify relevant regional, national, or global labor market trends. You need to look for any and all information that may impact development needs or career aspirations.

Looking ahead is critical for your employees' career planning and development success. After all, if they don't know what your company's business strategy and direction is, where your industry or profession is headed, or what's happening in the labor force, how can they identify future competency and skill requirements or align their development with the business needs? If they don't know what organizational changes are underway or where the future job opportunities are, or aren't, how can they set realistic career goals? Effective career planning and development demands information. The more reliable and current the information is, the better. So, where does all of this information come from?

Because you are a manager, you frequently have access to business information that your employees don't have. If this information relates to their careers and development, share it with them or point them in the direction to get it for themselves. If you know of company sources where relevant information may be found, educate your people about them. If you know of key people who might have useful information, you should do what you can to open the doors so that your employees can gain this information directly. When your employees know in advance that tough times are ahead or that changes are coming, they can prepare contingency plans. This is far better then being caught unaware.

The important point about looking ahead is that you work *with* your employees on an ongoing basis to identify and share information that would be useful for or relevant to career planning and development. Then, you help your employees use this information to prepare realistic plans that are aligned with the business direction, and you use it to provide them with better coaching, guidance, and support. This information sharing can also help you with talent retention. Frequently, just knowing more about what the future may hold will keep employees around. On the other hand, a lack of information and the uncertainty it brings may cause them to leave for imagined "greener pastures." You might ask these questions in a look-ahead conversation:

- Have you read the organization's annual report? What new directions stand out? Does this suggest any important skill areas that you need to develop?
- Are you optimistic about the organization's future? What are the specific reasons you feel this way? Do you see new opportunities for yourself?
- What do we need to get better at? Faster at? Smarter at? What implication does this have for your career?

LEVERAGE EMPLOYEES' OPTIONS AND GOALS

Behaviors 10, 11, and 12 in the assessment refer to the skill of leveraging. Leveraging is helping your employees identify multiple, realistic options for their career growth and development. Given the rapid pace of change in today's world, it is imperative that employees have multiple options and corresponding goals and plans. When employees have multiple options, and changes occur, they can simply switch gears and move to the next logical option. Without multiple options, employees risk running into dead-ends. So, how exactly can you leverage multiple options and plans?

First, you can help your employees understand that there are at least six ways employees can move their careers along.

1. *Enrichment or growing in place*: Future career aspirations will never be achieved if employees aren't keeping their competencies and skills current or aren't performing up to the standards of their current position. In today's world, all employees must include this as an option in their plans.
2. *Lateral or moving across*: This move involves a change in job, but not necessarily a change in level of responsibility.
3. *Exploratory or looking around*: This involves searching for the answer to questions like "What else can I do?" The goal is gathering information so better decisions can be made about next steps.
4. *Realignment or moving down*: Downshifting can be an effective strategy for balancing work/life priorities. It is also a great strategy for technical employees to consider when they move into a management position and discover they aren't happy.
5. *Relocation or moving out*: Leaving the organization may be necessary when an employee cannot find career fit where they are.
6. *Vertical or moving up*: The most traditional career goal. Yet, today more than ever, it may not be everyone's first choice. Balance and time for family and outside interests

have become more important to all age groups. Vertical moves often do not afford this.

As a manager, you also need to help your employees understand the importance of written career development plans. The best development plans list specific goals for learning and growth in the current positions as well as options for the future. All of the research that has been done regarding career success factors underscores the importance of establishing written goals with corresponding actions and timing. You need to ensure that your employees' goals are aligned with your business goals at the departmental, functional, and corporate levels. Alignment ensures that both employee and employer needs are being met, and it bridges the gap between jobs and careers, providing mutual benefits. Some questions to ask at this phase include

- What are some of the career goals you're thinking about?
- Which goals seem most in sync with where the organization is going?
- Which goals will position you best for the future?

LINK EMPLOYEES TO RESOURCES

The last three behaviors, 13, 14, and 15, relate to how well you link your employees to the resources they need to move their career aspirations from vision to action. They may need information, contacts, opportunities for growth, or channels for development. It is up to you to provide the guidance, encouragement, and support they need, but, once again, you can't do it for them.

The key to effective linking is for you to understand that your employees' ongoing growth and development is good for them, good for you, and good for the company. The employees keep their skills marketable and achieve their career goals. You establish a reputation as a development-minded manager, so talented employees want to work for you, and you have the right people with the right skills to achieve your business objectives. The company has a workforce that is continuously learning, growing, and developing in alignment with its strategy and direction. Hence, it is more competitive in the marketplace.

As a manager, it is important for you to help your employees grow in their current positions. You need to work with them to find ways to increase their career fit. You also need to ensure that the assignments that you give them provide opportunities for learning. One of the best ways to do this is to ask them questions as they complete their assignments, like a debriefing session. Ask them what worked and what didn't work. Ask them what they would do the same or differently in the future. Ask them how the tasks could be streamlined. Ask them if their customers are satisfied. The point is they need to reflect on what they have done so they can learn from the experience.

Another way you can help your employees grow and develop is to craft a learning assignment with them. We like to use a three-level learning process. Level 1 is *conscious observation*. Have the employee observe an experienced person doing the job, knowing that he or she will have to do it in the future, so they are really "tuned in" to what is being done. Level 2 is *selective participation*. Have the employee complete certain portions of the job, with the experienced person by his or her side, so the employee can learn it in manageable chunks. Level 3 is *key responsibility*. At this point, the employee is taking the lead responsibility for the job, and the experienced person is just there in case he or she is needed. This is an excellent way to cross-train your employees, increase their competencies and skills, keep them engaged and challenged, and simultaneously give seasoned employees a chance to pass on their knowledge. What better way to build succession plans then to see how people do in other positions before you need to move them there?

You can also help your employees grow by introducing them to your professional network or helping others who can serve as mentors or coaches. You may also have employees who need to learn in a traditional setting, namely the classroom. Perhaps your company provides the training, or the employee may need to complete a formal degree program. In any case, your job is to connect employees to the resources they need to succeed. These questions might help you to engage in this essential part of the career conversation:

- What training programs or educational opportunities most align with your goals?
- If you could give yourself the perfect assignment, what would it be?
- Who would you like as a mentor or coach? How can I help you enlist his or her support?

DEVELOPMENT PAYS OFF

Career discussions need not take a long time, but they should be regular and frequent. No one is exempt from concerns about their future. Individuals will interpret inconsistent attention to their career development as indifference on the part of their manager. When individuals feel that the organization doesn't care, they withdraw their commitment and energy. No longer is it possible to demonstrate this interest by making decisions for others, nor is it possible to have all of the answers. Employees are not asking for decisions or answers. The skill sets described here demand that managers truly understand their employees' talents and that they challenge and channel that talent appropriately.

You are expected to build a work environment in which your team can thrive, remain competitive, and develop specialized knowledge or skills. You construct the pipeline for the flow of talent in your organization. You build the pipeline; your employees traverse it. When your people feel that you care about developing their talent, they believe the organization cares. Their commitment and energy increase and their retention increases too!

16

THE NEWEST LEADERSHIP SKILLS

Randall P. White and Philip Hodgson

E ffective leadership is finding a good fit between behavior, context, and need. There is no one right way, no all-explaining theory, but theories do matter.[1] We all have theories of how our world works. Our theories help us anticipate and explain what might happen next. If you have a theory, you must continually chip away at it to see if there's a better way or if it can be made more comprehensive or thorough. This process can be applied to leadership theory.

Historically, the most useful question we could ask was: "Where did the leader come from?" When leaders were rare

---

[1] The authors wish to thank Stuart Crainer for his help with an earlier version of this piece. This chapter is adapted from R. White and P. Hodgson, *Relax, It's Only Uncertainty: Lead the Way when the Way is Changing*, London: Pearson Education, 2001.

and unusual beasts, many of them were chosen for leadership roles because of their background. So asking where they came from told you a lot more than asking questions about their skills, behavior, or personality.

Even today, there are some frequent suppliers of leaders—certain families, universities, etc. However, it would be wrong to suggest that the assumption that leaders are born remains strong. Today, leaders can come from anywhere. Everybody feels that they could be a leader, whereas in earlier times most people felt excluded irrespective of their talent, skills, or aptitude. Today, defining leadership is a complex matter. Before, it was simple: Leadership was what leaders did.

IDENTIFYING NEW LEADERS

It is arguable whether there was a single moment when there was a dramatic shift from choosing leaders because of their background to choosing leaders because of their skills, behaviors, and competencies. However, we would identify World War II as one of the most significant turning points in the progression of leadership understanding and development. Prior to that time, there was little research or structured work done on selecting leaders for their skills and competencies.

During the World War II, competing organizations needed to rapidly identify and understand what effective leaders did and then work out how to select them. Each side had to tackle the same problem. Where do we find new commanders who don't come from the traditional sources? Each camp approached the problem in remarkably similar ways. They developed various versions of what we now would call the assessment center. They analyzed the activities, behaviors, and attributes necessary to be an effective military leader, and then sought ways of identifying people who had those skills or that potential. Assessment techniques like the paper-and-pencil test, the psychological inventory, the structured interview, and so on were all developed around this time. The War Office Selection Board (WOSB) in the United Kingdom and the Office of Strategic Services (OSS) in the United States were early examples of the assessment center technology, which would go on to have a major influence.

THE TASK AND THE PEOPLE

After World War II, the researchers who had done this work went into industry or back into university psychology departments. What emerged became classically quoted cases. Scientists reported that the behavior of leaders could be categorized on a map. The leaders' behavior was composed of two main aspects: concern for the task and concern for the people who did the task.

There followed a series of debates about whether effective leaders were chiefly concerned with the task or the people. Eventually, it was identified that the situation the leader was trying to handle was the key influencer in the style and behavior that the leader should adopt. How then to identify the situation?

One popular method, situational leadership, described the development of the follower. The follower, who knew little on entry into the organization (or job), would need clear structure and instructions to perform well. The leader would take full responsibility for the task and would give clear instruction to the follower so that the follower could achieve useful output.

COMMAND AND CONTROL

This is command-and-control leadership. The effective leader can supervise his or her followers, because the leader knows at least as much about the task as the follower does. Because the leader knows a lot about the tasks, he or she can structure, support, coach, or delegate to followers appropriately. It has to be said that many managers, while aware of the need to change their style according to the followers' need, actually have strong preference for a particular style and often tend to use that one style inappropriately. This can lead to all kinds of problems and issues as followers receive too much or too little structure, for instance.

The command-and-control style can be a very effective way of thinking about leadership when known tasks are being done by people who know how to do them. Many consulting firms and partnerships employing specialists use this type of leadership because it is an information-based approach. The senior partner knows more than the junior partner, and therefore applies that knowledge to guide the junior. At the time when these ideas were first being discussed (in the 1970s), there was little distinction made between management and leadership. The words were for most purposes interchangeable. Now we notice that many people describe this type of leadership behavior as management.

I HAVE A DREAM...

What do you do if you don't know how to achieve your goal? What happens if you want to attain a dream? You have a vision. However, visions don't work unless the people who have to find their way to the vision are empowered to take the actions necessary to reach the vision without continually needing to refer back to their leader.

Compared with command-and-control leadership, empowering leadership was designed for a different context, offered different kinds of outcomes, and required very different behavior. People who had grown up with command-and-control leadership continued to expect predictability, accuracy, and the dominance of knowledge and experience. They were frequently disappointed. The true visionary leader allows followers to be highly empowered so that they have the flexibility to take the actions necessary to achieve the vision. Many leaders from the previous era were unwilling to give up their own power.

So, the two main forms of leadership used and understood in organizations are the command-and-control approach and the empowerment and visionary approach. Sadly, when we look around many organizations, what we find is empowerment words and control actions. This results in the worst of both worlds. We want people to be imaginative, risk-taking, and creative but still to return their project on time, and on budget. Organizations need to more clearly recognize which of these two leadership styles is more appropriate to which context. Both are fine in the right context. Both will work very badly in the wrong context.

Unfortunately, there is an emotional difficulty to be overcome. For the most part, people find the notion of being visionary leaders more attractive than being controlling managers. Hence, the command-and-control approach tends to have a poorer image than that of the empowering and visionary leader. However, both methods work well in their own contexts.

LEARNING LEADERSHIP

What do you do if you don't have a vision? After Lou Gerstner took over IBM in 1993, he observed: "The last thing IBM needs now is a vision." He knew that the company had a huge amount of talent, but he didn't really know what the talent was capable of or what opportunities there really were. What happens if you aren't ready for vision yet? What happens if, like Jeff Bezos when starting up Amazon.com, you really don't know what could be sold on the Internet? Could you have a clear vision of the future?

In such cases, people in leadership roles face huge levels of inherent ambiguity. They feel uncertain and stressed. However, they move towards the uncertainty—not away from it. There is a third style of leadership emerging—that of learning leadership—and its defining feature will be leaders who head towards uncertainty and ambiguity.

The visionary leader is normally quite clear and quite certain about what the vision should be. There is much uncertainty in interpreting the vision of the leader, but this now becomes a communication issue, not a direction issue. The visionary leader says to the followers, "Let's work together on how to make my vision happen." The leader in ambiguity says,

"Let's work together on how we can learn what the vision should be."

In our 1996 book *The Future of Leadership*, we defined the leader's role as "Identifying productive areas of uncertainty and confusion and leading the organization into those areas to gain competitive or other kinds of advantage." This is the situation in which many of today's executives find themselves. Many of their instincts are to avoid ambiguity and uncertainty, to install certainty by making clear and firm statements. The problem is that today's organizational world is in such a volatile state that it is much harder to accurately make clear and firm statements than it was 20 years ago.

The pressures on this new kind of leader is immense. First, to what extent can they really admit to their followers that they don't know? An equally tough requirement for learning leaders is to recognize that learning from their mistakes needs to be at least as public as learning from their successes. Everyone in the organization has to engage in continuous learning, and some of that learning may challenge existing concepts and require genuinely original solutions. Here the leader's job is to take the organization toward things it doesn't know in search of fruitful new ideas and original learning.

If you are a learning leader, then you want to spend much of your and your organization's time doing things that are difficult to learn but are of high value to the organization. The only thing that guarantees your success is the quality of learning that your organization can muster. Because you don't know how to do the things that you will come across, you must learn rapidly under tough conditions to survive and prosper. It is certainly not for everyone! But, people who operate at this level will describe it as thrilling, exciting, and challenging.

Do you want to test how much your organization is using the third model of leadership? Try this. Ask your people to name five important products, services, and production techniques now taken for granted, but which a previous generation of managers would not have known. Now list five trends in products, services, and production techniques that the next generation will take for granted but which you can hardly fathom. The pathway to installing those trends so that they become real is the amount of difficult learning that you and your colleagues face. If it is substantial, then develop your difficult learning skills or get out of the business.

A FINAL WORD

The leaders of today and tomorrow are both free and constrained. They are free to choose from a wider range of strategies and opportunities than has ever existed. At the same time, they are constrained as leaders to be responsible for the potential of the new and undiscovered. Their uncertainty skills will be fully tested if they are to be responsible for a continually coherent, improving, and relaxing world rather than a continually dysfunctional, unraveling, and stressful world.

17

WHEN GOOD PEOPLE DO BAD THINGS: THE ANATOMY OF A CORPORATE DISASTER

Ronald M. Green

☐ n October 1, 1999, Medhat Labib of Indialantic, Florida, was behind the wheel of his Ford Explorer, driving home after a niece's wedding rehearsal. His wife and two sons were with him, along with three friends who had joined the festivities. Just 10 minutes from home, the rear tire on the driver's side came apart at 70 mph. The 1996 Explorer rolled over three times, coming to rest in a mass of trees off Interstate 95. Labib's wife, Margaret, 42, died instantly. Their son, Andrew, 9, was thrown from the vehicle and killed. Labib, 49, was left paralyzed from the waist down. No others in the vehicle were seriously injured.[1]

---

[1] Anita Kumar. (2001, May 21). "A Special Report: Deadly Combination: Ford, Firestone and Florida." *St. Petersburg Times*, [Online]. Available: *http://www.sptimes.com/News/webspecials/firestone/qa.shtml.*

The Labib family tragedy eventually proved to be one of hundreds that would make the 15-inch, all-terrain, Firestone tires used on Ford Explorers the object of one of the most extensive product recalls in history. By the time the recall was completed over a year later, at least 174 deaths and over 700 injuries would be attributed to Firestone tire failures on Ford Explorers, and 6.5 million tires would be recalled.[2] In reaction to criticisms, the top leadership of both Ford and Firestone would step down. Both companies would face billions of dollars in liability suits. Another casualty would be the relationship between these two corporate giants. Begun almost a century earlier in a friendship between Harry Firestone and Henry Ford, it would end in a chorus of name-calling and mutual recriminations.

How can a corporate disaster of this magnitude be explained? Some obvious answers present themselves. On both sides corporate greed probably played a role. There is evidence that Firestone cut corners on design, manufacture, and testing in order to offer Ford a tire that would be cheaper than those offered by competitors. Ford apparently placed a higher priority on the affordability of tires than on customer safety. Both companies also displayed a stubborn inability—or unwillingness—to learn from experience. In the late 1970s, faulty design and manufacturing processes caused numerous failures in Firestone's "500" line of radial tires. During that same period, Ford came under attack for fuel-tank design problems in its Pinto automobiles. These problems caused scores of fatal accidents and earned the Pinto a reputation as a rolling incendiary bomb.

Nevertheless, this history tells us that greed and stupidity are probably too simple as explanations of the Firestone-Explorer disaster. Both companies had to be aware of the financial stakes of product liability in this sensitive area. During the 1980s, Firestone lost its corporate independence to Japan's Bridgestone Tire Company as a result of the financial difficulties caused by the earlier problems with its 500 line.

---

[2] Ibid.

Each manufacturer had to realize that it could incur billions of dollars in costs—in class-action lawsuits alone—if it were implicated in another string of fatal accidents. This suggests to me that we should look deeper for the causes of this episode. In fact, I believe that it was the result of a systematic and, unfortunately, very typical failure by both companies. It was systematic because it involved a variety of intersecting factors in the way the companies did business together. It was typical because the problems that came to light often make their appearance in other, less tragic instances of corporate negligence and misconduct. By analyzing the causes of this disaster, we can better understand why business managers sometimes make ethically poor decisions, and we can learn how to avoid such problems in our own professional life.

THE PARABLE OF THE SADHU

The quest for an understanding of the events that led to the Labib family tragedy takes us far from Florida to an episode that occurred in the Himalayan Mountains nearly two decades before. The central character in this story is a Wall Street investment banker named Bowen ("Buzz") McCoy. In 1982, Buzz took a 6-month sabbatical from his firm, Morgan Stanley, and decided to hike in Nepal. During the trip, he had a disturbing experience, which he described in an article for the *Harvard Business Review* entitled "The Parable of the Sadhu."[3] Buzz came to believe that what had happened on a mountainside in the Himalayas had relevance for the field of business ethics.

Three months into his trek, Buzz and his party were ascending to a mountain pass at 18,000 feet. Their destination was the holy city of Muklinath. The group included Buzz, his companion Stephen, an American anthropologist, and several Sherpa guides and porters. In order to get to Muklinath, they

---

[3] September–October 1983, pp. 103–108.

had to rise early and cross a series of snow steps that would melt later in the day as the sun rose. Buzz was already suffering from the altitude sickness that had caused him to experience pulmonary edema on a trip some years before.

As the group ascended to the summit of the pass, a New Zealander from a party ahead of theirs met them. He came toward them, carrying the body of a Sadhu, an Indian holy man, whom his group had found, barefoot and almost naked, lying unconscious in the snow. The New Zealander handed the Sadhu over to Buzz and his companions, saying, "Look, I've done what I can. You have porters and Sherpa guides. You care for him. We're going on."

In a few minutes, the Sadhu revived, but he was unable to walk or explain what he was doing at those heights without shoes and clad only in a skimpy garment. With the help of members of a Swiss group, the Sadhu was soon clad in warm clothing. Buzz and Stephen were unsure what to do. Below them, they spotted a Japanese party with a horse. Buzz told Stephen that he was concerned about the altitude and wanted to cross the pass. Without much thought, he took off after some of the porters who had gone ahead.

Several hours later, Stephen rejoined Buzz at the summit. Buzz greeted him, but Stephen was angry. He explained that the Japanese had refused to take the Sadhu. Stephen reported that he then proposed to the Sherpas that they carry the Sadhu down to safety, but their leader resisted the idea, saying that they needed all their energy to get over the pass. At Stephen's urging, the Sherpas carried the Sadhu down to a rock in the sun 500 feet below and pointed to a hut another 500 feet below. To this day, neither Stephen nor Buzz knows what happened to the Sadhu.

Buzz apparently wrote about this episode as an act of contrition. He wished to extract from this experience a moral lesson of broader import. As an active layman in the Presbyterian Church, he came to believe that he had unwittingly violated his own deepest values. He had read the parable of the Good Samaritan many times in his life, but when it came time for him to act as a Good Samaritan, he missed the opportunity. In Buzz's view, what happened to him and his companions also occurs in business organizations. Because of complex group dynamics, good men and women, "nice" people with solid values, often end up doing things they regret.

Buzz McCoy's experience on the mountain brings to light a series of key factors that contribute to poor and ethically irresponsible group decision making:

1. Stress
2. Goal obsession
3. Rationalization
4. Blaming the victim
5. Failures of leadership
6. Value conflicts
7. Buck-passing
8. Bad examples
9. Decision making by technicians
10. Alien cultural environments
11. Failures of individual moral responsibility

STRESS

The first item on this list is stress. For Buzz, stress took physiological form in the hypoxia at 18,000 feet altitude and the reduced physical and mental functioning associated with it. Stress can come in other forms, however, including serious organizational conflicts or acute financial pressures. Because stress reduces the quality of decision making, those responsible for organizations must manage it. They must make it part of their responsibilities to minimize the stress imposed on personnel. Since it is difficult to avoid stress entirely, they must also plan and train for handling stressful situations *before* they occur. The failure of Buzz and his companions to do this was a key contributing factor to their moral failure. Unlike skilled mountaineers, they never discussed how to respond to a life-threatening event on the mountainside. When they came upon the Sadhu, they had no prior guidelines or training to help them. Apprehensive and confused, they acted by instinct and ended by violating their basic moral values.

GOAL OBSESSION

Goal obsession is the occupational disease of hard-driving executives like Buzz McCoy. It is what makes them successful, but it can also set them up for personal and organizational disasters. A colleague of mine has coined a name for this prevalent mindset: *teleopathy,* literally meaning goal-sickness. It occurs when the goal owns you, not the other way around. Goal obsession has two very typical features. First, like a magnet, it gets stronger as we approach the goal, sometimes making it difficult or impossible to change direction to adapt to new circumstances. Second, it often involves a confusion of one's larger or longer term goal with some immediate objective. In Buzz's case, for example, his goal was to enjoy a sabbatical experience, to get a break from Wall Street, and in the process to learn something positive about himself. Instead, he and his companions became obsessed with the narrow objective of reaching Muklinath. Pursuing this objective, he missed his chance for the most valuable sabbatical experience of all. Imagine if Buzz had seen his goal properly. Returning to Morgan Stanley, when asked, "Did you finish your trek?" he could have replied, "No. We saved a human life instead."

RATIONALIZATION

Rationalization, the third item on this list, almost always accompanies unethical behavior. Rationalization has been described as "the compliment that vice pays to virtue." It seems that as human beings we are unable simply to do wrongful things. Instead, we try to justify them in ways that soothe our conscience. For Buzz, this took the form of various excuses and reasons why he could not stop to save the Sadhu, including risks to the group if the ice steps melted. In reality, Buzz and his colleagues weren't in any danger. All the perils would have vanished if they had chosen to turn around and bring the Sadhu to safety.

BLAMING THE VICTIM

Blaming the victim is a special form of rationalization. How easy it is, when I am about to neglect or harm another human being, to somehow justify this in terms of the victim's own fault. Are AIDS drugs priced too high for millions of people in our country or abroad? "Why did they get AIDS in the first place?" Does a poorly designed toy or piece of furniture injure a child? "Why weren't the parents more careful?" In Buzz's case, it was the Sadhu who was blamed. All those who might have saved him asked themselves why he was being so foolish as to wander, flimsily clad, high in the mountains. This led to the unfortunate conclusion that maybe he deserved to be abandoned.

FAILURE OF GOOD LEADERSHIP

The next item on this list, good leadership, is an essential factor if organizations are to steer their way through new and difficult challenges. Too often, however, appointed leaders are ineffective, or when unitary direction is needed, a multiplicity of conflicting voices is raised claiming attention. Buzz's group clearly lacked a leader. Buzz and Stephen had some authority, but neither was entirely willing to defer to the other. The Sherpas acted as paid employees. In the crisis, the group fractured.

VALUE CONFLICTS

Further compounding this problem of divisiveness was the value conflict that appeared in the situation. Sometimes, groups that lack a single leader can spontaneously unite around a shared set of values or goals. We see this when a volunteer "bucket brigade" forms in response to a fire. But, even formally organized groups can fracture if key personnel insist on acting on fundamentally different values. Value conflicts of this sort should not be confused with diversity of views. Open discussion and debate can enrich an organization. However, when key and core values are concerned, there must be unity, or the group will split and be unable to meet challenges. The fundamental disagreements between Buzz and Stephen had this effect. They pulled the group's two leaders in different directions. In the end, a problem that was not life threatening became one, as Stephen feared for Buzz's safety higher up on the mountain.

BUCK-PASSING

Buck-passing is another fatal factor in the erosion of organizational integrity and ability to respond. Buck-passing should not be confused with a proper division of labor. No member of a group can do everything. What characterizes buck-passing, however, is that no one takes responsibility for the outcomes and instead passes this essential duty onto others, often without their assent. In the case of the Sadhu, this phenomenon made its appearance when the New Zealanders peremptorily handed the Sadhu off to Buzz's group. From this point onward, it became a matter of "passing the Sadhu" to whomever was available. In the end, the Sadhu paid the price for everyone's failure to ensure that he was safe.

BAD EXAMPLE

The New Zealanders' conduct points up the next item on this list: bad examples. Much more than we realize, human beings are social animals. We are powerfully influenced by what others do. Good examples raise the standard of conduct of a group; bad examples have the opposite effect. In a matter of moments on the mountainside, the New Zealanders communicated the idea that all one had to do was pass the Sadhu along to others. Without thinking, Buzz and his companions followed that bad example.

DECISION MAKING BY TECHNICIANS

The next item on the list, decision making by technicians, needs careful explanation. Technicians come in many forms. In a business organization, they include the engineering, financial, or legal experts who are needed to achieve the company's purposes. For those trekking in the Himalayas, they are the Sherpa guides and porters who know the route and conditions. In all circumstances, the advice and skills provided by technicians are essential, but they should never be confused with or be allowed to replace the higher level, value-driven direction of the group's leaders. Buzz and Stephen succumbed to this problem.

Unable to see or set their own priorities, they deferred to the Sherpas. Since the Sherpas had only one objective—getting their charges to Muklinath and receiving their pay—this low-order priority became the "purpose" of the trek.

ALIEN CULTURAL ENVIRONMENT

Buzz and his companions were clearly operating in an alien cultural environment, a factor that entered into their poor decision making. All of the problems mentioned above are made worse when we are acting within circumstances outside the normal range of our experience. Ignorance about others' conduct or values supports our tendency to rationalize our own negligence or blame them for our difficulties. Not knowing what is expected can divide a group, puzzle its leaders, and lead everyone to defer excessively to local expert advice. In his very strangeness, the Sadhu invited all these responses. When Stephen later rejoined Buzz at the pass, he angrily accused Buzz of contributing to another person's death and asked whether Buzz would have similarly left behind a Western man or woman. Stephen's question brought home to Buzz how much the "otherness" of the Sadhu and his surroundings had distorted his judgment.

FAILURES OF INDIVIDUAL MORAL RESPONSIBILITY

The factors itemized here help explain why people with solid values sometimes go morally awry in complex situations of group conduct. Led by bad examples, pulled by the voices of conflicting authorities, misled by inappropriate technical advice, people like Buzz and Stephen can abandon commitments that are central to their own identity. Nevertheless, while these factors can explain individual misconduct when people are part of groups, they do not excuse it. No matter how bad the group dynamics we encounter, each person is always required to act on his or her own better values. Both Buzz and Stephen know that to some extent they are responsible for the

Sadhu's abandonment. By warning others of the causes of this episode, Buzz hoped to help others minimize the pressure to wrongful conduct created by group factors. However, the best group dynamics cannot replace the need for each person in a group to assume responsibility for his or her own conduct or the need to bring the group's behavior in line with one's own best values.

FIRESTONE AND FORD ON THE MOUNTAINSIDE

Accidents of the kind that devastated the Labib family resulted from the sudden failure of a Firestone all-terrain tire. A combination of heat, heavy load, and low tire-pressure caused the tread of the tire to peel off. Sudden failure of a rear tire could lead the top-heavy Explorer to roll over. Behind these immediate causes, however, were a series of decisions and actions by both Bridgestone/Firestone and Ford, stretching back over more than 10 years. Amidst these, we can see many of the factors identified by Buzz McCoy preparing the way for disaster.

STRESS

For Firestone, this was a persistent factor in the sequence of events leading up to the tire recall. Crippled financially by the 1978 recall of 13 million 500 tires, the company limped through the 1980s, until in 1988 it agreed to be acquired by Japan's Bridgestone. According to executives with Firestone and other tire companies, instead of bringing relief, the acquisition increased pressure on the company, because the new owners quickly made it clear that they wanted increased volume from their American unit.[4] The best way to do this was to expand business with the auto companies. As a result,

---

[4] "Road Signs: How Ford, Firestone Let the Warnings Slide by as Debacle Developed." (2000, Sept. 6). *Wall Street Journal,* pp. A1, A16.

Firestone competed aggressively to win the Explorer tire contract. It may have done so, in part, by hurrying into production a tire design and manufacturing process that skimped on materials, quality assurance, and testing.

Although Firestone won a large share of Ford's business, the demanding price and production terms that the company had to meet only increased the pressure. During this period, parent Bridgestone was also unwilling to invest heavily to upgrade its aging Decatur, Illinois, plant, where many of the defective tires would eventually be produced. As a result, during the early 1990s workers and plant managers experienced increasing production demands that led, in turn, to reduced quality controls. In the words of one line employee, "If you didn't make the numbers, you were in trouble." From 1994 to 1996, these problems were accentuated by a prolonged and bitter strike that forced the company to resort to poorly trained replacement workers. It was during these 2 years that most of the defective tires were manufactured.

GOAL OBSESSION

We can see the presence of this factor in the pressure-inducing business decisions just mentioned. An irony of goal obsession is that it can lead people to pursue some objective that is instrumental to achieving a larger goal, but in the process causes them to lose that goal. This is exactly what happened to Bridgestone/Firestone. Obsessed with winning the Explorer contract, the newly merged company imperiled some of the key sources of Firestone's long-term worth: its relationship with Ford and the established value of the Firestone brand name.

On its side, Ford also evidenced goal obsession. This was particularly apparent in the series of design decisions that went into the Explorer model. The Explorer was initially conceived during the 1980s to fill a growing niche that Ford had identified for a comfortable, family-style, sport utility vehicle to replace its more truck-like, stubby Bronco II model. Because of the high suspension required for off-road operation, the Bronco experienced rollover problems, and Ford engineers wanted to reduce this risk on the Explorer.

However, reports during final development weren't encouraging. During testing, the Explorer prototype demonstrated a rollover response not shown on benchmark Chevrolet Blazer models or even the older Bronco II. As a result, Ford engineers and managers scrambled for a solution. Instead of reexamining the whole idea of an off-road, truck-like vehicle that could also be widely used by families in high-speed highway driving, Ford remained stubbornly locked into the Explorer concept. Some Ford managers dismissed the problem, reasoning that the company intended to market the Explorer to buyers with "a less aggressive driver profile." Another solution involved reducing the recommended air pressure in the vehicle's tires to a low of 26 pounds (Chevrolet Blazers used similar tires, but at a recommended pressure of 35 pounds). This would not only ensure a softer more comfortable ride, one of the design objectives, but it would increase the vehicle's body roll and reduce cornering confidence, thereby discouraging aggressive driving. One commentator summed up Ford's "goal-obsessed" approach to the Explorer model when he observed, "In other words, two of Ford's responses to Explorer instability were to sell it to people who didn't drive hard and to make it scary for those who did, so they'd back off before getting into more trouble."[5]

RATIONALIZATION AND BLAMING
THE VICTIM

Against this background of manufacturing and design decisions, it is not surprising that denial was one of the first responses of executives at both companies to the early reports of tire failure and rollovers. Reports of accidents coming in from overseas subsidiaries in Saudi Arabia and Latin America were dismissed as resulting from the high heat and hard driving conditions in those countries. Victims, too, were blamed. Apparently, many drivers paid less attention to tire inflation guidelines than they should have. The problem was compounded by the fact that recommended inflation levels for the tires were already close to the

---

[5] James R. Healey. (2000, Dec. 26). "Firestone Leaves an Indelible Mark." *USA Today*, pp. 1B–2B.

point where increased friction with the road would cause heat to build up and the tread to separate. This combination of factors led Bridgestone/Firestone executives to point the finger at Explorer owners, who it accused of failing to maintain proper inflation levels on their tires. "Any problems associated with this tire," one manager explained, "are not problems resulting from any deficiency in the design or manufacture of the tire itself, but rather, from the maintenance habits of a large portion of American motorists."[6]

Ford had its version of this rationalization for its questionable design decisions. When excessive loading of the Explorer was implicated in heat buildup and tire failures, Ford issued a statement clearly blaming drivers: "With the Explorer or any other truck, it is the responsibility of owners to check weight labels posted on the inside of the doors and then limit the weight put inside, with particular attention to not putting too much weight on the back of the vehicle." However, safety experts critical of this position pointed out that few sport utility customers think of their vehicles as trucks, much less check the weight ratings on the label. Indeed, it was Ford's marketing objective to move the Explorer into a non-truck category in consumers' minds. Hence, although they tried to do so, both companies could not easily evade responsibility for poor decisions on the part of the end-users of their products. If Bridgestone/Firestone and Ford were to acquit themselves ethically, they had to anticipate how customers would be likely to use the tires and the Explorer and design products with comfortable margins of safety.

FAILURES OF LEADERSHIP
AND VALUE CONFLICTS

Both of these factors played a powerful role in this episode. Even under the best of circumstances, the merger of two corporate cultures is a difficult enterprise, but it becomes even more so when companies have different national identities and

---

[6] Cindy Skrzycki, "Agency Missed Early Tire Warnings," Washington Post, September 12th, 2000, pp. E1, E12. ©2000 The Washington Post. Reprinted with permission.

value systems. That Bridgestone/Firestone did not initially achieve a unified organizational culture is shown in the parent company's arms-length relationship to its North American unit and its excessive revenue demands during a stressful period of transition. Later, as tire problems developed, it was clear that this division of corporate cultures continued. In a surprisingly candid admission, Yoichiro Kaizaki, president of the parent Bridgestone of Japan, [explained at a] Tokyo news conference... [why] Bridgestone executives ignored signs of trouble. "If there was a problem with a Bridgestone tire," he explained, "our technology staff in Tokyo would rush to the site overseas to help out. But if a problem arose with a Firestone tire, they wouldn't do anything."[7]

Earlier, I remarked that diversity of cultures in business organizations can be a positive thing. This is particularly true if differing values enrich peoples' perspectives and educate them into alternate ways of doing things. The Japanese business presence in the United States had this effect during the 1980s and 1990s, as Japanese firms like Honda and Toyota brought a new emphasis on product quality and employee performance to the American workplace. What the Bridgestone/Firestone episode reveals, however, is just the opposite dynamic at work. Instead of coming together into a larger, more powerful whole, the undigested twin cultures led to divisiveness and neglect. Like Buzz's fractured group on the mountainside, components of the new company went separate ways, and the victim in this case was not a solitary Sadhu, but millions of people who relied on Firestone tires.

BUCK-PASSING

Post-event analysis of the Explorer-rollover episode shows that it resulted from the combined effect of independent decisions made by Bridgestone/Firestone and Ford executives. Few doubt that many of the all-terrain ATV and Wilderness tires manufactured by Firestone during the mid-1990s were substandard or

---

[7] David Barboza. (2000, Sept. 15). "Firestone Workers Cite Lax Quality Control." *New York Times*, , pp. C1, C5.

even defective. However, it was the use of these tires on Ford Explorers that created the recipe for disaster. In almost all cases, death or injury resulted when the heavy Explorer, with its imposed requirement of low tire pressure and high center of gravity, rolled over when a rear tire suddenly failed. Firestone tires on most other vehicles would not have failed so suddenly or, if they did, would not have had such a catastrophic effect. Ford Explorers equipped with sturdier or better-inflated tires would not have succumbed to their rollover tendency.

In the frenzy of name-calling that accompanied media coverage of the recall, Ford executives pointed to this latter fact in order to shift blame onto Bridgestone/Firestone. They observed that during the mid-1990s, nearly half a million Explorers had been equipped with Goodyear tires. These vehicles had not experienced significant tire failure or rollover problems. In the eyes of Ford executives, this "proved" that the Explorer was safe. Alluding to these facts, Jacques A. Nasser, Ford's chief executive, [stated flatly,] "We know that this is a Firestone tire issue, not a vehicle issue."[8] But, of course, this obscures the role that the Explorer design played in these events. Nasser and other Ford executives' stubborn refusal to admit their part in the tragedy, their consistent efforts to shift blame, first to customers, then to their supplier, epitomize corporate buck-passing at its worst.

DECISION MAKING BY TECHNICIANS

The experience of Buzz and his companions shows us how easy and seductive it can be for leaders to hand over decision-making responsibility to technical experts of one sort or another. In the Explorer episode, we can identify many examples of this tendency, although one in particular had tragic consequences. This involved decisions by both the tire and automaker to heed lawyers' advice to avoid exposing themselves to legal liability.

This tendency manifested itself as early as 1997, when reports of the failure of Firestone tires on Ford Explorers began

---

[8] Keith Bradsher. (2000, Sept. 16). "Margin of Safety on Ford at Issue." *New York Times*, pp. A1, B4.

to arrive from countries in the Gulf region, Venezuela, and other Latin American nations. These failures were a warning sign of what was to come, but lawyers for both firms cautioned managers not to alert U.S. government officials of the problem. As one journalist reports, "Memos showed that lawyers for the auto and tire makers worried that the U.S. government might see the action as evidence of a safety defect and insist on a U.S. recall. No law required either company to report the actions, and neither did."

With the wisdom of hindsight, we can see that an early opportunity was missed to report and identify a problem that would only grow. Focusing on their narrow duty of protecting the companies in the cases at hand, lawyers for both firms missed the larger picture. Managers who heeded them and failed to appreciate the importance of a growing problem served their companies poorly and contributed to the epidemic of U.S. accidents that would occur.

It is always difficult for a manager to override the advice of a skilled legal professional, or for that matter, any professional that the company relies on for counsel. The lesson here is not that we are to ignore our Sherpas. They are an essential resource for informed managerial decision making. It is rather that theirs cannot be the last word in a complex managerial decision with ethical significance. Their advice must be weighed against fundamental value objectives that define a company and shape its ethical responsibilities. If technical advice threatens or undermines those objectives and responsibilities, it must be reconsidered, and alternate ways of reaching appropriate organizational goals must be sought.

ALIEN CULTURAL ENVIRONMENTS

For Buzz and his colleagues, it was Nepal that posed the challenge of an alien cultural environment. For companies, however, "strange" or "new" environments come in many forms. The "alien" can arise when a Japanese company acquires a U.S. subsidiary, or vice versa.

New business opportunities, products, or technologies can also thrust managers into unfamiliar territory. In this case, perhaps the leading "alien environment" was Ford's effort to design and manufacture a new kind of sport utility vehicle. We've seen that engineers and designers accustomed to truck manufacture strained to develop a truck-based vehicle for a wholly new market. Their tendency to bring truck-based thinking to this endeavor, as evidenced by their approach to vehicle loading and suspension issues, shows how hard a transition from one sector to the next can be.

FAILURES OF INDIVIDUAL MORAL RESPONSIBILITY

It is clear that many organizational forces working together contributed to the events that led Bridgestone/Firestone and Ford to produce a vehicle and tires that unnecessarily killed scores of people and injured many more. Understanding those organizational dynamics does not excuse the individuals whose carelessness or indifference contributed to these outcomes. All these people bear a measure of responsibility, from the line managers at Firestone who allowed uninspected tires to leave the plant to Ford designers who rationalized the manufacture of unstable vehicle as a means of encouraging driver caution.

Does this mean that organizational factors are unimportant? No, it is just the opposite. Careful attention to organizational dynamics can help spare managers from being faced with acute or agonizing moral dilemmas. Furthermore, managers' individual moral responsibilities extend to the decisions they make, whether in the examples they set or the policies they select, that shape and mold the organization's culture. Organizational ethics and individual ethical striving are not alternatives, but mutually reinforcing aspects of business ethics.

CONCLUSION

Nobody will ever be able to restore wholeness to the Labib family or to the hundreds of others whose lives were marred by culpable neglect and mismanagement at Bridgestone/Firestone and Ford. This terrible episode, however, offers a cautionary lesson for all business managers and for each one of us in our personal lives as well. If we are to minimize or avoid ethical disaster, we must act differently than Buzz McCoy and his companions or the Bridgestone/Firestone and Ford managers. Specifically, we must

- Seek to reduce the stress we create within organizations and prepare and train for stressful situations. Key organizational values should be discussed and implemented *before* stress arises.
- Beware of goal obsession. When a single objective looms so large that we can't let go of it and we risk imperiling our most basic values in its pursuit, it is a warning sign.
- Avoid rationalization and victim blaming. When we find ourselves struggling to justify things that we sense are wrong, or when we become irked at people we are harming, this should be a sign that we may be on morally questionable ground.
- Develop good organizational leaders and make sure that in times of crisis the lines of responsibility are clear.
- Achieve organizational consensus on key values, especially those related to our ethical responsibilities. Diversity and decentralization are good, but not when they lead a company to act uncertainly or in opposing ways in the face of ethical challenges. On matters of ethical integrity, all the members of an organization, from top leaders to rank file, must speak with one voice.
- Refuse to tolerate buck-passing. Managers who accept responsibility for their decisions—and even for their mistakes—are better than those who try to offload responsibility on others.
- Reward those who furnish examples of good behavior and punish or fire those who do not. Nothing rots an organization quicker than keeping "bad apples" around.
- Avoid allowing technicians to make strategic decisions. We should always ask ourselves, who are our Sherpas and who are our leaders?

- Be careful when entering alien environments. This is not a geographical issue. Managers for a staid manufacturing company can tread on unfamiliar ground when they acquire a film production division and suddenly find themselves doing business in the fast-paced world of Hollywood. New terrain can stimulate and challenge a company, but it can also cause managers to lose their moral bearings.

Exercise moral responsibility. Groups can help us or hurt our moral performance, but in the end, we stand as individuals responsible for the organizations we shape and ourselves. Above all, we must never forget that our most important measure as human beings is whether we have lived our lives with integrity. We should try to avoid having Sadhus on our conscience, whether they are holy men left behind on a mountainside or innocent victims of our company's bad products.

18

RECRUITING SUPPORTIVE COACHES: A KEY TO ACHIEVING POSITIVE BEHAVIORAL CHANGE

Marshall Goldsmith

I have recently completed a research review on the unique challenges and strategies involved in helping successful people get even better.[1] One interesting finding of this research is that successful people are much more likely to accept coaching from those whom they respect and whom they see as successful. Successful people are less likely to value coaching from those whom they do not see as successful. This phenomenon tends to occur even if the content of the coaching from less successful people is very similar.

This point was made even more clearly when Beverly Kaye, Ken Shelton, and I asked great thought leaders and teachers to

---

[1] Article adapted from "Helping Successful People Change" in F. Hesselbein and M. Goldsmith (Eds.), (2001), *Leading for Innovation*. San Francisco: Jossey-Bass.

describe a key event when they learned something that made a significant difference in their lives. This led to our book *Learning Journeys*.[2] More than half of the respondents described a situation in which they had received coaching from someone that they deeply respected. In many cases, this coaching did not come from someone in a formal coaching relationship (like a consultant, manager, or teacher). Interestingly enough, most agreed that the same message would not have had much impact if a different person had delivered it. This made us realize that when dealing with successful people, the *source* of coaching can be as important as the *content* of the coaching.

Another clear finding of our literature search is that positive behavioral change is much more likely to last if the individual who is trying to change has a "support group" (or at least "support person") who is assisting in the change process. In order for these supportive coaches to be helpful, there needs to be a two-way respect relationship. They need to respect us, and we need to respect them.

In helping you achieve a positive, measurable change in behavior, your best coaches will not necessarily be outside experts (like me) who have credentials or training in this field. Your best coaches may often be people whom you respect and who impact your life on a daily basis.

A common misconception about coaching is that your coach has to be an "expert" to be helpful. This is not true. A helpful behavioral coach can be anyone that you respect. Your coach can be someone who observes your behavior on a day-to-day basis. Your coach can be a person who is part of any valuable relationship. Your spouse, friends, or partners may not be experts on interpersonal behavior, but they may be experts at understanding how your interpersonal behavior impacts them! They can usually describe the behavior that you need to demonstrate so that you can become more effective (at work) or happier (at home).

Who should your coaches be? In selecting coaches, you may wish to consider the key people who are impacted by your

---

[2] Goldsmith, M., B. Kaye, and K. Sheldon (Eds.). (2001). *Learning Journeys*. Palo Alto, CA: Davies-Black.

behavior. This list might include your manager, direct reports, colleagues, customers, friends, and family members. A key guideline is, don't ask for their advice if you don't want to hear it! Involve the people whom you believe can help you get better.

After determining who you want your coaches to be, it is important to gain their commitment to the coaching process. Have a one-on-one dialogue with each person whom you are going to recruit as a coach. Ask them if they would be willing to spend a few minutes each month during the next year to help you achieve a positive change in your behavior. When they respond, look closely at their faces; don't just listen to their words. Only involve people who are sincerely willing to try to help you.

Be honest and direct in these dialogues. Let them know that you are going to make a sincere effort to improve. Don't promise that you will succeed. Be realistic—let them know that you will probably "fall off the wagon" during the next year. Let them know that you will be very sensitive to the value of their time in this process.

I have found that the answers to the three simple questions that follow can be great predictors of their future success in being your coach and in helping you change.

1. Are you willing to "let go" of my past behavior and try to help me change my future behavior?

   One of the great mistakes that we make when we try to help others change is to focus on the past, not on the future. How many times have we been "helped" by a spouse, friend, or partner who is able to impress us with their near photographic memory of our previous "sins"? How much does this generally help anyone? None of us can change our past; all we can do is change our future. Focusing on the past can be demoralizing. Focusing on the future can be energizing.

   For better or worse, it is often useless to have a dialogue with successful people about what they have done wrong in the past. The successful person who receives the feedback often becomes defensive, denies the feedback, and tries to prove that the sender is "wrong" or "doesn't understand." The sender of the feedback may feel awkward, embarrassed, uncomfortable, or even afraid. Successful people tend to resist negative feedback about their past; they almost always appreciate constructive suggestions for their future.

By focusing on the future, the coach can usually cover the same material in a much more constructive way. Rather than focusing on "Let's talk about how you made an ass of yourself in front of the executive team!" the coach can focus on ideas for making more effective executive presentations in the future.

Having your coach focus on the future will make this process a lot more fun (and a lot less painful) for you. Do you really want someone pointing out everything that you have done wrong? Wouldn't you rather work with someone who is willing to forgive yesterday's sins and try to help you get better tomorrow?

2. Are you willing to be a supportive coach, not a cynic, critic, or judge?

Successful people tend to respond very well to future-oriented advice that will help them achieve their goals. Successful people tend to resist advice when they feel that they are being judged or manipulated.

Improving an interpersonal relationship involves a two-way effort. If we work hard to change our behavior so that we can have better relationships with others, and we only receive cynicism or criticism, we will generally give up on the process. Why should we work so hard to improve our relationships with people when we feel punished for our efforts?

The person whom you are recruiting to help you needs to understand that your efforts to change behavior (over the next year) will often result in failure. We all have a tendency to revert back to old behavior. The more stressful the situation, the more likely this is to be true. If your coach does not give up on you when you fail in the short run, you will be much more likely to succeed in the long run. If your coach expects you to fail and says, "I knew you could not change," your odds for successful change go down.

The people whom we respect can create either positive or negative self-fulfilling prophecies concerning our behavior. Optimism is a key ingredient in helping people change. If your coaches consistently communicate a belief that "you can do it," you will be much more likely to succeed. If they do not believe that you can change, they may do more harm than good.

3. **Will you commit to being honest with me when you give me suggestions for the future?**
   Coaches who are unwilling to be honest are generally not that helpful. If the coaches are unduly negative, the person being coached may become unnecessarily demoralized. If the coaches are unduly positive, the person being coached may be getting positive reinforcement for negative behavior. Neither option is useful. Just ask your coaches to tell the truth as they see it. Point out that they are the only people in the world who can accurately provide their assessments of your behavior.

In my corporate work, hundreds of my clients have asked their colleagues these questions. The huge majority of people say yes to all three. In some cases, people say no. Perhaps the relationship has been too strained too long for them to want to fix it. Perhaps they are uncomfortable providing honest suggestions. Perhaps they are too busy. It doesn't really matter. If they don't want to participate, don't force the issue. Just thank them for their honesty in telling you how they feel. In almost all cases, there will be more than enough people who are willing to help. Work with them.

FOLLOWING UP WITH YOUR COACHES

After recruiting your support group of coaches, ask them for their ideas on how you can improve. This can be done either formally (through 360° feedback) or informally (through merely asking for suggestions for the future).

Identify the one or two behavioral changes that can make the most positive impact. Realize that these behaviors may vary with different groups. Ask them for ongoing suggestions for improvement in these behaviors. Do not promise that you will do everything they say. Do promise to listen to their ideas, to understand their perspective, and to do what you can. Stick with the plan and make sure that you keep following up.

Results from thousands of people who have followed these steps demonstrate a clear pattern. If you recruit supportive coaches whom you respect, ask them for ongoing suggestions, listen to their ideas, and keep following up, you will almost always achieve a positive long-term change in your behavior. You will also improve your relationships with the most important people in your world!

GLOBAL LEADERSHIP AND GLOBAL EMOTIONAL INTELLIGENCE

Stephen H. Rhinesmith

THE NEED FOR GLOBAL LEADERSHIP

As the world economy becomes increasingly global, the demand for leaders who can think and operate on a global basis is sharply rising. The highly touted "War for Talent," documented by McKinsey & Company,[1] is nowhere more evident than in the search conducted each year by global corporations for the talent they need to staff their subsidiaries, manage joint ventures, build and lead global teams, and develop strategies based on an understanding of the complex dynamics of international operations.

---

[1] McKinsey & Company. (1998, Fall). "The War for Talent." *McKinsey Quarterly*.

There is evidence of a growing global economy everywhere. Swiss chemical manufacturers receive 90 percent of their revenues from foreign income; half the profits of Japan's automakers come from U.S. sales; and U.S. pharmaceutical companies receive, on average, 40 percent of their annual revenues from foreign operations.

Not only are foreign sales growing, but other global forces are at work. Cross-border mergers and acquisitions, strategic alliances, and the emergence of global and regional competitors are forcing companies to understand their foreign environments. Today, as never before, companies must respond to the complexity of a global marketplace.

As a result, the demand for global managers who are able to work across multiple boundaries is fast outpacing the supply of managers with global experience. To meet this demand, companies are not only examining possible sources of new global leaders, they are trying to determine what mindsets and skill sets are necessary for success in a complex global marketplace.

THE NEED FOR LEADERS WITH GLOBAL MINDSETS AND SKILLS

Recent research at Columbia University in New York has isolated two important dimensions of what the authors call a "global mindset."[2] In a wide-ranging review of literature about globalization and global management, researchers discovered a clustering of variables that they believe account for much of the success or failure of executives operating in foreign environments.

The first dimension, *cognitive complexity*, involves the degree to which a global manager has the basic intellectual capacity to deal with the complexities of a global world.[3] This begins with the technical and professional knowledge to lead

---

[2] Moynihan, Michael. (1993). *Global Manager: Recruiting, Developing and Keeping World Class Executives*. London: The Economist Intelligence Unit.

[3] Levy, Beechler, Taylor, and Boyacigillar. (1999). "*What We Talk About When We Walk About Global Mindset,*" Academy of Management Paper.

an organizational unit on a global basis and extends to the ability to manage the paradoxes that are part of operating in a global environment.

Jean-Pierre Jeannet, in *Managing with A Global Mindset,* describes what distinguishes domestic, multinational, international, regional, and global mindsets.[4] Fundamentally, a global mindset involves making decisions with increasing reference points. Domestic managers tend to make decisions within the context of their own domestic reference points regarding what is right or wrong, good or bad. Global managers, on the other hand, make decisions within multiple references, contrasting and comparing not only different worldviews, but also the interactions between these worldviews and social, political, and economic megatrends.

In my work with global leaders, I have discovered that there is a vast difference between leaders who can solve complex problems and those who can manage unsolvable paradoxes. Competing global and local needs present a classic paradox for global leadership. The constant drive for greater efficiency calls for global consolidation. While locally there are needs for local customization of products and the decentralized authority to make fast, speedy decisions, there is no final solution to the global-local dilemma. Global managers must learn to manage such issues on an ongoing basis. They must know how to dissect complex global and local interests; they must manage these in a fair and equal way; and they must exercise patience and understanding.

A second aspect of the Columbia criteria for a global mindset is what the authors call "cosmopolitanism," or the ability to look beyond yourself and beyond your own borders to understand and appreciate the differences that exist in many cultures around the world. Cosmopolitanism has long been associated with cross-cultural understanding. However, although substantial research has been conducted on cultural differences and cultural adjustment, no one has developed a way of integrating the following into one framework:

---

[4] Jeannet, Jean-Pierre. (2000). *Managing with a Global Mindset.* London: Financial Times Prentice Hall.

1. Self-awareness;
2. Knowledge of others; and
3. The capacity to work in and adjust to foreign cultures. Global emotional intelligence bridges this gap and fulfills this need.

For the last decade, I have been coaching and training executives on how to develop global mindsets. I also teach the same subject in Columbia Business School's Senior Executive Program. In my work, I have translated cognitive complexity and cosmopolitanism into what I call *global intellectual intelligence* and *global emotional intelligence*, borrowing from the recent work of Daniel Goleman and integrating it with my own experiences as a global manager. As can be seen in Figure 19.1, there are two basic components of a global mindset: global intellectual intelligence and global emotional intelligence. I have found that what distinguishes effective global leaders is their intellectual ability to operate globally. I have divided this global intellectual intelligence into two components: (1) *business acumen*, the knowledge of industry, business, profession, products, and services; and (2) *paradox management*, the ability to understand and manage the complexities of ongoing dilemmas that cannot be solved in a globally complex world.

FIGURE 19.1 Basic components of a global mindset.

I have developed the concept of global emotional intelligence as a way of describing the ability to work in and adjust to a changing world. Global emotional intelligence entails both *self-management,* the ability to work constructively with others, and *cultural acumen*, the ability to work across cultures. At our consulting firm, we work to develop leaders for a changing world and have developed programs that focus on the components of an effective global mindset. Through our coaching and action learning programs, we work on developing the intellectual and emotional capacities that managers need to execute winning strategies in the global marketplace.

GLOBAL EMOTIONAL INTELLIGENCE

In his groundbreaking book, *Emotional Intelligence,* Daniel Goleman examines why some leaders with high IQs fail in their responsibilities.[5] Interviewing hundreds of leaders over a 5-year period, he discovered that the key to executive leadership is more emotional than intellectual. In other words, he found that the higher someone is on the ladder of corporate responsibility, the more important it is to be able to work with and through people.

This is not to say that basic IQ is unnecessary, but the defining factor that distinguishes those leaders who are effective at the top of organizations and those who don't make it is most often related to their emotional rather than their intellectual intelligence.

This emotional intelligence, as defined by Goleman, is the ability of leaders to understand and regulate their emotions. There are four components to it: (1) self-awareness, (2) self-regulation, (3) empathy, and (4) social skills. In developing the concept of global emotional intelligence, I have extended each component to a global level in the following manner:

---

[5] Goleman, Daniel. (1995). *Emotional Intelligence.* New York: Bantam Books.

Emotional Intelligence	Global Emotional Intelligence
Self-awareness	Cultural self-awareness
Self-regulation	Cultural adjustment
Empathy	Cross-cultural understanding
Social skills	Cross-cultural effectiveness

I have also examined the impact of these global components on cross-cultural leadership to see how each becomes a building block for global executive success. I will more fully explore the implications of each factor in the rest of this chapter.

CULTURAL SELF-AWARENESS

Emotional intelligence begins with self-awareness. People with high self-awareness are aware of their strengths and weaknesses and have realistic assessments of the circumstances in which these strengths and weaknesses will either help or hinder them in their careers. It is important for leaders to understand and accept their strengths and weaknesses, because this is what enables them to ask others for help when they need it. This self-awareness also enables them to make contributions based on their unique skills and abilities.

Cultural self-awareness is the awareness of what it is to be from the country you are from. This includes an understanding of the characteristics, values, and behaviors peculiar to your country, and especially those that may prove helpful or pose problems in working with people from other countries. Cultural self-awareness includes an understanding of your values and prejudices. These values and prejudices are not necessarily right or wrong, but they can create difficulties when you operate in radically different cultures.

Cultural self-awareness is hard to develop without spending time outside your native country. Many companies have learned that leaders sent on overseas assignments better understand the merits and difficulties of transferring knowledge and skills across borders, cultures, and values. They can also better understand different worldviews and appreciate the impact these have on marketing, advertising, human resource management, product development, strategic planning, and leadership activities critical for success in a global world.

CULTURAL ADJUSTMENT

As important as it is, cultural self-awareness is only the first element of global emotional intelligence. Global leaders must be aware of their strengths and weaknesses and be able to "self-regulate" their emotions so that their feelings do not negatively affect those with whom they work. An often-cited example of the lack of self-regulation is the executive who is "moody," or worse, yells at his or her colleagues when frustrated and upset. This lack of consistency ultimately undermines leadership effectiveness.

In my experience coaching and training executives from around the world, I have found that self-regulation is much more likely to be troublesome than is self-awareness. With 360° feedback training, many executives become aware of their strengths and weaknesses; however, it is one thing to be aware of a weakness and quite another to regulate it.

The extension of self-regulation to a global context involves *cross-cultural adjustment.* This is the ability to enter a new culture with different values and patterns of behavior and adjust to the "shock" that occurs when you're faced with managing yourself and others in an environment in which expectations may be largely unknown.

Culture shock has been defined in the psychiatric profession as a "transient personality disorder." When I was president of the American Field Service International Student Exchange Program, we sponsored 10,000 high school students a year from 60 countries. The students lived with a family in a foreign country for up to a year. Each year, a very small percentage was unable to adjust to new circumstances. In some cases, students returned home with psychotic disorders. Amazingly, however, after 2 or 3 months at home, they were perfectly normal again. They had realigned themselves to familiar surroundings and were able to regain their normal capacity for living.

When examining the cause of their cultural maladjustment, we discovered that some of the students were unable to adjust to new cultures because they had never experienced failure in their own culture. When entering a new culture, it is inevitable that you will not perform at the level you achieved at home. Many fully functioning, achievement-driven executives in their 30s and 40s find themselves regressing to the behavior of 6- or 7-year-olds when they go abroad. They don't speak the language well, don't know how to act, and don't know how to manage effectively in their new environment.

Having the emotional capacity to self-regulate under these conditions requires you to have a strong self-concept, great personal discipline, and a basic faith in yourself and others that allows you to look at the positive over the negative and adjust quickly to the demands of the new situation. This is, of course, more easily said than done. When you're in a foreign environment, the landscape is filled with the potential for personal, professional, and business blunders. To make matters worse, you don't have the personal and organizational capacity to make the complex tradeoffs that are involved in managing the paradoxes of different value systems. Although rates of success vary, failure rates of 25 percent to 50 percent have been documented for U.S. expatriates on overseas assignments, with cost estimates of $50,000 to $250,000 per failure. This is a powerful incentive for companies to develop executives who can operate on a global basis.

CROSS-CULTURAL UNDERSTANDING

The third aspect of Goleman's emotional intelligence is empathy. This is the basis for what I call *cross-cultural understanding*. Without empathy, it is difficult for leaders to place themselves in another person's shoes. If you cannot identify with another's situation, it is difficult to supervise, motivate, or develop people, or to sell, negotiate, and work with customers or clients.

Many executives have told me that they feel guilty for not taking the time to understand the needs of those who report directly to them. When CDR ran a leadership integration program for the merger of Bank of America and NationsBank, we discovered that many executives defined the purpose of the new Bank of America as being able to "help people realize their dreams." While this may sound like hyperbole, there is a great deal of evidence to support the contention that helping people fulfill their dreams is a powerful leadership idea. This, however, requires leaders who are willing to take the time to understand the dreams, hopes, and fears of others. While many executives have come to better understand the needs of their clients and customers, many of them consistently report that they fail to allocate enough time to understand the needs of their colleagues and the people who report directly to them.

There is no question that empathy and cross-cultural understanding constitute critical aspects of global emotional intelligence. Without empathy, it is impossible to truly understand people, to gain their trust, or to provide products and services that are responsive to their needs. Empathy is also required to understand the strategy of competitors, to negotiate with governments, and to have credibility with the people with whom you work on a day-to-day basis.

In recent years, many cultural factors influencing global leadership have been examined. These include an understanding of group-oriented versus individually-oriented cultures; differences in perception of time and space; differences in attitudes toward hierarchy and authority; differences in communications and language; and differences in business and personal relationships. All of these cultural variables affect the way in which people work together across borders and need to be understood by those hoping to lead effectively in a global organization.

One example of a cultural factor that impacts global leadership is the difference between "doing-oriented" versus "relationship-oriented" cultures. Doing-oriented cultures, like the United States, Canada, Australia, the United Kingdom, and Scandinavian countries, tend to sell products and services based on technical and performance criteria. People from relationship-based cultures, like Latin America, the Middle East, and many African countries, tend to sell products and services based on relationships, personal compatibility, and chemistry.

When companies from a doing-oriented country try to sell products and services based mainly on technical criteria in a relationship-oriented country, they may encounter difficulty closing business deals, because they have not spent enough time developing a personal relationship with their clients or customers.

CROSS-CULTURAL EFFECTIVENESS

Finally, the fourth element in emotional intelligence is what Goleman identified as social skills, or what I call *cross-cultural effectiveness*. This includes a range of interpersonal skills associated with working with others, such as communications, decision making, motivating, negotiating, and conflict management.

The final challenge of cross-cultural effectiveness (assuming you now have the ability to understand differences between your culture and others) involves achieving business objectives that may conflict with cultural values in other countries. Welcome back to paradox management, the intellectual side of global mindset!

Managing cross-cultural paradoxes in business ethics is one of the most challenging aspects of cross-cultural effectiveness. In this instance, a global manager must (1) analyze and understand cultural differences (cross-cultural understanding); (2) self-regulate against the frustration that comes from not being able to solve conflicts between local values and business ethics (cultural adjustment); (3) maintain a balance between business interests and local needs (cross-cultural effectiveness); and (4) understand his or her strengths and weaknesses in dealing with other cultures (self-awareness).

In her book on this subject, Eileen Morgan advises global managers to create "maps for cross-cultural ethical navigation."[6] She recommends that managers use these paradox grids in all aspects of global intellectual and emotional intelligence to (1) understand cross-cultural challenges from different perspectives

---

[6] Morgan, Eileen. (1998). *Navigating Cross-Cultural Ethics: What Global Managers Do Right to Keep Them from Going Wrong.* Boston: Butterworth-Heinemann.

(self-management); (2) analyze the force of these perspective (business acumen); (3) manage the contradictions of the conflicting perspectives (paradox management); and (4) learn to work effectively in developing what she calls "communities of practice" to manage these conflicts on an ongoing basis (cultural acumen).

Cross-cultural effectiveness is very simply the ability to put it all together. It is the ability to translate knowledge, mindset, and skills into appropriate leadership behavior and a style that enables you to achieve business objectives in challenging cultural situations.

So, we conclude that global emotional intelligence, with its self-management and cultural acumen, is as important for global leadership as global intellectual intelligence, with its business acumen and paradox management. What does this mean for the development of global leaders?

DEVELOPING GLOBAL EMOTIONAL INTELLIGENCE

Almost all companies use international assignments as a method of developing global emotional intelligence. Coca-Cola, Colgate Palmolive, IBM, Philips, Matsushita, Sony, and Nestle have long used foreign subsidiaries as a source of executives to fill corporate management ranks and as a training ground where home country executives learn to operate from a broader perspective.

But now, more and more global executives are needed not just for international assignments, but for global task forces, joint venture teams, globally functional roles in company headquarters, and a variety of other jobs that require a global mindset and skills. Companies like IBM, Philips, and Matsushita have begun to track people on a global basis to develop a worldwide talent pool. NEC has a talent system that evaluates all executives every 3 years specifically on "their ability to adapt to international environments." [2]

GE's Medical Systems Group in Milwaukee derives more than 40 percent of its income outside the United States. To ensure that it had the leadership necessary to manage these wide-ranging operations, GE developed a Global Leadership Program. During this multi-year process, managers from Europe, Asia, and the United States worked together on action-learning projects to solve globally complex business problems. At the same time, as individuals, they learned to more effectively work with their colleagues across cultural and functional differences.

These global action-learning programs are a popular way to develop global intellectual and emotional intelligence. Using 360° feedback as well as extensive executive coaching, they emphasize cultural acumen as well as self-management. Over time, this results in managers who have an intellectual understanding of global management and a better understanding of their emotional and personal capacity to manage in a global marketplace.

Manfred Kets de Vries and Christine Mead point out that there are three fundamental variables that affect the development of global managers.[7] The first, *childhood development,* affects people's ability to adapt to new situations and the self-confidence they need to handle difficult circumstances. There is little companies can do to affect these capacities. These are characteristics that should be included in executive selection processes.

The second factor is *professional development.* Here, corporations can use a wide range of management training and coaching experiences to help managers understand and incorporate new mindsets and skills that will increase their global emotional intelligence.

The third factor influencing global leadership success is *organizational development,* or the degree to which a company is well run as a global organization. I have watched many leaders fail because they were in organizations that did not understand globalization. As a result, they placed people in

---

[7] Kets de Vries, Manfred, and Christine Mead. (1992). "The Development of the Global Leaders within the Multinational Corporation." In Vladimir Pucik, Noel Tichy, and Carole Barnett (Eds.), *Globalizing Management,* New York: John Wiley.

positions that were untenable, unsupported by the cultural values or the management process and systems needed to operate a global company.

All of this calls for an integrated approach to globalization. In my book, *A Manager's Guide to Globalization,* I advocate supporting a global strategy and structure with a global corporate culture and managers who have the global mindset and skills needed to manage world-class competitive organizations.[8] By working with many companies on globalization, I have learned that the key to globalization is not *where* you do business, but *how* you do business. Globalization is ultimately the business of mindset and behavior change.

I have found *global emotional intelligence* a useful way to summarize the critical characteristics of effective global leadership. Within the concept of global mindset and skills lies a cluster of four essential components: *cultural self-awareness, cultural adjustment, cross-cultural understanding,* and *cross-cultural effectiveness.* As global leaders around the world recognize these components and work to develop them, they will come to understand themselves and others in a way that will contribute to their business success and their greater personal fulfillment in a global world.

---

[8] Rhinesmith, Stephen. (1996). *A Manager's Guide to Globalization: Six Skills for Success in a Changing World,* 2nd ed. New York: McGraw-Hill.

20

IS YOUR ORGANIZATION DRIVEN BY DYNAMIC LEADERS?

Larraine Segil

A crisis of meaning has morphed the Western world in the first decade of the millennium. Every leader or aspiring leader is reevaluating the meaning of his or her own life and the purposes of his or her organization. Although outwardly, not much may have changed, internally, every person has been touched in some way or another by a multitude of earth-shattering events that occurred in this first decade of what some predict will be the century of the human clone, human habitation of Mars, and the complete digitization of the workplace. The events of terrorism of September 11, 2001, festering wars, and tribal battles, all of which create global effects of local terrorism; the economic challenges for Argentina; the business opportunities in China that continue to be elusive for some and explosive for others—these are just some of the events that are beginning to shape this century.

Some new leaders grew out of panic and fear; other anointed leaders failed to live up to expectations. However, in every organization, group, or community, we consistently applauded the characteristics of those quiet heroes who showed great versatility, flexibility, determination, and focus of purpose—those who promoted change.

Are you someone who wants to identify the issues that need to be changed not only in your organization, but also in the lives of those around you? Are you willing to make change happen? If so, the challenges you will encounter are real—but not insurmountable.

The problem is that most people don't want to recognize or accept change. Many organizations ignore the issues that prevent them from profitable change As such, today's manager must exhibit a special kind of leadership; he or she cannot avoid or deny the issues that are most difficult. This special kind of leadership must exist not just in the person at the top of the organization, but at all levels of management.

Over the past 10 years, my work helping clients to develop strong alliances has identified the trickle-down effect of these challenging relationships from CEOs and senior management, to middle and evolving managers, to supplier and purchasing groups, to all functions of the organization (including sales and marketing, human resources, engineering, research), and to a variety of service organizations and functions.

I began to examine what kind of special leadership could be applied to both simple and complex tasks and relationships. Based on my research into more than 250 companies, I have pinpointed the traits these change agent leaders possess—what I call "The Ten Essential Traits of a Dynamic Leader."[1] These personal characteristics include

- Fearlessness
- Completion

---

[1] Segil, Larraine. (2002). *Dynamic Leader, Adaptive Organization*. New York: John Wiley and Sons.

- Commitment
- Inspiration
- Assuredness
- Penetration
- Intelligence
- Energy
- Integrity
- Perception

In this chapter, I focus on the intersection between commitment and alliances.

Nothing will destroy a good alliance faster than a deficiency of leadership. In alliance parlance, we call it *executive sponsorship.* This means that there is a senior executive in the organization who is going to put his or her reputation and power of persuasion on the line with the middle managers who are implementing the alliance. However, too often, senior executives participate in the alliance formation stage—for example, as golf partners! These are high-level discussions in which all appears possible and much is promised, but when it comes to the nitty gritty of implementation, these same senior managers and their support systems are nowhere to be seen.

Recently, I was advising the alliances group for a Fortune 500 company. A talented perceptive leader, a vice president who had been with the company for a number of years, led the team. She understood the corporate resource games that were played and had reached the end of what she could tolerate.

"Its all about commitment," she said. "Senior management gives the mandate for an alliance—and appear to be behind it. However, once the deal is done, the announcements are made, the glory moment is over, and we are giving our troops their marching orders, resources just dry up. Where is everyone when the press conference is over and the hard work begins?"

What was upsetting this executive was not the work or the alliance. Certainly alliances can be aggravating, since one cannot control the behavior of the alliance partner. However, in this case, it was not the partner that was the problem. The issue was that when this vice president looked for the support of a senior manager to provide the resources that would back up the "golf course" commitment, it was not there. This is not uncommon. The result? Two outcomes, neither of which were good for the company.

FIRST: THE ALLIANCE ISSUE

The only reason to have an alliance is to achieve a result. That result has to be clearly defined by all parties. This may sound simplistic, but it is remarkable how few alliances are governed by clear, flexible, and mutually negotiated metrics. A few examples of metrics are

- Time to bring the product or service to market;
- Amount of revenues or market share increase (or not!);
- Specifics regarding capital invested by each side;
- Actual products shipped;
- Knowledge transferred—a difficult intangible to measure, but it can be done; and
- The ability to sell more to the common customer of both or all partners.

These metrics will support the definition of success for every partner. The metrics need to be changed as the parties change. For example, measuring the market opportunity means also understanding the opportunity cost of not doing the alliance. As new competitors enter the marketplace or other competitors drop out, the picture changes for all players, and the metrics mapping the costs and benefits from a relationship must be adjusted—that is, if anyone is paying attention to the strategic implications of an alliance.

This brings me to the second issue. In the example above, the disappointed vice president had given representations to the partner, as had her senior executive. As a consequence, the partner (a smaller company) was thrilled to have such a large and prestigious partner and had dedicated a high-energy team to the alliance. However, the vice president could not deliver. She did not have the senior executive's mandate to those in sales who would be held accountable for the relationship. In fact, they were not accountable. This partner had not been considered by them to be an important partner, although the customers that both partners were hoping to get more business from were significant. The problem lay at the feet, not the head, of senior management. Only the corporate alliance team had been told to go forward and make the alliance, not the sales team, who had responsibility for actually implementing it. Thus, the larger company could not deliver. The result? The smaller company became extremely frustrated, the larger company's reputation as a partner worth having was sullied, and the vice president, after many similar events in years past, left her employer and took years of contacts and expertise to its competitor.

This was a completely avoidable outcome. Had there been alignment between the verbal commitment of the executive sponsor, the allocation of resources and metrics, and the sales team that would be charged with implementing, the corporate alliances group would not have been left hanging. This happens rather too often with many groups at corporate levels.

What could have been done differently? The senior executive should have obtained buy-in and given a clear mandate to the sales group that this alliance was important, was expected to bear results, and that budgetary allocation of resources had to be dedicated to its fulfillment. His unwillingness to do that sent a clear message: This company is not serious about partnering, so "caveat, partner!"

SECOND: THE LEADERSHIP ISSUE

The vice president in the example above was a fine leader. She embodied many of the personal characteristics examined in my book *Dynamic Leader*. What she did not have, however, were many of the organizational characteristics that would have made her successful in that company, or in any company. Without the organizational characteristics to support and reward, nurture and encourage dynamic leaders, the personal frustration level grows so high that those desirable, hirable people leave. This is exactly what happened. A competitor was willingly standing by to snatch up this valuable resource, and soon she was in a new position at a higher salary.

The lack of leadership is manifest in many acquisitions. After one false start in the integration of two large automobile companies, it looks as if the second attempt at integration is going to work.

In March 2001, DaimlerChrysler was in a mess. Jurgen Schrempp, the company's outspoken CEO, had made some unfortunate statements about Daimler's acquisition of Chrysler that caused the morale in the U.S. operations to plummet. Although many consider that an acquisition is not an alliance, I prefer to classify it as the most integrated of all alliances. In my first book on alliances,[2] I describe in detail a management tool called "The Pyramid of Alliances."[3] On the very top is the acquisition or merger. Since our definition of an alliance is "a business relationship for mutual benefit between two or more parties who have complementary and compatible business interests and goals," the acquisition becomes the most intimate of those business relationships. The major failure statistics of acquisitions (over 80 percent fail to give the results expected by the parties, according to my research into 250 companies in January 2001) leads to the firm conclusion that post-merger integration issues are generally poorly planned and even more poorly implemented; hence our characterization of an acquisition as a highly integrated alliance.

In the DaimlerChrysler example, Dieter Zetsche, the new CEO of the U.S. division, took immediate and aggressive action. He knew that they could no longer pretend that this was a merger of equals. Instead, he bet on honesty and went forward with the takeover. He closed down a number of plants, changed the senior management, inserted some of his own key people, and started to change the culture. He ate in the cafeteria and shared some of his own personal challenges in being away from his family. He was a man comfortable with his own convictions

---

[2] Segil, Larraine. (1996). *Intelligent Business Alliances*. New York: Times Books, Random House.

[3] The Lared Group is an Alliance Advisory Group in Los Angeles: *www.laredgroup.com* and *www.lsegil.com*; phone (310) 556-1778; email *lsegil@lsegil.com*.

and with a belief in self that carried him through the tough decisions that would affect the lives of so many people. His willingness to be fearless was tempered by his ability to be "of the people." The very appointment of Herr Zetsche to his position indicated a strong commitment from corporate headquarters in Germany. They had to make this acquisition work. Two of the versatile traits of dynamic leaders were strongly in play in this example—fearlessness and completion.[4] The organizational characteristics were there to bolster the individual efforts: a good management team, a mandate from corporate, communication to the middle managers, and although the news was difficult to accept, the moves were in the direction of saving and turning around the company. Most people would rather have a job than not, so complaining and poor morale started to diminish as the turnaround plan evolved.

COMMITMENT

Dynamic leaders care intensely about what they do. For these leaders, commitment is about emotional vesting, perseverance, and passion. The sense of reward they derive from their accomplishments feeds more than their pocketbooks—it feeds their souls.

The word *emotion* is used with restraint in business, because it is often equated with weakness and instability. Emotional vesting does not mean losing emotional control. It means that the individual has strong and passionate expectations for positive results. It means working with commitment and using multiple resources, such as internal alliances. It means that the desire for success is high—and so are the rewards.

Cal James, CEO and president of Kaiser Permanente Company's Permco, was ready to retire when the opportunity came to lead the organization. He was a most unusual leader in what had been a hierarchical organization. He did away with

---

[4] Segil, Larraine. Dynamic Leader, Adaptive Organization. (2002). New York: John Wiley and Sons.

the two administrative assistants who had worked for the CEO before him and took care of basic tasks like email himself. He asked for most communications to be on line. He sat in the back in the meetings. I presented a program on alliances for his top management team, and he was there the whole time. He set an example, not by words, but by actions. A quiet, intense, and intellectual person, he saw himself as an extension of the corporate commitment to doing good things for the community—whether it was their health, as was the mandate of the organization, or their general well being. Cal donated his weekends (bringing his family along) to community outreach for the homeless and less fortunate. His employees saw his commitment, and many of them joined him.

Commitment does not evidence itself necessarily with what a leader does only at work—it is what that person stands for as a human, as a member of a community, as well as a corporate citizen. In the first decade of the millennium, the world seems to have become a much smaller place. Wars and feuds thousands of miles from home touch the very center of all of our beings, and leadership in a company, whether domestic or global, cannot turn its attention from community and macro-events, or those same events will come to roost in our own backyards. So too, Cal James felt his involvement with community was key to his participation in a health services organization.

Similarly, Royal Dutch Shell is committed to the world in which the company operates. Shell is the largest corporate investor in multiple diverse locations worldwide. Hundreds of its executives participated in the custom-designed alliance programs that I presented at Shell USA. When I expressed my delight at the commitment to the company to Jerome Adams, then president of the Shell Learning Center, he agreed.

"Shell has always taken care of its people. This is a tradition that goes back many years to early in our history. Many of our employees are placed in difficult parts of the world, uncomfortable living conditions, to say the least, and they are committed to the company and our mission. We must take care of them. That is why you will see people with very long tenure here at Shell, it's a mutual relationship, under your definition, a real alliance!" All the companies that partner with Shell are exposed to the integrity that the company brings to those they serve, both internal and external to the organization.

Consider these insights from Nigel Newton, chairman and CEO of Bloomsbury Publishing PLC in London, England, publisher of *The Harry Potter Series.* "If you try too hard to improve your failure rate, you become afraid of your inbox, terrified by the proposals made by authors and their agents. You end up either having no output or a book that is so bland that no one will want to read it. Discovering J. K. Rowling has reminded me of the sheer fun of knowing long before anyone else that you have something that will change the world." Newton's commitment to unknown authors and his ability to attract and inspire entrepreneurial, risk-taking editors has meant that this independent publisher is competing successfully on a global level.

Becoming a dynamic organization like Bloomsbury Publishing is critical to motivate people to work smarter, happier, and more productively. These are the reasons everyone is searching for ways to reward, inspire, and provide opportunities for innovation.

Commitment means applying patience. George Fisher, former Chairman and CEO of Eastman Kodak, had a vision of where he wanted Kodak to go, but even he could not control the changes in the market, and adapting a large and still-political organization is like turning a destroyer on a dime. Says Joerg Agin, former president of the entertainment division of Kodak, "He knew what it takes and went through the rigors of making sure everyone in the organization was committed to making that happen. He dedicated the resources and he had the patience to wait. That was one of his most important capabilities. He had patience. He never lost sight of the end and the vision."

In my many conversations with George Fisher, it was clear to me that his commitment went much further than just turning the company around. He was committed to his employees to the extent that he delayed terminating large numbers of them until he could give them and the company the very best chance for success.

"I feel good about the fact that thousands of our employees had jobs for another two years, and that terminating them earlier would not have made the difference. Top-line growth is as critical as cutting expenses. Sometimes it is as important not to do something as it is at other times to take decisive action. I believed, some may disagree, that this was the right thing to do at the time."

A man of solid ethics, strong commitment, and well-reasoned cautious beliefs, George Fisher contributed a great deal to Kodak in his sojourn there. Yet, one of the most lasting parts of his legacy was what he left behind at Motorola where he had been Chairman and CEO: his unwavering belief in what was right and what was wrong—and actions that followed his belief system. I examine this characteristic in my book *Dynamic Leader* as well as in *Fast Alliances: Power your E-business*, which deals with the world of alliances online—integrity.

You cannot succeed in relationships with other companies or with your employees over the long term if you or your organization lacks integrity. That means you say what you are going to do and you do it. It is indeed the real meaning of trust in alliances. Since many partnering arrangements involve partners who may collaborate in one sense while competing in another, you may never totally trust a partner/competitor. However, if they say what they are going to do and they do what they said, you can have a very successful alliance with them! Look, for example, at Lotus/IBM. It partners with competitors all the time, and in order to do so effectively, it separates the partner teams from physically walking around Lotus/IBM's ordinary operations—the result is that partnering can take place with all team members knowing what they should and should not be talking about or working on and no knowledge is transferred by "walking around."

Alliances and leadership are inexorably intertwined. My research in alliances through my work at Caltech, where for the past 20 years I have presented the two-day alliances program for its executive education group, has proven that alliances require alignment with corporate goals and clarity of direction. This can happen only where leadership is established—but more importantly, where that leader and his or her team are held accountable for their actions, not their words. Further recent research into leadership issues at Caltech leads me to conclude that leadership accountability, as well as the metrics of the alliance and the resources to support it, are essential elements of both organizational and alliance success.

21

EFFECTIVE CRISIS MANAGEMENT: NOW MORE THAN EVER

Idalene Kesner

Ever since the incidents involving Johnson & Johnson and the Tylenol poisonings in 1982, corporate executives have been keenly aware of the need for effective methods to deal with organizational crises. Indeed, following the Tylenol incidents many firms established crisis management programs. Although these programs vary from firm to firm, the overriding message of crisis managers has been that effective crisis management begins with prevention.

Experts agree that the best-handled situations are the crises that never happen—the crises that are averted because of outstanding detection mechanisms both inside and outside affected organizations. And, although crisis prevention remains the mantra of all good crisis managers, managers also know that not every crisis can be prevented. The terrorist actions of September 11, 2001, that destroyed New York City's World Trade Center Towers and damaged the Pentagon in Washington D.C. are tragic reminders of this fact. These events confirm that effective crisis management is also about effective crisis preparation and response.

What has changed in the way we think about crisis management today? What steps can managers take to better prepare themselves and their organizations? These and other questions will be answered as we explore the realities of managing crises in an environment that too often presents situations that are unexpected and unpreventable.

WHAT IS A CRISIS?

While not all crises are alike, most have several features in common. Specifically, crises are situations that run the risk of escalating in intensity, interfering with normal business operations, jeopardizing a company's positive public image, damaging a company's bottom line, and falling under close media and/or government scrutiny.[1] Crisis management, therefore, is about employing effective management techniques to minimize the damage and negative impact on a company and to gain control of the situation.

A well-handled crisis is one in which the problem disappears quickly; there is minimal media or governmental attention; the company's sales, profits, and productivity are not severely negatively affected; and the company's reputation and credibility remain unscathed among key constituents. On the other hand, a poorly handled crisis can cause numerous negative outcomes, such as significant damage to the firm's reputation or credibility, and it can result in litigation, fines, or penalties. Some crises can lead to changes in senior-level personnel and/or a loss of employees, employee loyalty, or employee productivity.[2]

---

[1] Fink, Steven. (1986). *Crisis Management.* New York: American Management Association.

[2] Caponigro, Jeffrey. (1998). *The Crisis Counselor.* Southfield, MI: Barker Business Books, Inc.

CRISIS PREVENTION

Over the years, managers have learned firsthand that crises come in all shapes and sizes, including product failures, plant accidents, industrial relations incidents, cash and financial problems, succession events, and even public perception crises. In most cases, crises begin with one or more warning signals. In fact, the earlier a manager detects these signals, the more likely he or she is to prevent the situation from escalating to the level of a full-blown crisis. The key, therefore, is putting signal-detection mechanisms in place throughout the organization.

Why aren't these mechanisms prevalent in all organizations? One reason is that managers sometimes labor under the misconception that a crisis will never impact their company or industry. This misconception is particularly acute if a company and its industry have been unaffected by prior crises. Of course, in today's environment almost no company can make such a claim. The interconnectedness of organizations and the pervasiveness of media coverage challenge managers in even the most insular organizations from claiming they are invulnerable.

Companies may fail to set up early-warning systems because of cost. Signal-detection mechanisms can be expensive to install and maintain. Yet, if one compares the costs of detection to the costs associated with handling a full-scale crisis, investments are more than justified. However, short-term financial concerns often override long-term investments, especially when the cost savings from averting a crisis cannot be directly identified or easily quantified.

Nevertheless, it is impossible for even the most prepared organization to implement a system that will detect *every* conceivable crisis. The best response, therefore, is to conduct a *crisis vulnerability audit.*[3] This audit begins with identifying the full range of crises that may affect an organization. Next, managers in each division, product area, or functional area assess their department's vulnerability to each type of crisis. Figure 21.1 provides a representation of this type of audit.

---

[3] This is sometimes referred to as a *crisis susceptibility audit.*

Type of Crisis	Division/Functional Area/Product Area				
	A	B	C	D	E
1.					
2.					
3.					
4.					
5.					

Cells can be filled in using the following ratings: H = high vulnerability; M = moderate vulnerability; L = low vulnerability; X = crisis not applicable for this area.

FIGURE 21.1 Crisis vulnerability audit.

While the actual audit includes far more detail, the end objective is the same. Managers must uncover areas in which their company is most susceptible and invest in early-warning devices in the areas of greatest vulnerability, where the damage caused by potential crises is the greatest.

Overall, when it comes to crisis prevention, experts often refer to the *crisis management paradox*. Simply put, this rule of thumb suggests that the less vulnerable managers think their firm is, the fewer crises they prepare for and the more vulnerable their firm becomes. Conversely, the more vulnerable managers think their firm is, the more crises they prepare for and the less vulnerable their firm becomes.

CRISIS PREPARATION AND CRISIS RESPONSE

Every organization must weigh the costs of early-warning detection systems against the likelihood that a crisis will occur in a given area and the seriousness of the damage that could result. Yet, there are some situations for which warning signals are undetectable by management, and there are some times when, despite detection, the crisis cannot be averted. Under these circumstances, the best managers can do is have sufficient crisis-management response systems to minimize resulting damage, especially loss of life. The most common crises in this category are natural disasters, such as earthquakes, hurricanes, or tornadoes; yet, following September 11, 2001, we now include on this list acts of domestic and international terrorism.[4]

When this type of crisis hits, how does the role of crisis manager change? Perhaps the most significant change is a shift in focus from crisis prevention to crisis preparation and response. Fundamentally, crisis preparation involves identifying the processes and procedures one will use during the crisis. Disaster-response manuals, for example, can be used to detail immediate actions, including evacuation plans, succession procedures, and even communication steps. These items minimize the need for contemplation and debate in the event of a crisis, thereby shortening decision-making and response times. This in turn can minimize the trauma and potential damage. Of course, signal detection is still important even when crises cannot be prevented. The sooner managers detect crises, the sooner they can launch response plans.

Determining a firm's preparedness requires a different type of audit than the crisis vulnerability audit. A *crisis capability audit* explores how well a firm is equipped to respond. For this type of audit, each area of the firm must evaluate its ability to detect, to respond, to repair, and to incorporate lessons learned.[5] This type of audit might also involve highlighting specific weaknesses so that they can be targeted for improvement. Figure 21.2 provides a representation of this type of audit.

Another important part of crisis preparedness is the establishment of a crisis management team.[6] This small team helps plan for and manage the crisis. An effective team is one that includes appropriate senior managers, representation from key areas (e.g., legal, financial, human resources), as well as communications experts. Other functional or divisional executives

---

[4] Terrorism experts suggest that with sufficient early-warning detection mechanisms, even some terrorist actions can be prevented. However, from an organization's perspective, most acts of domestic and international terrorism are difficult to detect and thus difficult to prevent.

[5] Meyers, Gerald C. (1986). *When It Hits the Fan.* Boston, MA: Houghton Mifflin Company. pp. 218–221.

[6] Ibid, pp. 221–225; Caponigro, pp. 109–114.

Division/Department/Area: _____		Type of Crisis: _____
Crisis Stage	**Evaluation**	**Areas of Weakness**
Detecting crises early		
Managing the immediate effects of crises		
Repairing the damage resulting from crises		
Incorporating lessons learned from crisis response		

Divisions or areas of the firm can be evaluated using a three-point scale where H = high capabilities; M = moderate capabilities; L = low capabilities.

FIGURE 21.2 Crisis capability audit.

might need to be included depending on the nature of the crisis. Some organizations even go so far as to establish multiple teams, with each team focusing on a unique area of vulnerability. Each team often includes different experts inside the organization as well as external counselors available on demand.[7]

While it is important that crisis management teams have strong representation from key areas of management, the characteristics of its members may be even more important. Because their role involves both preparation and response, team members must be knowledgeable about the company, the industry, and the situation. They must demonstrate good judgment and the ability to maintain perspective even under extreme pressure. They must possess sufficient authority and capability to make decisions quickly. In addition, members must be able to manage time effectively, to delegate, to communicate, and to work well in a team setting.

The role of the crisis management team varies depending on the stage of the crisis.[8] In the *pre-crisis period,* the team is responsible for

---

[7] Examples of outside counselors include attorneys, insurance carriers, public relations experts, temporary employment agencies, external law enforcement and security services, and governmental disaster response teams and relief agencies.

[8] For a more in-depth discussion about these various responsibilities at each stage, see Meyers, p. 226.

- Intelligence gathering and information monitoring;
- Threat assessment, scenario development, and testing;
- Episode investigation;
- Simulation training; and
- The establishment of communication channels.

During the *crisis period* the team's responsibility shifts to the following:

- Fact gathering about the actual crisis event;
- Situation evaluation;
- Options assessment;
- Action selection;
- Issuance of instructions;
- Establishment of spokesperson responsibility and maintenance of effective communication channels; and
- Progress monitoring.

Finally, in the *post-crisis period* the team's role includes the following:

- Scenario reconstruction;
- Improvement of early warning systems, information systems, and communication systems;
- Implementation of damage limitation and long-term recovery mechanisms; and
- Development of a new strategy.

CRISIS COMMUNICATIONS

While crisis preparation and crisis response have increased in importance as the environment has become more hostile, the greatest change for crisis managers has come in the area of communications. More than ever before, managers rely on their communication strategies to minimize the potential damage to their companies' reputations and turn the negative aspects of bad situations into positives.

The pervasiveness of the media and the constant search for news stories has created explosive coverage of events. Even minor incidents can become crises when under the spotlight of media coverage. Moreover, television and electronic media are used more extensively than in the past, creating coverage that is instantaneous and constant.

Perhaps the most significant change in the area of communications is the increased need for full disclosure. Crisis managers should be wary of advice to keep a low profile or hide information. Similarly, advice that encourages managers to treat reporters as adversaries during times of crisis can prove damaging. While advice such as this might have been appropriate in an environment of limited media coverage, today it is unlikely to protect a firm. Accessibility to information from sources such as the Internet means that the media can and will uncover information about the crisis even without the firm's cooperation. Therefore, it is better to be the source of information, especially if one can influence the tone and substance of the message.

Full disclosure is critical if future injury or fatalities are likely as the crisis unfolds. Moreover, full disclosure can be helpful when the fictions surrounding the crisis are worse than the facts or when the organization shares the role of victim—as is often the case in unpredictable crises. In these instances, it is important to communicate the facts early and to a broad audience.

Crisis communications today means more than just sharing information with people inside the company. It means the firm must take responsibility for delivering its message externally to key constituents and to the public at large. Considering the public's interests requires managers to balance the advice of lawyers with the advice of public relations experts. Now more than ever, crisis managers must understand the role of reporters as well as educate them about their company, its industry, and the facts surrounding the crisis. As such, crisis managers at all levels can benefit from advanced crisis-communications training.

Overall, one must remember that a crisis can destroy a company not simply because of what takes place in a court of law, but also because of the damage to the firm's reputation in the court of public opinion. An effective communications strategy is one of the most important tools a manager can use to mitigate this damage. Table 21.1 lists past and present communication strategies.

TABLE 21.1 Crisis Communication Strategies

PAST STRATEGIES	PRESENT STRATEGIES
■ Use partial disclosure or nondisclosure whenever possible; adopt a reactive posture releasing information only when the company is forced to do so.	■ Use full disclosure with an aim of having better control over content and tone of messages; adopt a proactive posture releasing information before being forced to do so.
■ Keep a "low profile" to avoid communication errors that could be used in a court of law; allow legal counsel to shape the message; adopt the company's viewpoint in all communications.	■ Adopt a higher profile, recognizing that the company is impacted both by the court of law and the "court of public opinion"; balance the advice of legal counsel with that of public relations/communications experts; accept the public's "right to know" when planning the company's communications during crisis.
■ Focus mostly on internal communications with employees.	■ Focus equally on internal communications with employees and external communications with key constituents (e.g., customers, suppliers, local community members, the public-at-large).
■ Treat reporters as adversaries and minimize contact if possible.	■ Treat reporters as respected professionals and work to educate them about the company, its industry, and the issues surrounding the crisis; if possible build relationships with reporters in advance of crisis situations.
■ Provide crisis-communications training only to the individual who is designated as company spokesperson.	■ Provide crisis-communications training to a broad group of managers; recognize that with the pervasiveness of media coverage today, many organizational members will be asked to respond (internally and externally) to the situation.

CONCLUSION

It is no secret that effective crisis management can be a career maker or a career breaker for the managers who must handle these tense and often chaotic situations. The same extremes are also true for organizations. Firms that handle crises well can survive and perhaps even thrive, while those that handle crises poorly may face permanent damage or even bankruptcy. The complexities of today's environment remind us that managers can no longer take for granted the predictability or preventability of crises. They can no longer take for granted that they will know what to do when the unimaginable happens. Handling these situations requires steady nerves, excellent judgment, and strong communications skills. For firms that have not begun developing managers for the uncertainties that lie ahead, it is time to take notice—the wake-up call has been sounded.

IV

CREATING COMPETITIVE ADVANTAGE: STRATEGIES FOR SUCCESS

PART

MARKETING THROUGH RECONCILIATION: GLOBAL BRAND, LOCAL TOUCH

Fons Trompenaars and Peter Woolliams

M arketing professionals are becoming increasingly aware of the need to take account of culture when working in diverse markets. The issues of branding for different cultures and how to develop a marketing strategy for the global market are current fundamental questions for us all. Based on our recent research with Dr. Charles Hampden-Turner, we can now offer a new and effective proven methodology that addresses these challenges.

Let us first note that fundamental mistakes are still being made even at the most basic level of cultural differences, originating, for example, simply from language. When General Motors introduced the Chevy Nova, it hadn't checked that *no va* means "no go" in Spanish. Red, representing danger in Western cultures, can send different messages about a product to the Chinese, for whom it can represent success. Similarly, the color yellow in marketing promotions may be offensive to Arabs, yet may convey freshness and summer to Western cultures.

More important than these overt aspects of culture are differences that derive from the subtly different meanings given by different cultures to apparently the same things. For instance, U.S. Americans may purchase a Sony Discman, because it enables them to "listen to their favorite music *without being disturbed by others.*" The Japanese may purchase the same product in order to "listen to their favorite music *without disturbing others.*" The product may be technically identical, but the purchasing motive is different because of the different meanings and priorities given to oneself and other's privacy. Kodak introduced an advertising campaign based on capturing "memories" in the physical form of photographs. In contrast, for European cultures, "memory" is a much more sentimental construct and may be tainted if represented in the explicit format of a photograph that omits the higher levels of the experience. Procter and Gamble successfully developed a new generation of highly absorbent Pampers with the unique selling point that they could be changed less frequently. This approach failed in Japan, where frequent changing of diapers/nappies is perceived as fundamental to keeping baby clean.

Our new marketing paradigm is based on the three R's: recognize, respect, and reconciliation.

1. **Recognize:** While we can easily recognize explicit cultural differences, we may not be aware of these implicit cultural differences. This explains why cultural due diligence is often absent from management agendas and many of the classic marketing models, such as Porter. Thus, the first step is to *recognize* that there are cultural differences.

2. **Respect:** Different orientations are not right or wrong; they are different. It is too easy to be judgmental about people and societies that give different meanings to their world than we do. Thus, the next step is to *respect* these differences and accept customers' rights

to interpret the world (and our products and marketing efforts) in the way they choose.

3. **Reconciliation:** Because of these different worldviews, we have two seemingly opposing views of the contrasting cultures: those of the seller and those of the buyer. The task of the marketer is to *reconcile* these seemingly opposing differences.

We can categorize the different dilemmas that arise in each of several dimensions based on our earlier research on cultural differences.[1] These dilemmas include

1. universal or particular?
2. individualism or communitarianism?
3. specific or diffuse?
4. neutral or affective?
5. achievement or ascription?
6. internal or external control?
7. time: sequential or synchronic?

UNIVERSAL OR PARTICULAR?

Do we follow a single global approach or particularize to each market? The dominant dilemma originating from this dimension is the global–local dichotomy (see Figure 22.1). The question is, Shall we have one standardized approach (identical product range and associated identical marketing support) or shall we go for a local approach (different products and local-based marketing in each destination)? In other words, are our customers best served by becoming nearly globally universal and alike, or by becoming more influenced by particular national or local cultures?

The answer lies in *transnational specialization*. Here we reconcile the seemingly opposing extremes. We integrate best

---

[1] *Riding the Waves of Culture*, Trompenaars and Hampden-Turner.. New York: McGraw Hill © 1998. Reprinted by permission.

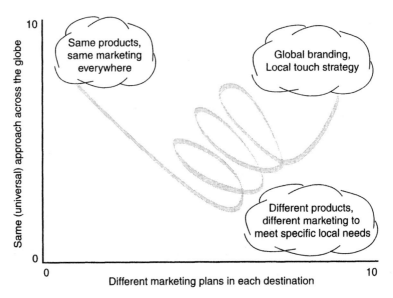

FIGURE 22.1 The global–local dilemma.

practice and satisfy customer needs by learning from the diversity of adopting, adapting, and combining the best.

McDonalds successfully achieved this integration by branding the Big Mac universally across the globe. The big M represents the universal corporate identity with standard furnishings and fittings in all their restaurants. Yet, in the Middle East, the Big Mac is a veggie-burger, and it is served with rice rather than fries in the Asiatic. Even smaller local variations are promoted, such as the croquet variant in the Netherlands.

Heineken alters the temperature at which its beer is served to follow local tastes, but also positions its same product differently in different markets—to reflect the different meaning that drinkers ascribe to the product. In Europe, it is sold as "Beer, as meant to be drunk." In the Caribbean, it is positioned as "cosmopolitan." The (almost identical) TV advertisements for each island show the same shots of Paris, London, and Tokyo (to represent the global branding of Heineken), but with an easily recognizable island-specific building or monument to locate the global brand in the local context.

In some situations, the marketing strength derives from the universal world branding. Thus, Coca-Cola is Coca-Cola everywhere and represents the American dream, although ingredient details on the can or bottle may be in a local language. Similarly, British Airways sells safe, reliable, quintessential Englishness, supported by local agents in the destinations it serves.

INDIVIDUALISM OR COMMUNITARIANISM?

This second dimension also gives rise to a number of key dilemmas. Is marketing concerned with satisfying individual customer needs and preferences, or is the focus on creating a trend or fashion that is adopted by the group? Individuals then purchase to show that they have joined the group by following the shared trend.

From the customers' perspective, do we relate to others by discovering what each one of us individually wants, or do we place ahead of this some shared concept to which we can identify and feel part of?

Simply rejecting the other viewpoint or adopting it as a compromise will not yield the best market return. In our new marketing paradigm, we can follow the same logic for each dimension by starting from one extreme but integrating with the needs of the other.

Although marketing to an individualistic culture might see the individual as an end, marketing benefits from a collective arrangement as the means to achieve that end. Conversely, marketing to a communitarian culture sees the group as the target market, yet can use feedback and suggested improvements from individuals. The marketing relationship should be seen as circular. The decision to focus on one end is arbitrary.

Microsoft Windows and its associated office products software offer the benefits of a group approach. Documents can be shared and exchanged because they adhere to common file formats. Yet, individuals can tailor the configuration of their system to satisfy individual preferences, such as the screen zoom-level to meet their individual eyesight capabilities.

Jaguar and Mercedes owner-drivers take pride in being members of their fellow club of drivers of prestige cars (belonging to their peer group). However, when they insert their individual key in the lock of their own car, the seats and driving mirror configure to their own preference, even though someone else may have altered these settings.

At the metalevel, we see how Richard Branson has successfully reconciled the personalities of David and Goliath in the branding of Virgin. He successfully creates public sympathy in favor of the wronged individual confronting the collective assailant (the establishment).

Specific or Diffuse?

What is the degree of involvement of the customer? Do we see the customer as a "punter," someone from whom we can make a fast buck, or is a customer a series of relationships over time? Do we need a relationship first, before he or she becomes customer, or do we easily do business from which a relationship may or not follow?

In our work with British Airways and American Airlines, we can examine how they define their relationship with their customers differently. It is typically American to emphasize "core competencies" and "shareholder value." In contrast, British Airways (and Cathy Pacific) emphasize service: hot breakfasts, champagne, and the like. In a "one-world" alliance, it may appear that the options are limited to the following:

- Serve the "cattle" with Coke and pretzels.
- Serve hot breakfast, champagne, and add in-flight massage and shoeshine (and go bankrupt in the process).
- Compromise and sell the "hot pretzel," thus upsetting (and losing) customers.

Marketing through reconciliation is more than this. It is the craft of defining those specific areas to provide a more personal service and thereby deepen the relationship. Jan Carlson of SAS calls this the "moment of truth." The future success of an alliance depends on one particular reconciliation: the competency of the marketing team to identify those circumstances in which specific moments can be used to deepen the relationship. A single brief 30 second interaction that a passenger has with a member of the cabin crew staff on a long haul flight, can influence their whole perception of the service provided and therefore their decision to stay loyal to the same airline or not. Such brief interactions are 'moments of truth'.

NEUTRAL OR AFFECTIVE?

What part does the display and role of emotion play and/or is the display of emotion controlled? Typically, reason and emotion are linked or combined. When customers express satisfaction (or dissatisfaction), they are trying to find confirmation in their thoughts and feelings—and trying to show they have the same response as others. ("I have the same view of this product or service as you"). Customers whose responses are neutral are seeking an indirect response.

Michael Porter said that Germans don't know what marketing is about. In his American conception, marketing is about showing (overtly) the qualities and features of your product without inhibition. Germans might see this as bragging and the sort of tactics expected from second-hand car dealers. The way you express positive things in Germany needs to be subtler. As Tom Peters said in Atlanta in 1999, "It's cool to be emotional nowadays."

ACHIEVEMENT OR ASCRIPTION?

Does the customer want a functional product that achieves the utilitarian purpose, or is he or she buying status? You can tell time from a $1 LED digital watch as well as with a $10,000

Rolex Oyster. But, a Rolex Oyster is not simply a watch. It is a symbolic representation of status.

All societies give certain members higher status than others, signaling that unusual attention should be focused on those persons, the products they own and display, and the services they consume.

In achievement-oriented cultures, the emphasis is on performance. In ascribed status cultures, such as Asia, status is ascribed to products that naturally evoke admiration from others, such as high technology and jewelry. The status is less concerned with the functional capabilities of the product.

We can see this dilemma in action between the achieved and ascribed status in the profit-oriented versus nonprofit status of BUPA and reconciled successfully by Val Gooding. Should she set a goal of a 25 percent profit to shareholders to compete on the stock exchange, or make enough return to serve the sick and the weak? To care about people you serve is a precursor to success and you must ascribe status to them. The provident status of BUPA reconciles the need to achieve business growth with providing primary healthcare. Care for your employees through a strong successful business base, and they pass that care to the clients (patients).

INTERNAL OR EXTERNAL CONTROL?

Are we stimulated by an inner drive or do we adapt to external events beyond our control? The issue here is to connect the internally controlled culture of technology push (sell what we can make) with the externally controlled world of market pull (make what we can sell).

Nobody will deny the great knowledge and inventiveness of Philips in its technologies and the quality of its marketing. The problem is that these two major areas didn't seem to connect. The push of the technology needs to help you decide what markets you want to be pulled by, and the pull of the market needs to help you know what technologies to push.

TIME: SEQUENTIAL OR SYNCHRONIC?

Do we view time as sequential or synchronic? In *sequential cultures*, time is an objective measure of passing increments. The faster you can act and get to the market, the more effective will be your competitiveness. In contrast, *synchronous cultures* like doing things "just-in-time," so present ideas converge on the future. The better your timing, the more competitive you will be.

Keeping traditional products that made your name in the first place can jeopardize the creation of new products. Karel Vuursteen of Heineken successfully integrated the (past) traditions of the Heineken family with the future needs of the company, and the traditions of the Heineken product with the need for (future) innovation—for example, in the area of specialty beers. Process innovation sought new methods of creating the same result (traditional product), while product innovation allowed new drinks from scratch without involving Heineken's premium product in the experiments.

SUMMARY

Our new marketing paradigm requires a mindset that reconciles these continuing dilemmas. It is the result of linking learning efforts across each dimension with the contrasting viewpoint.

The new concepts described here are explored further in the new book *21 Leaders for the 21st Century*.[2]

---

[2] Trompenaars, Fons, and Hampden-Turner. (2001). *21 Leaders for the 21st Century*. United Kingdom: Capstone; United States: McGraw Hill.

23

THE EFFECTIVE USE OF SCENARIO ANALYSIS TO SUPPORT RESEARCH AND DEVELOPMENT

Peter Schwartz and Gerald Harris

INTRODUCTION

During the past 5 years, we have worked with companies interested in applying scenario analysis techniques to their research and development (R&D) plans over the medium-to-long term (generally 5-year to 10-year timeframes). These engagements involved companies in a range of industries—computer hardware and software, telecommunications, and power generation—as well as people in various roles from business development and marketing executives to pure researchers, engineers, and scientists. Based on our experience, we have identified a number of best practices that produce the most useful results. They include

1. Involve a diverse team of people and perspectives.
2. Put a "stake in the ground." (In other words, take into account that which senior management or key decision makers consider as vital aspects of the *company's strategic intent*—the company's vision or sense of "who it wants to be."
3. Maintain openness about the uncertainty of customer needs and wants.
4. Make the path from ideas to the creation of products and services clear by incorporating a strong technology roadmap.
5. Establish a well-functioning connection between R&D and business development, marketing, and manufacturing departments.
6. Embed a continuous learning loop and focused scenario analysis at the market entry point and beyond.

USING SCENARIO ANALYSIS TO GUIDE R&D PLANNING

The purpose of R&D is to enhance the product and service offerings of a company. This may mean incremental or revolutionary improvements to current products as well as the introduction of completely new offerings. However, in a successful business, R&D is not solely the job of the technical people who sit in the laboratory, invent things, and throw them over the wall. Superior R&D requires a connection to customer needs and desires and to how products and services might be priced, positioned, and sold relative to the competition. This is a complex process involving many people with different roles and priorities, which inevitably gives rise to communication challenges.

It is in managing such communication challenges that scenario analysis techniques can provide real value. A diverse team of people, drawn from across the organization and seeded with knowledgeable outsiders (maybe even customers), can open up the strategic conversation about the intent and direction of R&D spending. In other words, it is useful to bring together key stakeholders from marketing, customer relations, business development, and finance as well as R&D to ask a broader set of questions: What is R&D trying to achieve, and over what timeframe? What will enhance competitiveness? How will it support meeting important aspects of the customer's total value proposition? The R&D department's technical staff cannot answer these questions alone. A well-managed scenario analysis provides a process through which diverse stakeholders can explore the uncertainties behind these questions in an open and learning-oriented way. Ultimately, this can generate exciting new insights, deepen the shared understanding of R&D decision making, and build lasting, cross-organizational relationships.

A COMMON R&D SCENARIO FRAMEWORK

To explain more about scenario analysis in R&D, we will share a scenario framework that arose consistently in our work. In developing scenarios, it is useful to establish the framework by isolating two highly uncertain, but very important, variables that may drive change in the future. In our R&D work, we found two recurring variables: (1) the pace or direction of technology innovation, and (2) changes in customer needs or wants. In most cases, the scenario teams felt that the underlying technology (or technologies) they were working with could either accelerate or stagnate, be open to sudden breakthroughs, be shifted by wildcards, or be largely out of their control. Despite edicts to "know thy customer," the teams felt that customer demand could be fickle—affected by competitive offerings, substitutes, economic conditions, peer pressure, and a host of other factors. This typically led to different versions of the scenario framework displayed in Figure 23.1.

This framework was only a starting point for detailed and well-researched scenarios. Its strengths lay in the divergent and challenging worlds that each quadrant suggests. Typically, the northeast quadrant produced a "Brave New World" scenario, where many big changes—and opportunities—challenged companies to keep up and to innovate. The southwest quadrant, by

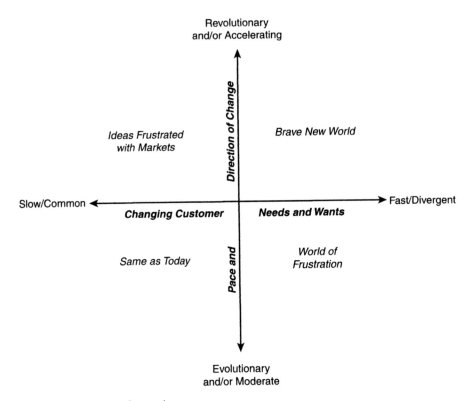

FIGURE 23.1 Scenario framework.

contrast, tends to produce scenarios with a "same-as-today" feeling; participants were either satisfied that their companies were well positioned or frustrated that a lot of good ideas would go undeveloped. Scenarios for the southeast and northwest quadrants seemed counterintuitive, and the teams found that making them work in the real world was challenging and exciting. The southeast quadrant typically involved a "world of frustration," as customer needs went unmet and a series of inadequate solutions were tried and usually failed. In the northwest quadrant the scenario was often a variation on "ideas frustrated with markets"—participants worried that new technologies would not match customer needs and wants and therefore wouldn't find profitable markets. In many cases, the southeast and northwest quadrants introduced unexpected, but plausible, real-world contradictions into the conversation.

ELEMENTS OF A GOOD SCENARIO ANALYSIS

Whether scenarios are developed to guide R&D plans or to inform other strategic decisions, a number of basic steps should be followed. Once a divergent and sound (well-researched, convincing) set of scenarios is created, they should be used to test, or "wind-tunnel," existing strategies— what the organization is actually doing or positioning itself to do in the areas of concern. Then, the scenarios should be used to create new strategic options. In order to do this, members of the stakeholder team should "live" in each scenario— assume it is true—and determine what strategies or actions might lead to success. Then, the options for each scenario should be tested for robustness: Do some work in all scenarios? Those that are robust should become high priority. Those that are not, but have great appeal if certain events unfold, should be looked at closely in two ways. First, are there low-cost and low-risk actions that the stakeholder team can take that will allow the organization to quickly move to this option? Second, can the team identify and scan for early indicators that give a signal to move that option to the forefront? Making strategy development proactive rather than reactive, and dynamic instead of static, is among the most valuable dimensions of scenario analysis.

GETTING THE MOST FROM R&D SCENARIOS

In our experience, a strong, well-facilitated team will create challenging and useful scenarios. The real differences lie in the level of participation and in how the scenarios are ultimately used and shared within the organization, as demonstrated by the following three examples.

In one of our most successful cases in the telecommunications industry, a joint team from business development and R&D initially requested the scenarios. This team worked together throughout the process and at a key point introduced and wind-tunneled a technology roadmap through the scenarios. The conversation exploded with insights and ideas. The team was able to pinpoint specific technical advances that would support high value-added or competitive product features specific to each scenario. The path to commercializing products was also made clearer and more concrete. Importantly, this team enjoyed clear senior management support and direction, including an attitude that there were no failures. Instead, if a chosen path didn't succeed in meeting its objectives, there was still an opportunity to capture the learning for future efforts. The 5-year timeframe for evaluating results allowed the team to be patient, and the scenarios provided the context for deeper, more focused analysis. Years after we concluded the project, focused scenarios were used to consider pathways to market entry.

In a moderately successful effort, a company involved in heavy manufacturing succeeded not so much in radically shifting the direction of R&D spending, but in getting a wide range of parties involved. As a result, the ultimate decisions were well understood and supported across the organization. Relationships were built internationally across several groups. Finally, the team isolated some key uncertainties for longer term scanning and monitoring that could portend a change in direction. This project would have been much more valuable if there had been deeper research on and openness toward changing customer needs and wants. Integrating more customer perspectives would have added more content in the strategic option development stage of this project.

Our least successful effort involved a consortium of companies and resulted, we feel, from confusion and a lack of cohesion around the strategic intent of the key stakeholders. These companies were mostly involved in computers and information technology, and fit in different places along the value chains of those industries. In this situation, R&D results had to be shared with multiple and sometimes competing firms. Competitive concerns kept many participants from being explicit about their true strategic interests and made it impossible to test existing or potential strategies within the context of the scenarios. Eventually, this handicapped the lead organization's ability to articulate viable options and share results. However, this project did have a powerful impact in terms of using the scenario-development process as a tool for sharing perspectives across a diverse group. Many participants expressed appreciation at the opportunity to see how companies at various points in the industry value chain perceive issues and problems differently. Based on these and similar projects, we recommend following the process map (shown in Figure 23.2) in order to ensure that scenario analysis is successfully applied.

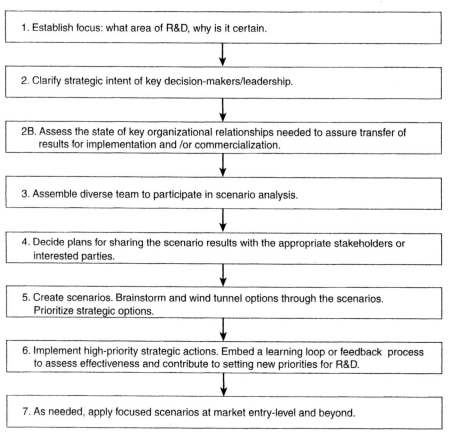

1. Establish focus: what area of R&D, why is it certain.

2. Clarify strategic intent of key decision-makers/leadership.

2B. Assess the state of key organizational relationships needed to assure transfer of results for implementation and /or commercialization.

3. Assemble diverse team to participate in scenario analysis.

4. Decide plans for sharing the scenario results with the appropriate stakeholders or interested parties.

5. Create scenarios. Brainstorm and wind tunnel options through the scenarios. Prioritize strategic options.

6. Implement high-priority strategic actions. Embed a learning loop or feedback process to assess effectiveness and contribute to setting new priorities for R&D.

7. As needed, apply focused scenarios at market entry-level and beyond.

FIGURE 23.2 Process map for applying scenario analysis to R&D planning.

CONCLUSION

In conclusion, scenario analysis can enhance and guide R&D efforts by engaging a broader range of stakeholders; leveraging their experience and knowledge to create divergent and challenging future worlds that illuminate risks and opportunities; and creating a context for evaluating existing and potential strategies in an uncertain world. Ultimately, scenario analysis can enrich the organization's ongoing strategic conversation about the purpose and increasing importance of forward-looking research, development, and innovation.

24 MORPHING MARKETING: DISSOLVING DECISIONS

James M. Hulbert and Pierre Berthon

M arketing in the 21st century is in a process of rapid metamorphosis. We will identify the shift from the material economy to the information economy as the primary driver in the evolution of the key divisions, distinctions, and boundaries that constitute the practice of marketing. We will explore the rise of the information economy and its impact; identify some of the key divisions, distinctions, and boundaries in marketing that are being dissolved, and with each, suggest how the practice of marketing will change; and we will argue that this process of dissolving of old distinctions and the concomitant creating of new ones will lead to an age of unprecedented uncertainty: The rules of the games are being redrawn; marketing is metamorphosing.

FROM MATERIAL TO INFORMATION

The transition from the material to the information economy entails a change in location of economic value. Simply, economic, psychological, and social value is less and less located on the physical level, and more in the virtual realm of information and ideas. A number of prominent authors anticipated the emergence of this postindustrial economy, the characteristics of which are the rise of service and information as the critical factors of carriers of industrial value.[1] The critical role of knowledge in the late 20th century is cogently illustrated in the words of T. A. Wilson, chairman of Boeing, who stated that Boeing was in the knowledge business—and that it was incidental that airplanes were the end result.[2] This typifies the increasing importance of knowledge, for physical materials, processes, and techniques are no longer a sustainable source of competitive advantage.[3] We show this transition graphically in Figure 24.1 and document the shifting expenditure pattern in Figure 24.2.[4]

For this transition to occur required a convergence of the process of conversion and the process of conveyance. As Table 24.1 indicates, there is an interesting parallel between the process of industrialization and that of the information revolution. Computers have been around for a long time, but until the advent of the Internet and the World Wide Web, the full impact of increases in information-processing capacity could not be manifest.

---

[1] Bell, D. (1973). *The Coming of the Post-Industrial Society*. New York: Basic Books.. Emery, F. E., and E. L. Trist. (1973). *Towards a Social Ecology*. New York: Plenum.

[2] Achrol, R. S. (1991, Oct.). "Evolution of the Marketing Organization: New Forms for Turbulent Environments." *Journal of Marketing, 55*, 77–93.

[3] Glazer, R. (1991).. Marketing in an Information-Intensive Environment: Strategic Implications of Knowledge as an Asset." *Journal of Marketing, 55*(4), 1–19.

[4] A greater elaboration of this phenomenon can be found in Berthon, P., M. H. Holbrook, and J. M. Hulbert. (2000). "Beyond Market Orientation: A Conceptualization of Market Evolution." *Journal of Interactive Marketing, 14*(3), 50–66.

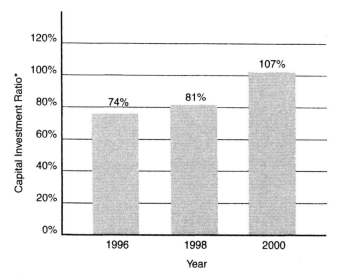

* Ratio of capital spending on computer hardware, software and communciations gear to capital spending on machinery and equipment (US data from *The New York Times*, December 18, 2000).

FIGURE 24.1 The transition to the information economy.

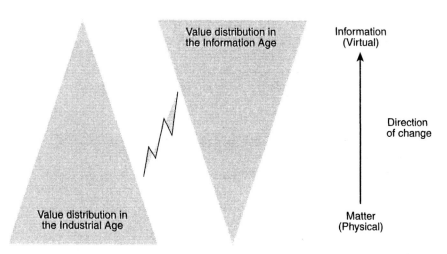

FIGURE 24.2 Changing investments: Ratio of informational to material spending.

TABLE 24.1 Matter and Symbol

	AGE OF THE MATERIAL	AGE OF THE SYMBOL
Raw material (contents)	Physical goods, and services	Informational goods, service, and experiences
Processing (converting- transforming)	Mechanisms (which process matter/energy)	Computers (which process symbols)
Transmission (conveying- transmitting)	Transportation (of matter/energy)	Telecommunications (of symbols)

With the transition to the information economy, however, new distinctions become important. Increasingly, the source of competitive advantage will lie in the *creation* of these new distinctions. For example, B. Arthur has pointed out that economics has traditionally used an assumption of diminishing returns to scale.[5] Yet, many information-based products do not fit these assumptions. Rather, they are subject to flat or increasing returns, sometimes dubbed "network economics," wherein the prize to the winner can be immense (witness Wintel!), but with little or nothing for other competitors. The importance of setting standards (the creation of new distinctions) for many of these new markets is so great that leading competitors in high technology go to enormous lengths to protect their opportunity to become a standard. The premium for being the information standard is likely to continue to increase in the 21st century.

Thus, with the rise of the virtual, traditional physical boundaries, distinctions, and divisions that delineated and constituted the practice of marketing are being dissolved and new ones created. We now consider a few of the more pertinent.

---

[5] Arthur, B. (1996, July–Aug.). "Increasing Returns and the New World of Business." *Harvard Business Review*, 100–109.

THE DISSOLUTION OF DIVISIONS

The dissolving boundaries we focus on are within the firm (marketing versus the rest of the firm: marketing dissolves into the firm); among firms (disintermediation, reintermediation, alliances, co-ventures, networks, clusters); between firms and customers (creation and co-creation); among offerings (products, services, and experiences), and among countries (national dissolves into regional and global marketing).

WITHIN THE FIRM

With the rise of the virtual, the ideas that constitute a practice become more important than the traditional physical demarcations of organizational specialization. Thus, the marketing department becomes the marketing philosophy.

For much of the 20th century, a departmental view of marketing sufficed. As competition intensifies, however, firms will find that they cannot and will not solve their marketing problems by delegation to a traditional marketing department.[6] This recognition is already leading to a growing chorus of voices calling for change in the way that we think about marketing.[7] We have coined the phrase *total integrated marketing* to describe the required change of outlook. The change will pose many difficulties in implementation—because it constitutes a change in *mindset*.[8] As McKinsey found working with Kraft General Foods:[9]

---

[6] Hulbert J. M., and L. F. Pitt. (1996, Feb.). "Exit Left Center Stage? The Future of Functional Marketing." *European Journal of Management, 14*(1), 47–60

[7] Lehmann, D. R., and K. E. Jocz (Eds.). (1997). *Reflections of the Futures of Marketing: Practice and Education.* Cambridge, MA: Marketing Science Institute.

[8] Hulbert, J. M., N. Capon, and N. F. Piercy. (2002, in press). *A Guide to Total Integrated Marketing.* New York: Free Press.

[9] This excerpt is taken from Rodger Boehm and Cody Phipps, "Flatness Forays." *The McKinsey Quarterly, 1996 Number 3.* The full article can be found on the publication's Web site, *www.mckinseyquarterly.com.*

The sources of customer value were no longer just marketing-based. The entire organization, from R&D to marketing, to packaging, to manufacturing and distribution, to the field sales representatives working the customers, was essential to identifying and delivering value to consumers.

Thus, a significant change of in the role of marketing is inevitable. Lehmann comments, "Focus on customers is now at least discussed by people in R&D, design, quality departments, operations, and even finance. While this is potentially very good for business, it is not good for the marketing function per se."[10] As a more appropriate and broader view of marketing evolves, the outlook for marketing managers with a more traditional, departmental view of marketing is likely to deteriorate significantly. To get marketing out of the department and into the business will prove a significant challenge both for managers within the marketing function and elsewhere.[11] To work across the boundaries of traditional functions will demand high levels of interpersonal skill as well as a holographic understanding of the business.

AMONG FIRMS

Disintermediation (reintermediation), alliances, co-ventures, networks, and clusters are all representative of an evolving vocabulary that reflects changing relationships among firms.

With the rise of information, the boundaries—both spatial and temporal—between firms are dissolving. Ten years ago, the typical large company shunned joint ventures, cooperative agreements, and anything that smacked of less than complete control. Today, large companies are engaged in many such

---

[10] Lehmann, D. R., and K. E. Jocz (Eds.). (1997). *Reflections of the Futures of Marketing: Practice and Education.* Cambridge, MA: Marketing Science Institute.

[11] Indeed, some are concerned that if marketing expertise is viewed as something to be diffused through the firm as a whole, laudable as this may be, there is a danger that the more specific professional skills associated with first-class marketing departments may wither away.

alliances, new words such as co-opetition have been created,[12] and many firms have venture capital operations. One way to view these changes is that they reflect attempts to hedge against increasing uncertainty.[13] However, these new approaches change and complicate the job of managing relationships with suppliers, customers, and competitors in ways quite alien to the more simplistic approaches that characterized much of the 20th century.

Vertical marketers act simultaneously as retailer, wholesaler, and manufacturer, in effect disintermediating products and markets. Dell Computer, Ben and Jerry's, Starbucks, and The Body Shop all made obsolete the traditional distinctions between channel members.

As old distinctions dissolve, however, new ones are created. Thus, with the rise of the virtual and the information economy, new intermediaries (or, as they are sometimes called, *infomediaries*) with powerful brand names such as Amazon, AOL, and Yahoo! have arisen.

An extension of the between-firms theme is that of between-industries. The Internet has reduced entry barriers in many industries. Deconstruction of value chains, combined with the growth of outsourcing and contract manufacture, create a dramatically more complex milieu than that of the traditional "industry." Further, the Internet means that constructing a low-cost virtual presence is possible for entrepreneurs anywhere in the world, even though lack of brand recognition still presents them with a serious problem. Yet, managing and eliminating customer risk will be important to the success of new Internet-based businesses and may provide opportunities for branded intermediaries. Information-based products and services will almost certainly gain most from the Internet revolution, since physical products, particularly if they require direct experience, will always require some form of conventional distribution system.

---

[12] Brandenburger, A. N., and B. J. Nalebuff. (1996). *Co-opetition.* New York: Doubleday.

[13] Courtney, H., J. Kirkland, and P. Viguerie. (1997, Nov.–Dec.). "Strategy under Uncertainty." *Harvard Business Review,* 67–79.

BETWEEN FIRMS AND CUSTOMERS

With the switch from physical products and services to informational products and services, the distinction between producers and consumers, firms and customers, is blurring. Both produce and transform information, and this is leading to new forms of relationships and interaction.

Traditionally, there has been a sharp demarcation between a company and its customers. These distinctions are clearly becoming increasingly blurred. As we have documented elsewhere, co-creation with customers is an increasing facet of economic activity.[14] Recognition of this interplay is also implicit in much of the research about first-mover and pioneering effects. Classical marketing treated customer preferences as endogenous, but in newly developing markets it is clear that they should be treated as exogenous.[15] As Peter Drucker pointed out, customers are not found but created, and the logical extension of this concept is the co-creation of value by customers and companies.[16]

In the information economy, the Internet is facilitating this change by transforming the process of marketing communication. Historically, in consumer markets, information has been primarily sent one-way in undifferentiated one-to-many mass communication. Not only does the Internet allow consumers to be addressed relatively cheaply as individuals, they can also easily communicate with their suppliers and with other consumers, both enthusiastic and disaffected. Thus does yet another barrier dissolve.

Further, as a result of intensifying competition, the ability to create and sustain competitive advantage by practicing the

---

[14] Berthon, P., J. M. Hulbert, and L. F. Pitt. (1999). "To Serve or to Create? Strategic Orientations Toward Customers and Innovation." *California Management Review, 42*(1), 37–58.

[15] Carpenter, G. S., R. Glazer, and K. Nakamoto. (1997). *Readings on Market-Driving Strategies: Towards a New Theory of Competitive Advantage*. New York: Addison-Wesley.

[16] Berthon, P., J. M. Hulbert, and L. F. Pitt. (1999). "To Serve or to Create? Strategic Orientations Toward Customers and Innovation." *California Management Review, 42*(1), 37–58.

tried and true principles of neoclassical marketing will undoubtedly diminish in the future. Of course, we do not argue that one should not listen to customers and attempt to fill their articulated unmet needs and wants. Yet, in a world in which all surviving competitors will subscribe to such a view, the prospect of attaining more than a fleeting advantage from such strategies seems remote indeed. We have elsewhere pointed out the limitations of this essentially responsive or adaptive view of the marketing task.[17] In the 21st century, instead of responding to existing customer wants and needs, successful firms will have to create them; this is not only a distinctly challenging task, but also one alien to traditionally trained marketers. Indeed, as the barrier between the firm and its customers dissolves in this way, traditional marketers are likely to become discomfited if not obsolete.

The shift in emphasis to more basic, even disruptive, kinds of innovation and away from the evolutionary "flanking" efforts, for which marketers have become notorious, toward market development rather than market servicing, will also pose new questions for marketers, many of whom will be ill-equipped to deal with them. Indeed, customers will increasingly be highly informed and in a very different bargaining position. Historically, information acquisition was difficult and expensive; today, the electronic revolution is rapidly transforming the situation. This process has already occurred in financial markets where real-time information is available on virtually a global basis. Similarly, the World Wide Web is providing a low-cost means of accessing information about product and markets. As inefficiency is driven out, the only sustainable price differences will be those reflecting differences in customer perceived value; those due to lack of information will disappear. Not only will information technology lower costs by permitting vicarious search, it will increasingly permit the buyer–seller matching via intelligent search engines. Disintermediation will certainly increase as a result.

---

[17] Ibid.

AMONG OFFERINGS

Boundaries that are in the process of dissolving are the distinctions that have traditionally been made among products, services, and experiences—information constitutes yet transcends each.

The product–service–experience distinction is essentially arbitrary inasmuch as offers purchased by the majority of buyers comprise a mixture of tangibles and intangibles. Indeed, structural changes in the economy and company strategies often transform products into services, services into experiences, and so on. For example, an activity conducted inhouse by a manufacturer is typically counted as value-added in the product sector; that same activity (unless manufacturing) conducted by an outsourcing supplier, is counted in the service sector. For example, because McDonald's operates restaurants, the government classifies it as a service business; however, its strategy of growing take-home sales (local manufacturing of sales for later consumption) has been so successful that in the United States, 60 percent of revenues are attributed to product removed from the premises before being eaten. As our children have birthday parties at McDonald's or play in the playgrounds at these sites, they are also involved in co-producing experiences that accompany the products and services.

Durable goods manufacturers also provide interesting illustrations. For example, commercial jet engine manufacturers traditionally made little profit on engine sales; profit was made on spares and maintenance. However, as engine quality and performance has improved, the revenue yield from these activities is declining and manufacturers are actively discussing pricing on a per-hour of operating life basis. Furthermore, products as diverse as automobiles, railroad cars and engines, computers and copiers, light bulbs, and furniture are now offered as "services" to market segments comprising customers who prefer to avoid the initial capital outlay by renting or leasing. The really important distinction is now recognized to be that between the marketing of tangibles and the marketing of intangibles, but as any successful brands manufacturer will tell you, the latter is as central to their success as it is to major services companies.

AMONG COUNTRIES

With the rise of global information networks, the time–space barriers that are so real for physical products and services are rendered irrelevant for informational offerings.[18] Under the influence of GATT and WTO, as well as regional groupings such as NAFTA, the EU, and MERCOSUR, the national boundaries that so clearly demarcated markets are themselves blurring and dissolving. The growth of global branding and marketing has forever changed the nature of marketing strategy and contributed to the necessity to take an organizational rather than a departmental view. Global marketing requires a high level of cooperation and alignment along the whole supply chain, and marketing can make no sensible contribution to these decisions if it restricts itself to a narrow view of its responsibilities. General Electric is noted, among other reasons, for its drive to become "boundaryless,"[19] and the 21st century marketer must truly strive for no less.

MORPHING MARKETING

Marketing faces enormous challenges in the years ahead. Globalization is driving ever more intense competition, and the viability of market positions is everywhere threatened. Yet, as competition intensifies and the weak succumb, surviving firms are correspondingly smarter and more sophisticated. The ability of surviving firms to win via traditional marketing practices will undoubtedly diminish. Indeed, as customers become more sophisticated and better informed, much higher standards of creativity and strategic insight will be mandatory for success. The very foundations upon which many managers' livelihoods rest will be shaken by the profundity of

---

[18] Cairncross, F. (1997). *The Death of Distance: How the Communications Revolution Will Change Our Lives*. London: Orion Business Books.

[19] Devanna, M. A., and N. M. Tichy. (1990, Winter). "Creating the Competitive Organization of the 21st Century: The Boundaryless Corporation," *Human Resource Management, 29*(4), 455–471.

the resulting changes. Yet, whether we look to the practitioner or academe, we find that marketers are often suspect in the eyes of others. Fixed in their paradigms, often frighteningly narrow in perspective, too many seem oblivious to the fact that both the theory and practice of marketing are approaching a crisis. If marketing fails to morph, there may be no marketing! The call is clarion clear: let us hope that marketers rise to the challenge.

SUMMARY

The shift from the material economy to the information economy is the primary driver in the evolution of the key divisions, distinctions, and boundaries that constitute the practice of marketing. We have explored how some of the classic distinctions that are implicit to the traditional practice of marketing are dissolving. Looking within the firm, among firms, between firms and customers, among offerings, and among countries, we charted some of these changes. The *generation* of informational distinctions (symbols, languages, standards, and processes) will increasingly constitute the primary sources of competitive advantage.

25

CREATING OBNOXIOUSLY DEVOTED CUSTOMERS

Chip R. Bell

They wear ugly razorback hog hats! They paint their faces red and holler, "Woo pig sooey!" in the most obnoxious, uncivilized way. Most are completely sober. Many wore business suits to work the day before. But on a Fall Saturday afternoon at the University of Arkansas, these normally sane people engage in the insane ritual of devotion...for a football team. They are more than simply fond of their Arkansas Razorbacks...they love 'em! The same is true for Cheese Heads, Deadheads, Yankee fans, and so on.

What if these enthusiasts were your customers? What would "wear-a-funny-hat-and paint-your-face" fidelity look like for your enterprise? And, what would you need to do to inflame such zealous commitment? How do you unleash obnoxious devotion from your customers?

The last question started a serious discussion about levels of devotion. Loyal customers come back, buy more, pay more, forgive more, and champion more. But these are actions appropriate to a fan...not a lunatic, go-nuts, follow-you-to-the-ends-of-the earth type zealot! Is there a level of devotion beyond loyalty? We labeled it "customer love" and set out to uncover its anatomy.

"Who are the customers you would label the devoted zealots of your organization?" we asked a number of companies. Surprisingly, some required a rigorous definition of this upper devotion stratum only to discover that they probably did not have any. Others, like the Ritz Carlton, Nordstrom, USAA, Harley Davidson, Disney World, and the Marriott could easily identify their borderline groupies. Interviewing these aficionados provided a basis for an understanding of customer love.

The pursuit of customer love is not just about one-to-one personalization, although that can certainly be a component. The quest for customer love is not simply about the economics of lifetime value, although customers who love you are more likely to stay with you over time. The "love" strategy is an attitude that starts with a deep allegiance to the very nobility of service. It is the perspective the merchant in your hometown used when treating you as a valued neighbor, not a valuable consumer. While not a complex strategy, it can be difficult to implement, particularly in an organization with many, many customers and frontline service people. Making the strategy work requires a special culture and uncommon methods. That is where our story begins.

SEEING THROUGH THE EYE OF THE BEHOLDER

My dad was a big fan of the *Mutt and Jeff* comic strip. When I was a little boy, I remember him reading it religiously. One of his favorite strips portrayed Mutt saying to Jeff, "If everybody saw like I did, everybody would want my wife." To which Jeff responded, "If everybody saw like I did, nobody would want your wife." It was my early introduction to the "eye of the beholder" idea.

Customer love is as complex as any other type of love. Like Mutt and Jeff, what attracts me to a service or product provider might be completely different than what attracts you. I have a friend whose idea of the perfect hotel check-in is to be able to get from the curb out front to the room upstairs in less than 30 seconds without conversation with a living soul. For me, unless it is super late or there's a long wait, I would rather chat with the front desk clerk, build a personal bond I might need later, influence the choice of the room I get, and make someone smile.

Customer love is not about a sure-fire formula guaranteed to be a hit simply by mixing the elements and stirring with enthusiasm. That said there were consistent parts of the anatomy reported frequently by these "obnoxiously devoted customers." Figure 25.1 provides the parts required to maximize attraction; the strength of any part is dependent on the customer. Remember Mutt and Jeff!

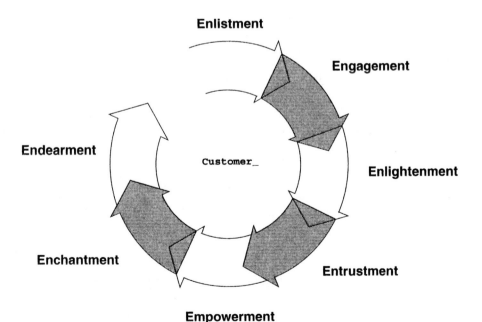

FIGURE 25.1 The anatomy of customer love.

ENLISTMENT: CUSTOMERS CARE WHEN THEY SHARE

"Dinner on the ground" was code for participation when I was growing up. While the event went with all family reunions, this special form of community most often occurred after certain church services. It was an event for little boys to run and holler unsupervised, since their caretakers were occupied with setup and cleanup. Women got to show off new recipes; men compared their prowess with baseball trivia. You went home after eating way too much fried chicken and homemade ice cream. This "everyone bring something" event helped people feel more interdependent. It was a sad day for this love feast when someone got the bright idea of "just calling Big Al and having him bring the barbecue with all the trimmings."

Devotion toward a service provider can ratchet up dramatically when customers get an opportunity to put some "skin in the game." Inclusion not only captures the creativity and competence of customers as they serve with you, but their commitment and allegiance rise as well. Sometimes, customers are not interested in participation; sometimes the inclusion of customers is inappropriate. The secret is knowing when and how to include. Wise service providers attract customer love by making the "dinner on the ground" side of service as fun, memorable, and wholesome as a church picnic.

ENGAGEMENT: THE POWER OF STRAIGHT TALK

Research in the retail industry shows that customers who have a problem and complain spend, on average, twice as much with a store as customers who have a problem and don't complain. The percentage might be different in other industries, but the principle remains the same. Complaining customers are loyal customers. But how do you get customers to absolutely level with you?

Eliminate any defensiveness when querying customers. No matter what they tell you, ask for more feedback rather than explaining. Instead of asking customers an evaluation question

("How was everything?"), try a problem-solving question ("What is one way we might improve our service to you?"). When you make a change—even a partial one—due to a customer's input, follow up and let him or her know. It's like this: If you were on trial for being a poor listener, would your customers have the evidence that would get you acquitted? It means listening to your customers in a way that makes them experience that their input was valued and made a difference.

Dramatic listening is a contact sport, not a research project. Market research and survey results give you data, not loyalty; they give you information, not devotion. Stanley Marcus, co-founder of Dallas, Texas-based Neiman-Marcus once said; "A market never purchased a single item in one of my stores, but a lot of customers came in and made me a rich man!" Think about the most important relationship in your life today. Can you imagine using a survey to get feedback in that relationship? "Honey, in the morning when you come down for breakfast, beside your cereal bowl you'll find a comment card." If your "important relationship" were like mine, you would wind up eating that survey for breakfast! Customer love is built on face-to-face engagement laced with straight talk and swift responsiveness.

ENLIGHTENMENT: GROWING CUSTOMER LOVE

Customers have learned that their ability to thrive is anchored in their capacity to keep up. They seek learning in practically every facet of life. As customers, we want software that not only instructs in application, but also offers insights into possibilities. When products come with assembly instructions, we also want to know about maintenance, add-on features, and access to information on upgrades. Call-center employees get dinged by customers much more quickly for inadequate knowledge than for rude interchange. In fact, we'd rather have a surly expert than a polite idiot. The service provider able to implant enlightenment into the experience will win customer devotion.

Larry Lehman manages the Eagle Postal Center near my office. It's where I go to mail packages, office supplies, and a graduate education on office efficiency. Larry noticed that I had mailed several items over a 2-month period to my publicist. "Why don't I have you a rubber stamp made with her name and address?" he asked. "It'll save you time, and I can do it in your same type style." His special attention-to-detail feature did not stop there. He went back to all my mailings for the previous year, ascertained the high-frequency items, calculated the time it took for me to type mailing labels, and suggested I have four more rubber stamps made. "These are the ones that'll be cost effective for you to have done," he advised. It was smart service at its best.

My financial consultant ends every phone consultation with the words: "Here's a question I want you to think about between now and the next time we talk." She starts our next financial-review session with a discussion of these thought-provoking questions. When I purchased my last car, the salesperson gave me a complete tour of every feature, knob, and gadget. After a recent surgical removal of a small skin cancer, my physician armed me with articles about my condition from her medical journals. While I did not understand much of the medical jargon, her concern for my wisdom as well as my well-being gave me confidence...and loyalty. Grow your customers and you'll grow your customer base.

ENTRUSTMENT: AFFIRMING THE COVENANT

Reliability, according to customer research, is the attribute critical to customer satisfaction. But there is a level above reliability...it is the stuff trust is made of. *Reliability* is what we do to convince the customer that *we* can be trusted. Customer service is an implied covenant—a promise to exchange value for value. Covenants are brokered on two-way trust. One side is obvious: The customer trusts the organization to do what has been promised. Yet, the other side is equally important: actions that tell customers *they* are trusted. It's the leap-of-faith that service and product providers take that involves some level of risk with customers.

Love starts with trust; love is solidified through betrayal. Customers are often gun shy of service providers until they witness service recovery. Before service failure, there is only hope; after service failure, there is proof. It is through the effective management of betrayal that customers come to truly trust. Think about it. Recall all the great service stories you have heard in your life. Most were about heroics when things went wrong.

This does not imply that service providers should intentionally screw up so they can fix a problem for their customers. It does mean that we take enough risk to create a likely potential for a mistake, and then handle the service betrayal with the care of a great friend. Such powerful restoration takes a culture in which service people view mistakes as a chance to learn and customer complaints as a valuable gift. As there is a dark side to "for better" and "in health" in life relationships, there is often one for customer relationships. Customers do not expect you to be perfect; they do expect you to care. How service providers demonstrate that caring can make a major difference in the adoration of those served.

EMPOWERMENT: CUSTOMER CONTROL THROUGH CONSISTENCY

Customers feel a sense of power when they feel in control, and "in control" happens through consistency. As customers, we would be knocked off our in-control platform should McDonald's suddenly sport tablecloths, candles, and fine china without warning, or should a five-star restaurant serve our gourmet meal in a Styrofoam container with a plastic fork. It is the unpredictability of negative surprise that robs us of the sense of control that gives us power and confidence.

What empowers customers is delivering first-rate reliability and "you-can-take-it-to-the-bank" consistency around the core offering—the basic need the customer hopes to fill. Sure, you can include a pleasant surprise with some value-added nonessential—but you should not change the core offering. A McDonald's employee can dazzle a customer by remembering him or her from a previous last trip, giving a free order of fries if there's a wait, or refilling a coffee cup with a smile and without a request. But if that employee puts jalapenos on the customer's Egg McMuffin, it throws the customer a curve ball that causes him or her to strike out...and you lose the customer loyalty ballgame.

Keep the constancy of the core offering absolutely sacred. If you were an airline, that means not tinkering with the basic proposition of getting passengers from point A to point B, safely, on time, and with their luggage arriving on the same day. All the frequent flyer points and smiling flight attendants in the world won't make up for late flights and lost luggage. When someone considers a new feature or technique, ask yourself if this addition will leave customers insecure about the reliability of the core service. Craft a simple vision with clear values and communicate them in a way that helps all employees see the link between the big picture and their roles. Model allegiance to the core offering and protect it with the same aggression that Disney uses to safeguard Mickey Mouse or that Coca-Cola uses to not weaken its brand name.

ENCHANTMENT: MAKING THE PROCESS MAGICAL

It goes by many handles: delight, dazzle, and knock your socks off! Regardless of the modifier, service with a surprise still builds customer devotion. We cannot rely on "wowing" the customer as our mainstay—at some point we run out of room trying to one-up the last experience. But most of us still enjoy an occasional unexpected gesture or the thrill of making a moment unique with candles, champagne, or a backrub.

Enchantment is a surprise created in a way that keeps the mechanics a secret. It is a service arrow aimed straight at the heart. At it's best, it is simple and pure. It is a housekeeper at a Disney hotel moving a Mickey Mouse stuffed toy around the room to make a young guest think "Mickey's been playing while we were gone." It's a nurse remembering that you like your coffee black and managing to have a big cup waiting for you right after the blood test you fasted to have performed. It's your pharmacist leaving a "meow, meow" message on your answering machine telling your cat to remind you to pick up a prescription ordered by the vet. It is the mechanic who writes on your car repair ticket, "Noticed your pressure valve was worn down, so I replaced it—no charge."

A key advantage of the pursuit of enchantment is what it does to the frontline person. Like planning a surprise birthday party, the creators gain as much as the recipients. The pursuit of enchantment helps associates think differently about customers. Connections are more personal; communications more attentive. When associates are a part of a culture that supports customer enchantment, there is a sense of joy that is passed on to customers who reciprocate with their affirmation, gratitude, and loyalty.

ENDEARMENT:
GIFTING WITHOUT A TOLL

This is the era of the short term. We expect results to happen faster and faster. The taxi does not go fast enough; the stock market is not open long enough; the sales graph is not steep enough. The frenetic raising of all standards evokes a greed mentality. "How can I help?" has been too often replaced with "What have you done for me lately?" We think far more about squeezing margins than we do about extra helpings.

Customers adore those service providers who are not preoccupied with keeping score. Such service providers know that generosity works like love: The more you give the more there is. The giver mentality is what makes marriages work, partnerships prosper, and customers fall in love. The wisdom of generosity lies in its being laced with authenticity. This suggests a culture in which associates are treated with the same endearment they are encouraged to demonstrate to customers.

Customers who like you come back. But customers who *love* you go out of their way to take care of you. They don't just recommend you; they insist their friends do business with you. They not only forgive you when you make mistakes, they defend you to others who have bad experiences with you. They give you candid feedback when they spot a problem, even if you take their feedback for granted. They never sue or threaten to sue. And, because they feel committed to you and see value in emotional terms, they will pay more for what they get from you...because they're convinced it is worth it.

Issuing funny hats and face paint to customers or teaching them the company fight song won't yield the enthusiastic fervor that you witness at the stadium, in the stands, or on the tube. Customers are not attracted by the cosmetics of customer love. But include customers, connect with them, teach them, trust them, reassure them, wow them, and care for them, and they will passionately reward you with their devotion, their advocacy, and their funds.

26

THE STRATEGY OF BUNDLING

Barry Nalebuff

O ne of the distinguishing features of our modern economy is the competitive success achieved by product bundles. There are many reasons why bundling is an extremely effective strategy. Yet, the advantages of bundling are not well understood. This chapter provides some of the intuition for how bundling works—and when it doesn't.

The advantage of bundling was first recognized by Augustin Cournot.[1] Further advances were discovered by Stigler;[2]

---

[1] Cournot, Augustin. (1838). *Recherches sur les principes mathematiques de la theorie des richesses*. Paris: Hachette. English translation: (N. Bacon, trans.), *Research into the Mathematical Principles of the Theory of Wealth*. Mountain Center, CA: James and Gordon, 1995.

[2] Stigler, George. (1968). "A Note on Block Booking." In G. J. Stigler (Ed.), *The Organization of Industries*. Homewood, IL: Irwin.

McAfee, McMillan, and Whinston;[3] and Nalebuff.[4,5] Only recently has the theory moved from the academic journals to the public policy arena. Its debut was dramatic. In 2000, the $45 billion proposed merger between General Electric and Honeywell was blocked by the European Union Merger Task Force. A primary reason for their objection to this combination was a concern over bundling.

It will help to define bundling right at the outset. Many items are sold as a package. A car is a bundle of seats, wheels, engine, transmission, gas pedal, cup holders, and much more. An obvious explanation for these types of bundles is that the company can integrate the products better and cheaper than the customers can. While cost savings and product improvements offer powerful motivation to offer a bundle, it is not the focus of this chapter.

For our purpose, a *bundling* is a combination of products that is sold at a discount relative to the individual items.[6] We imagine that the customer can put the items together as well as the seller. Thus, we are interested in exploring bundling as

---

[3] McAfee, R. Preston, John McMillan, and Michael Whinston. (1989, May). "Multiproduct Monopoly, Commodity Bundling, and Correlation of Values," *Quarterly Journal of Economics 104*, 371–84.

[4] Nalebuff, Barry. (1999). "Bundling." Working paper. [Online]. Social Science Research Network Available: http://papers.ssrn.com.

Nalebuff, Barry. (2000). "Competing Against Bundles." In P. Hammond and G.D. Myles (Eds.), *Incentives, Organization, and Public Economics*. Oxford University Press: London.

Nalebuff, Barry. (2001). "A Bundle of Trouble: Bundling and the GE-Honeywell Merger." Yale SOM working paper.

Stigler, George. (1968). "A Note on Block Booking." In G. J. Stigler (Ed.), *The Organization of Industries*. Homewood, IL: Irwin.

[5] Stigler and McAfee, McMillan, and Whinston show how bundling reduces customer heterogeneity and thereby allows a firm to do a better job at pricing. Nalebuff (1999) shows how a multiproduct incumbent can use bundling to deter the entry of a single product rival. Nalebuff (2000, 2001) emphasizes bundling complements, the theme of this chapter.

[6] We assume that the items are sold individually as well as in the bundle. This case is typically called mixed bundling. If the items are sold only as part of a bundle, this is called pure bundling.

a pricing strategy. If the package is simply priced at the sum of its component prices, we do not call this bundling, as there is no strategic impact of the bundle pricing.

Microsoft Office is our motivating example of a bundling strategy. The 2001 list price for Office XP Professional was $547. You could buy the components separately, but you wouldn't. Word, Excel, PowerPoint, and Access each cost $339, and Outlook is a bargain of $109. The total adds up to $1,465. The software package came at a 60 percent discount compared to the individual items. This made it very hard for someone with just one product to compete, and indeed Microsoft has come to dominate most of these product categories.

Microsoft Office's success was achieved in spite of the fact that prior to its arrival, there were successful firms each selling individual software applications, such as WordPerfect, Quattro or Lotus, Adobe PageMill, and Harvard Graphics. While no single factor explains Microsoft's success, one advantage gained via a bundle discount strategy can be found in the writings of Cournot.[7]

Cournot considered a market in which consumers are interested in buying a collection of several complementary products. Modern examples include hardware and software, ski rentals and lift tickets, and aircraft engines and avionics. When determining whether or not to purchase a bundle, the consumer takes into account the aggregate cost. Thus, a computer user examines the cost of hardware and software; a skier considers the price of lodging, transportation, lift tickets, equipment, and lessons; an airline looks at the total cost of equipping a plane. In Cournot's words:[8]

---

[7] Other explanations for the success of MS Office include the delay by Novell and others in updating their products to be compatible with Windows in its migration from DOS.

[8] Cournot, Augustin. (1838). *Recherches sur les principes mathematiques de la theorie des richesses*. Paris: Hachette. English translation: (N. Bacon, trans.), *Research into the Mathematical Principles of the Theory of Wealth*. Mountain Center, CA: James and Gordon, 1995.

We imagine two commodities, (a) and (b), which have no other use beyond that of being jointly consumed in the production of the composite commodity (ab). ...Simply for convenience of expression we can take for examples copper, zinc, and brass under the fictitious hypothesis that copper and zinc have no other use than that of being jointly used to form brass by their alloy.

Cournot considered the case where each component that goes into the bundle is produced by a monopoly. His key insight is that if the two monopolists get together, they will make more money by pricing the bundle of their goods *lower* than if they acted individually.

While it is not surprising that coordinated pricing leads to higher profits, what is surprising is that coordinated pricing leads to a *reduction* in prices. Both consumers and firms are better off. The reason is that the two firms are complementary—each firm's product makes the other's more valuable. Thus, when one firm lowers its price, the other firm's sales increase, an externality that is not taken into account with uncoordinated pricing. There is an advantage to bundling when two firms each have market power, but each is missing one of the complementary products.

Here, we take the next step. We examine what happens when there is competition between the component products that go into the bundle. Our objective is to better understand what happens when a player in the market aggregates a collection of complements and sells them as a bundle, while the competition remains independent or uncoordinated.

Following the intuition of Cournot, it will not be surprising that the bundler does better than the collection of independent competitors. But the scale of the advantage is remarkable. Table 26.1 gives some numbers based on a linear demand specification.[9] Firm A sells all the items as a bundle, while the Firm B acts in an uncoordinated fashion. Once there are four or

---

[9] The full model can be found in Nalebuff (2000). For simplicity, the total market is fixed at size 1 and Firm A offers its goods only as part of a pure bundle. Allowing for market expansion and mixed bundling only increase the incentive to bundle.

TABLE 26.1 Bundler vs. Independent Competitors

NUMBER OF GOODS	FIRM A'S BUNDLE PRICE	FIRM B'S COMPO- NENT PRICE	FIRM A'S MARKET SHARE	FIRM A'S PROFIT	FIRM B'S PROFIT	COMBINED FIRM B PROFITS
2	1.45	0.86	0.63	0.91	0.32	0.64
3	2.09	0.88	0.70	1.47	0.26	0.78
4	2.84	0.92	0.76	2.15	0.22	0.88
5	3.63	0.94	0.79	2.88	0.19	0.95
6	4.48	0.96	0.82	3.69	0.17	1.02
7	5.40	0.99	0.84	4.56	0.15	1.08
8	6.36	1.02	0.86	5.48	0.14	1.12

more items to the bundle, the bundle aggregator has captured 75 percent of the market and 71 percent of total profits.[10] By the time there are eight items in the bundle, Firm A has 86 percent market share and 83 percent of the industry profits.

This suggests that a firm that creates or simply aggregates a bundle of complementary products would have a substantial pricing advantage over its rivals and thereby achieve a leadership position in the market. This is especially true as the bundle grows in scale.

Moreover, the advantage is long lasting. The rivals do not have an incentive to emulate this strategy, as this would lead to even more ferocious competition. The resulting competition of bundle against bundle would leave the independent sellers even worse off than they are in their present disadvantaged position. Thus, it might seem that the first firm to bundle has a large sustainable advantage over its rivals.[11]

---

[10] Firm A's profits are slightly lower than its market share due to the bundle discounting. Bundling leads to essentially equal profits for Firm A compared to non-bundling with three items; with more than three goods in the bundle, bundling leads to higher profits.

[11] This, of course, doesn't take into account that forming a competing bundle would also destroy the rival firm's profits. Misery loves company. Or, more to the point, firms may prefer not to be in such an asymmetric position relative to a rival when there are issues of research and development financing or similar dynamic issues in long-term competition.

However, like all results, the advantage of bundling depends on some key assumptions. A crucial assumption required for this result is that the *sellers charge a single price to all consumers in the market.* This is a quite reasonable assumption for a typical consumer good, such as Microsoft Office. But it is not a reasonable assumption for most commercial products, where the two parties typically engage in extensive negotiation as part of the sale process.

When price negotiation is possible—the firm can charge different prices to different customers—then it is no longer clear that the Cournot effect will be present. (This is the heart of the argument for why bundling is neither empirically or theoretically relevant to the aviation and aerospace industry.) The ability to negotiate differently with different customers depends on information quality. In a world in which vendors know their customers' valuations and charge differential prices, there is no gain from bundling, either in profits or in market share.

Consider the case of three firms, one A and two B firms. (As will be clear, the results apply to any number of firms and any number of products.) Firm A can sell its products individually or as a bundle or both ways, a mixed bundle. The B firms can only sell their products individually. Marginal costs are symmetric at c.

These firms are selling to a customer whose preferences are known. For example, consider the competition for the customer who has a strong preference for A on good 1 and a weak preference for A on good 2. Imagine that the customer would pay an extra $6 for Firm A's version of good 1 and an extra $2 for Firm A's version of good 2. In this case, A should win both competitions. The customer has a preference for both its products. Before the B firms will concede defeat, they would be willing to price down to marginal cost, c, on each component. That means that A can charge up to c + 6 for the first component and c + 2 for the second and still make the sale. Firm A can also charge 2c + 8 for the bundle and make the sale.

Profits of the A and B firms are exactly the same when A bundles as when it does not. In each case, the B firms earn zero (which is the efficient outcome, as their products are inferior in this case) and the A firm earns 8. *The results are exactly the same when firms compete on a component-by-component basis. The option to bundle has no effect on prices, market share, or profits.* Thus, firms have no incentive to offer bundle discounts and consumers have no incentive to demand them.

When the customer valuation is known, there are no positive effects of bundling. However, bundling can be costly on two accounts. First, including inferior products in the bundle diminishes the product offering. Second, there is a reduction in product differentiation and thus increased competition in the market.

Firms make profits only to the extent that their products are differentiated. Profits exist to the extent that the firm has an advantage with the customer. When a firm bundles two good products or bad products together, the advantages (or disadvantages) sum up. and there is no impact. However, when a firm mixes good and bad products together and only sells a bundle, this mitigates the advantage. and profits fall accordingly. With mixed bundling, no one would buy the bundle and so there would be no effect at all.

Bundling is a powerful tool when applied in the right context. The advantage of bundling applies when the seller sets a single price in the market for all buyers. In some environments, every customer will pay a different price, while in other environments a firm will charge one price to all customers. There are three general situations under which a firm will set one price in the market to all of its customers.

The first case is one of necessity. If customers are numerous and small, no firm has the time to set a price to each customer—the costs of negotiation would outweigh any possible benefit. This would be the typical case for consumer goods. Most retailers, from movie theaters to corner stores to superstores such as Wal-Mart, use posted prices. Customers accept the price as fixed. There is no one to negotiate with.

The second case is when a firm is ignorant as to the customer's valuation. If the vendor doesn't know the customer's valuation, then there is no basis upon which to charge one customer more than another. A cell phone provider might like to charge a different price based on whether the call is being used to discuss a business deal or a date, but without any way of knowing, it must price based on the number of minutes and not the value of the call.

The third case is when firms are contractually required to give each customer the best price given to any customer, what is sometimes called a most-favored customer clause. Firms commit themselves to a one-price rule through a contract.

There is a second concern that a firm should explore before pursuing a bundling strategy. Due to the risks involved, we should consider more carefully the nature of the competitive response before advising that a firm embark on this path. *Whatever advantages may exist, they quickly disappear if the rival firms coordinate and offer a competing bundle.* While the rivals do not have an incentive to offer a competing bundle, there are two factors that suggest that a bundle competing against uncoordinated components would not be a stable outcome in this market.

First, customers would stand to gain a great deal if they could create a bundle-against-bundle competition. To the extent that customers are not passive in this market, it is in their interest to induce the creation of rival bundles.

Second, rivals stand to lose very little by offering a competing bundle. The big loss comes out of the incumbent bundler. If firms are worried that the bundler will use its profit advantage to better position itself in research and development, then they will want to lower the incumbent's profits.

Any advantage of bundling assumes that other firms will not match. However, buyers are put in the best position of all if they can pit one bundle against another. Thus, firms should be concerned that rival firms will be induced to form competing bundles. Sometimes this is a greater threat than other times, depending on the coordination required (technical and strategic) and even whether all the components exist to form a rival bundle.

CONCLUSIONS

Bundling can help a firm significantly increase its profits and market share. It is best used when a firm must set a single price in the market and faces heterogeneity in customer valuations. Even here, it is not without risk if competitors are able to form a competing bundle. Bundling is less valuable when firms negotiate prices with each customer. When the risks are understood and if used in the right environment, bundling is one of the most powerful and least appreciated strategy tools.

V

TAKING THE LEAD: ORGANIZATIONS OF THE NEW MILLENNIUM

Anatomy of an Innovation Machine: Cisco Systems

Vijay Govindarajan and Chris Trimble

Introduction

The Innovation Imperative

The twin forces of globalization and the digital revolution are transforming the world economic landscape at an unprecedented rate. Formerly state-dominated economies are becoming globally integrated. As a result, competitors can be anywhere on the globe. Furthermore, new Internet-based technologies are rendering traditional business processes obsolete and at the same time creating opportunities for completely new ventures that threaten long-stable corporations.

No corporate strategy lasts indefinitely, because no competitive advantage can be sustained forever. But in the current environment, characterized by discontinuous change, corporate strategies begin to die on the day that they are born. That's why now, more than ever, the companies that will stay on top over the long run are the strategic innovators—those that regularly introduce completely new or dramatically improved ways of doing business.

Following a decade of focus on reengineering and process improvement, many corporations run supremely efficient operations. One unintended consequence of the aggressive slimming down is that there is little slack time for managers to escape the demands of the present to think about the future. This must be recognized as a vulnerability.

How can CEOs build organizations that simultaneously manage the present and create the future? How can they turn their organization into innovation machines? What does the organization that has the ability to periodically transform an industry with a completely new approach to business look like?

This chapter outlines a framework for implementing the key components of an innovation machine. The framework is illustrated with a description of the innovative efforts of Cisco Systems, the Silicon Valley Internetworking giant, through the 1990s. Cisco has been one of the most aggressive and creative companies in fully leveraging Internetworking technologies to revolutionize core business processes. This chapter concludes with an analysis of the implications of the Cisco experience for other corporations.

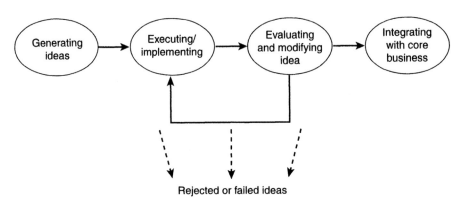

FIGURE 27.1 Process design.

COMPONENTS OF AN INNOVATION MACHINE

An *innovation machine* consists of two components: a process design and an organizational design. The process design, shown in Figure 27.1, consists of four generic macroprocesses: generating ideas, implementing, modifying, and integrating with the core business. Depending on the idea being implemented, the details within each process might be very different. Nonetheless, to regularly generate strategic innovations, senior executives must manage these processes as components of an overall system.

They must also energize the innovation processes with an appropriate organizational design, the components of which are shown in Figure 27.2.[1] Organizational design

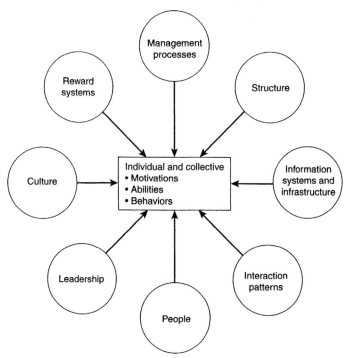

FIGURE 27.2 Organizational design: An organization's *social* ecology shapes motivations, abilities, and behavior.

1 This description of organizational design is adapted from: Vijay Govindarajan and Anil K. Gupta, *The Quest for Global Dominance*, San Francisco: Jossey Bass, 2001, Chapter 6.

extends far beyond reporting structure. It includes all elements of an organization's social system that influence individual and collective motivations, abilities, and behaviors. These elements, each of which can be directly or indirectly influenced by senior management, include structure, information systems and infrastructure, social interaction patterns, people, leadership, culture, reward systems, and management processes.

INNOVATION NOMENCLATURE

WHAT IS A STRATEGIC INNOVATION?

Strategic innovation is quite different from product innovation or technological innovation in that, unlike the latter types of innovation, which are generally the responsibility of corporate research and development departments and often the result of unpredictable random discovery, unexpected meetings, or a sudden creative inspiration, a structured approach to strategic innovation is both possible and necessary.

Strategic innovations transform industries by altering one of the four key elements of the prevailing business model: (1) Who is the customer? (2) What is the value proposition that appeals to the customer? (3) What is the system of business processes that delivers value? (4) What assets or resources must be assembled to enable the business processes, and how is ownership of these resources configured? (See Figure 27.3.)

Unlike product or technology innovations, which generally rely on a scarce expertise, ideas for strategic innovations might come from most anywhere in an organization. The challenge for CEOs is to energize the identification and execution of the best of the possibilities.

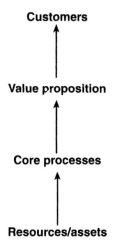

Customers

↑

Value proposition

↑

Core processes

↑

Resources/assets

FIGURE 27.3 Strategic innovators create new business models by redefining at least one of four business model elements.

NOT ALL STRATEGIC INNOVATIONS ARE ALIKE

Designing an innovation machine starts with describing the desired output. We distinguish two categories of strategic innovations: those that create identifiable new business ventures (those with new customers or value propositions) and those that make dramatic and discontinuous improvements to existing ventures (those that substantially alter the system of business processes and resources).

In addition, it is necessary for designers of innovation machines to characterize their risk tolerance. High-risk innovation machines generate multiple projects in parallel and seek the fastest possible implementation. Low-risk innovation machines focus on one or a small number of projects at a time and emphasize cost or quality of implementation over speed.

Figure 27.4 illustrates the four possible types of innovation machines, which we identify as the Cautious Process Revolutionizer, the Incubator of Process Revolutions, the Cautious Entrepreneur, and the New Venture Incubator.

WHY STUDY CISCO?

Although the fall of the dotcoms has been sobering, the challenge of reinventing large corporations to take full advantage of the Internet still preoccupies many of today's CEOs. The unrealized potential of Internetworking technologies is tremendous, and we are far from understanding their full impact on the economy. Managing the Internet transformation will likely remain a challenge for CEOs for at least another decade.

Looking for companies to learn from, many executives find inspiration in Cisco. During the dotcom run up, Cisco was often held up as an exemplar of everything that was right about the new economy. True, Cisco's shine was tarnished following a dramatic and unanticipated downturn in its business in early 2001. Nonetheless, its operations have been revolutionized by numerous information technology initiatives, and it remains well ahead of most corporations.

For a while, it seemed as though the Internet was transforming the business world at breathtaking speed, but Cisco's transformation hardly happened overnight. Cisco's innovation machine succeeded steadily over a long time period. In fact, Cisco used email virtually from the day it was founded in 1984, and it began investing in networked software applications for core business functions as early as 1991. More than a decade later, the extent to which Cisco has succeeded in improving its business processes through innovative use of the Internet is impressive. Underlying Cisco's accelerated progress in generating and implementing Internet innovations is Cisco's innovation machine—its well-constructed coupling of an innovation process design and an organizational design. However, Cisco's approach is not appropriate for every company. Cisco's innovation processes are characteristic of the Incubator of Process Revolutions approach (Figure 27.4). Companies that desire a machine producing different types of innovations will require a different approach.

By reviewing Cisco's successful series of initiatives, and then "lifting the hood" of Cisco's innovation machine, we'll see the logic of its design. Then, based in part on articulated concerns from Cisco executives, we'll suggest some alterations to

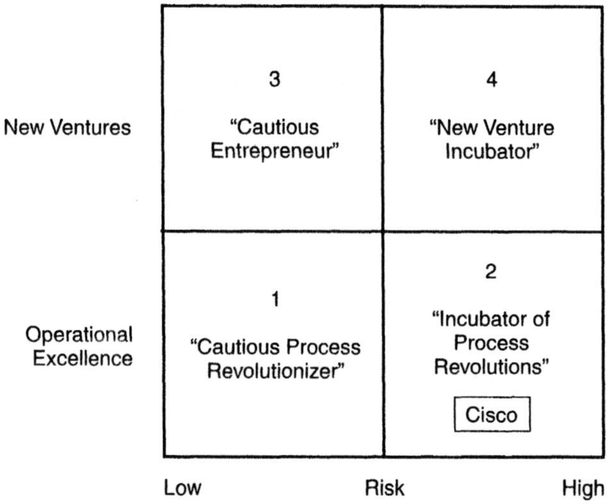

New Ventures	3 "Cautious Entrepreneur"	4 "New Venture Incubator"
Operational Excellence	1 "Cautious Process Revolutionizer"	2 "Incubator of Process Revolutions" Cisco

Low	Risk	High

FIGURE 27.4 What kind of innovation machine?

Cisco's approach that would be appropriate for companies seeking to become Cautious Process Revolutionizers, Cautious Entrepreneurs, or Incubators of New Ventures.

THE EVOLUTION OF CISCO'S USE OF INTERNET TECHNOLOGIES[2]

THE FIRST E-MARKETERS?

Cisco was founded in 1984 by two former Stanford University computer scientists, Sandy Lerner and Leonard Bosack. At Stanford, Lerner and Bosack focused their efforts on improving a computing infrastructure consisting of hundreds of distinct computer systems and 20 disparate email systems.

---

[2] The Cisco case study is based on extensive field research, including interviews with executives, reviews of internal documents, and public sources. For more detail, see "Cisco Systems (A): Evolution to e-Business" and "Cisco Systems (B): Maintaining an Edge in e-Business." Both case studies are available at *www.tuck.dartmouth.edu/cgl*.

After succeeding at piecing together hardware, which connected previously incompatible systems (including running cables through the universities sewer pipes!), the pair decided to start their own company. Email was part of their initial marketing strategy, and they succeeded in building a word-of-mouth reputation among other university computer scientists who were enthusiastic users of early forms of email.

THE GROWTH CRISIS

By 1991, under the leadership of CEO John Morgridge, Cisco struggled with a serious growth crisis. With sales of $183 million in 1991, a 2.5X increase over the previous year, Cisco could not hire enough talented engineers to keep up with its customer-service demands. Cisco's customers were implementing complex computer systems on the leading edge of technological development, and their technical support needs were substantial.

This situation persisted over the next several years. Cisco would have severely limited its growth had it not started creatively using information technology to satisfy customer needs directly. Between 1991 and 1996, Cisco implemented the following:

- Provided product information and company information online (1991).
- Added remote diagnostics capabilities into its support package (1991).
- Created online technical assistance bulletin boards (1992).
- Added capability to download software upgrades, and added email customer service (1993).
- Created the Cisco Connection Online, a Website that allowed customers to reprint invoices, check the status of service orders, and configure and price products (1995).
- Added order-status capabilities and interactive training modules (1996).

However, there was more to be done. As of early 1996, even with all of the above functionality, customers still had to make a phone call when they wanted to place an order. Because of the complexity and customizability of Cisco's product line, 25 percent of Cisco's orders were in error when they entered the order queue.

CISCO AND E-COMMERCE

Cisco's next move was to create one of the first e-commerce sites. Its site included an automated product configurator, which would ensure that the set of feature enhancements that customers chose was a compatible combination. By 1997, more than 25 percent of Cisco's orders were coming in over the Internet—by September 2000, the figure was close to 90 percent. Customer satisfaction ratings increased dramatically, and order errors dropped to 1 percent.

Since building this e-commerce site, Cisco has collaborated with a few large customers to take the purchasing process to an even higher level of automation. This involved integrating Cisco's e-commerce site with its customers' purchasing systems. Because no two customers had identical systems, this required the development of customized software for each customer. By 2000, Cisco was working closely with e-commerce software providers and industry standards-setting organizations to provide standardized solutions.

THE CISCO EMPLOYEE CONNECTION

Not all of Cisco's Internet efforts involved automation of communications with customers. In 1995, it turned to routine communications with employees. The motivation was similar—the rate at which Cisco could hire was limiting the rate at which it could grow. To accelerate hiring, Cisco automated routine human resources paperwork. This effort was frustrated by technological limitations—in particular, the lack of the Java programming language.

The next year, Cisco succeeded in automating the expense-reimbursement process. Employees now submit expenses online and get reimbursed by direct deposit within a few days. Subsequently, Cisco retackled the digitization of standard HR forms, and directly integrated hiring and benefits forms into the Cisco Employee Connection (CEC), the company's Intranet. This included the ability for managers to review and sort applicants for specific positions in a number of ways, including by capability and by the competitor they came from. Employee use of the CEC was solidified when Cisco partnered with Yahoo! to create a front page, which included access to such items as weather, sports scores, and headline news in addition to Cisco company announcements and personalizable company directory entries. Senior managers also heavily use internal systems, thanks to impressive management information systems, including a capability to "virtually close" the books within 48 hours, at any time.

THE MANUFACTURING CONNECTION ONLINE

By 1999, Cisco was focusing on digitizing many of its routine communications with suppliers and manufacturing partners. Cisco had increasingly chosen to outsource manufacturing, a further strategy to enable rapid growth. In June 1999, it launched the Manufacturing Connection Online (MCO), an Extranet that enabled partners to have ready access to inventory and order information. In fact, when customers made purchases on Cisco's Web site, its supply and manufacturing partners were notified immediately. The MCO also streamlined communications with Cisco's logistics partners, such as Federal Express, and it eventually incorporated an automated testing capability that enabled products to be delivered to customers without Cisco ever taking physical possession of them.

UNBUNDLING CISCO'S INNOVATION MACHINE

It is tempting to dismiss Cisco's ability to innovate strictly as a function of its technology expertise. Who but an Internetworking company could be expected to make the quickest work of finding new ways to innovate using the

Internet? Its technology expertise and an extremely sophisticated IT infrastructure did, in fact, have a major impact on its ability to innovate.

After a major acquisition in 1993, Cisco faced the technology labyrinth that many corporations currently face. Its infrastructure was ineffective, because there were numerous incompatible systems, no consistent standards, and no centralized data source. In particular, Cisco benefited from a bold and expensive decision in 1994 to completely rebuild its IT infrastructure. The move required a major investment in an Oracle database and resulted in a fully networked, fully scalable, standards-based enterprise system. Because Cisco tackled this problem early in its growth phase, the fix wasn't nearly as difficult as it might have been. Still, to complete the project, Cisco spent roughly $100 million—a sizable percentage of its 1993 revenues of $649M!

Achieving just this enabling condition is a seemingly never-ending headache for many corporations, tied up in a complex and tangled web of disparate, function-specific legacy systems. Cisco was lucky to make the transformation while it was still a small company—just 2,000 employees.

Cisco's success cannot be ascribed to its technology infrastructure alone. In fact, in a survey of 110 senior executives in global corporations, 88 percent indicated that human and organizational barriers were either as limiting or even more limiting than technology barriers in the effort to take full advantage of the Internet. This would suggest that those who seek to replicate Cisco's digital business sophistication need to understand more than the layout of Cisco's servers, databases, and routers. They need to understand its innovation machine. We'll now look at how Cisco's organizational design (summarized in Table 27.1) energized each of the four generic innovation processes.

CISCO'S APPROACH TO IDEA GENERATION

Cisco's approach to generating Internet business innovations involved engaging employees to think creatively, building capabilities and knowledge to generate high-quality ideas, and sustaining motivation.

TABLE 27.1 Cisco's Organizational Design

LEADERSHIP

- Chambers: Encourage others to be innovative and provide their own leadership, but provide broad direction.

CULTURE

- Values: Frugality, initiative, risk, responsibility, trust, teamwork, importance of staying connected. Not valued: Bureaucratic politics.
- Attitudes: Internet is the key to unlocking growth constraints, reducing costs, and improving customer satisfaction. Network and the data on it are shared resources. All responsible for thinking about how the Internet can improve the business.

PEOPLE

- Technological savvy throughout organization.

INFORMATION SYSTEMS

- Convenient to stay connected, share ideas.
- Modern, networked, enterprise IT infrastructure.

INTERACTION PATTERNS

- IT department trained to keep organization up-to-date on possibilities with new technologies.
- IT department helps connect people working on similar projects.

MANAGEMENT PROCESSES

- Funding for projects decentralized to each business unit. Relatively simple process to get ideas vetted, funded. IT investment decisions made by those close to customers.
- Favor projects that leverage the Internet and those that have a short-term payback period (<1 year).
- Fund multiple small projects in parallel. No limit (as a percent of revenues) to the amount invested.
- In evaluating progress, speed of implementation is valued more highly than cost minimization.

REWARD SYSTEMS

- Significant bonuses, spread deep into organization, to encourage rapid implementation.
- Bonuses based on customer satisfaction, revenue growth, and income growth.

STRUCTURE

- Technology staff in each business-unit implement projects; partnering with IT department, who ensured new applications were standards based and scalable and coordinated with related efforts.

Generating as Many Ideas as Possible. Every innovation begins with a flash of inspiration. At Cisco, everyone shared in the responsibility for generating ideas to further leverage the Internet, cut costs, and improve customer satisfaction. This sense of responsibility, driven from the top by CEO John Chambers, was a central element of Cisco's culture. Cisco's widely distributed stock options (40 percent of its stock options were spread beyond management ranks), combined with its location in the Silicon Valley, further embedded respect for initiative and risk in Cisco's culture. As a result, there was no shortage of creative thinking.

Channeling Creative Energies. While Chambers encouraged leadership and risk-taking, he felt that unfocused creativity was counterproductive. "You've got to have mavericks...however, the mavericks have to follow within reasonable bounds the course and direction of the company." Too much creativity could lead to an inability to execute.

Cisco focused creativity on the Internet. Because John Morgridge, Chamber's predecessor, had instilled frugality as a core value, Cisco looked for ways to save money. When it did, the first question asked was "What can be automated through the use of the Internet?" Cisco has constantly reinforced the notion that maximizing use of the Internet was the key to unlocking growth constraints, reducing costs, and improving customer satisfaction. (In fact, the Internet is meant to be so central in the operational mindset of Cisco employees that new hires are told that if they have a question, they should seek the answer on the network first.)

Cisco's history suggests a strategy of achieving further focus by sequencing major projects according to the constituents they were designed to serve. The Customer Connection Online was built in the early-to-mid 1990s, followed by the Cisco Employee Connection in the mid-to-late 1990s, followed by the Manufacturing Connection Online in the late 1990s.

Finally, Cisco focused creative efforts by identifying a small number of critical performance drivers: revenue growth, income growth, and customer satisfaction. Because significant bonuses were awarded, employees tended to suggest ideas that they anticipated would have a probable and short-term impact on these metrics.

Assuring High-Quality Ideas. In addition to motivating many ideas in a focused fashion, Cisco's organizational design assured high-quality ideas. Most importantly, the technological savvy of Cisco employees is unparalleled. Because many technologists are more motivated by the opportunity to work on innovative projects at the leading edge of technology rather than on older systems, high-quality ideas were generated by highly motivated employees. Cisco assigned the responsibility of keeping its employees knowledgeable to the IT department.

Quality ideas are often not the inspiration of a single person, but the result of sharing ideas within a community. As such, Cisco executives inculcated a belief in the importance of "staying connected." Because Cisco invested in such sophisticated information systems, it was convenient to find the right people to get involved in new initiatives. The IT department was a "central node" in the social network, and it assisted in making connections between employees.

Sustaining Motivation. Cisco's entrepreneurial spirit could have been squelched had there not been a sensible funding mechanism in place to support new initiatives. Many companies fund IT as a fixed percentage of revenues and manage it as an expense to be minimized. In 1994, Cisco moved away from this conventional approach and initiated what it called the Client Funded Model (CFM). "Client" in this case refers to the IT department's internal customers, the business units. Because funding of new IT initiatives was decentralized, getting creative ideas vetted and possibly funded was more straightforward than it could have been if a long process of approvals been required.

CISCO'S APPROACH TO IMPLEMENTATION

Allocating Resources. Given many solid ideas, Cisco managers must select the subset of those that are worth implementing. Because there is so much uncertainty in evaluating innovative project ideas, resources are generally allocated on the basis of judgment, often shaped by thumb rules, values, or the biases of the decision makers.

In many companies, funding authority for Internet initiatives rests within the IT department, which generally has relatively little exposure to customers and tends to focus internally and on costs. By decentralizing the funding process to each business unit, Cisco ensured that the decision makers were as close to the customer as possible. This created a decision-making bias that matched Cisco's balance of emphasis between customer satisfaction and costs. Each business-unit manager was encouraged to make whatever Internet-related investments in new applications that were sensible to improve customer satisfaction and profitability. Further, decision makers were encouraged to manage multiple investments in parallel. To manage risk and complexity of integration, they were encouraged to invest in each project incrementally and to make sure that each project paid off within one year. There were few tremendously large IT implementations going on at Cisco at any one time. In fact, typical projects involved no more than 5 to 10 people.

Implementation Roles. In addition to advising business-unit managers on the prioritization of competing projects, technology experts within each business unit would take a lead role in implementing new applications. They coordinated with the IT department, whose primary role was to ensure that each application followed a specific set of IT standards and was scalable so as to support the company's continued domestic and international growth. Because multiple projects were implemented in parallel, it was critical to coordinate efforts. Also, the IT department was responsible for trying to identify overlaps of functionality among multiple ongoing projects.

Interestingly, at the time the CFM was implemented, the reporting structure was altered such that a new group, Customer Advocacy, managed the IT department. This ensured that as applications were developed, even the IT department maintained a focus on the needs of the customer. As Doug Allred, the SVP of Customer Advocacy, put it, "Every past step that has worked arose from close customer intimacy...from being really well connected to customers and understanding what they are trying to do, and then addressing their needs in the form of what we would now call e-business functionality."

Cisco Culture. Implementation of innovative projects can easily engender conflicts over who gets the credit, or the blame. Cisco constantly reinforces attitudes of trust and teamwork, and maintains a pronounced disdain for bureaucratic politics. Another of Cisco's critical cultural attitudes is that Cisco's network, and all of the data on it, is a shared resource that nobody owns.

CISCO'S APPROACH TO EVALUATION AND MODIFICATION

Executives emphasized speed. Software applications with much of the same functionality that Cisco was creating from scratch were being developed and commercialized by enterprise software companies, so competitive advantages were likely to be short lived.

Cisco's approach to funding dictated its approach to ongoing evaluation and modification of innovative projects. Because investments were made incrementally, Cisco managers frequently revisited progress of their initiatives, deciding each time the merit of expending additional resources. Since Cisco's innovation machine produced multiple projects in parallel, frequent reviews were a necessity to keep costs under control.

CISCO'S APPROACH TO INTEGRATION

Cisco's IT department took on the most critical role in ensuring new applications were integrated seamlessly into the company's operations. To streamline this process, it initiated oversight of projects on day one, providing coordination with overlapping projects and ensuring that a common set of software standards was followed. Without Cisco's sophisticated IT infrastructure, integration of so many parallel projects would have been extremely difficult. As mentioned previously, the IT department's reporting relationship—to the Customer Advocacy group—helped create a customer-oriented mindset that influenced how new applications were integrated.

LEARNING FROM THE CISCO EXPERIENCE

LIMITATIONS OF THE CISCO APPROACH

While Cisco's record of innovation is impressive, executives within Cisco haven't let themselves become complacent about whether or not their innovation machine will continue to serve the company well in the future. Amir Hartman, formerly the managing director in Cisco's Internet Business Systems Group, described the angst: "What was innovative yesterday in many ways becomes the standard way of doing business tomorrow. You've got software packages and applications out there in the market that have ninety-plus percent of the functionality of the stuff that we custom built for our own company. So...how do we maintain and/or stretch our leadership position vis-à-vis e-business?"

Of greater concern to some is the type of innovations that the system is generating. Because of its relentless focus on customer satisfaction and a bias for making investments in initiatives with short-term paybacks, Cisco may be passing over opportunities for even more revolutionary efforts. Further, most of Cisco's initiatives focus on only one aspect of its business system—business processes. (See Figure 27.3.) Cisco is a leader in making business processes more efficient simply by automating routine information flows. The Cisco Connection Online, the Manufacturing Connection Online, and the Cisco Employee Connection all focused on exactly that—automating recurring transactions between Cisco and its three most significant constituencies: customers, production partners, and employees.

Innovations in the other three aspects of Cisco's business system are not as easily identified. True, Cisco's initiatives clearly enhanced its existing value proposition, but it is a stretch to say that Cisco used the Internet to create entirely new products and services or to reach entirely new customer segments. There were no "Internet startups" incubated at Cisco.

Although Cisco is an example of a company that outsourced and coordinated over the Internet, the outsourcing approach existed before the Manufacturing Connection Online—a system that simply streamlined existing operations. Cisco had the luxury of being able to implement its supply-chain Extranet when it was clearly the most powerful player in the chain. Had this not been the case, it might have found it much more difficult to get its suppliers and manufacturing partners to adapt their business processes to Cisco's Extranet.

The challenge for vertically integrated manufacturers to transition to a more "virtual" structure through the use of B2B commerce technologies would clearly require a different approach, one that involves designing applications in close partnership with supply chain partners—something Cisco admits it is still figuring out how to do.

These observations are not intended to detract from Cisco's tremendous level of accomplishment in using the Internet. Executives attempting to turn their organizations into innovation machines must decide if the output from Cisco's machine is what they require.

BUILDING YOUR INNOVATION MACHINE

Determining the best design of your innovation machine starts with choosing an approach to innovation (see Figure 27.4). Do you desire to be like Cisco, an Incubator of Process Revolutions? Or is one of the other quadrants in the matrix more sensible for your organization? Studies of other companies will allow more concrete conclusions, but based on the above analysis, adapting Cisco's innovation machine in the following ways for other quadrants appears appropriate.

Incubating New Ventures. The most revolutionary ideas are often generated by creating interaction between people who don't normally cross paths. At Cisco, the IT department was the "marriage broker," who looked for related initiatives throughout the company and sought to improve them by getting the technologists to work together. This approach seemed to keep Cisco ahead of the game in terms of automating business processes. But different types of interactions may have generated more grandiose ideas. For example, ideas for new startups are more likely to be generated by linking business managers, both inside and outside the company, to each other.

Other components of Cisco's innovation machine may not be ideal for companies interested in encouraging entirely new ventures. For example, the IT department may play a less central role, with heavier leadership burden on managers who regularly interact with customers or potential customers. In addition, for more revolutionary ideas, the ease with which the new systems will integrate with existing systems and scale is a much lower priority.

Furthermore, Cisco's focus on customer satisfaction and frugality are likely to discourage revolutionary ideas, which often cost too much initially and don't yet inspire interest from mainstream customers. It follows that customer satisfaction is also not an appropriate performance measure. Furthermore, the best funding mechanism for generating new business models is unlikely to involve managers who have a full-time responsibility for existing business units. Such ideas may be best evaluated by a separate corporate ventures group that is encouraged to take bigger risks.

Generating Process Innovations More Methodically. At Cisco, speed of implementation was heavily emphasized. This was reflected in its funding approach and decentralized style. Of central concern to Mr. Hartman is whether or not the company has simply become too large for this system to work. As the company becomes bigger, the task of coordinating the various initiatives becomes much more difficult. As a result, implementation times tend to rise. Costs also rise because of the increased likelihood that multiple initiatives are solving closely related problems.

For the largest corporations, it may not be sensible to generate so many Internet-related business initiatives in parallel. Centralization of the innovation process, at an earlier stage in the development of initiatives, is key. This will slow things down, but it is also likely to avoid excessive costs as duplicative efforts are minimized. To the extent possible, all employees should be energized in the idea-generation process, but this is difficult when the immediate next phase, receiving funding for the idea, requires a more centralized approval process.

CONCLUSION: SO YOU WANT TO BE LIKE CISCO?

Having considered your strategic priorities, suppose you conclude that you want an innovation machine like Cisco's. This is an admirable choice! After all, as many corporations learned from failed dotcom ventures, revolutionary ideas only succeed sometimes, and staying ahead of the game in terms of costs and efficiency can be a critical source of competitive advantage.

As a caveat, keep in mind that it can be a short-term advantage. It lasts only until enterprise software companies are able to build the same functionality into the packages that they offer and competitors successfully implement the new functionality. Cisco was able to stay ahead of software vendors in part because of its high level of technological savvy at all levels of management. Industries that have difficulty achieving this level of savvy will win competitive advantages of even shorter duration. (On the other hand, every industry has peculiarities that will never be included in software packages—so there is some subset of business activity where an innovation machine like Cisco's can generate advantages.)

Imitating Cisco's innovation machine won't be easy. For starters, getting through the process of updating computing infrastructures and installing enterprise software solutions can easily take 2 or 3 years, and that just provides the technology foundation. Furthermore, changing attitudes towards the importance of the Internet is much harder for an existing corporation than a growing one. Mature corporations turn over just a small fraction of their employee base each year, while in startups there is more opportunity to create and recreate culture as fresh and impressionable minds are rapidly hired.

Cisco was a great story of the 1990s, and its approach to leveraging the Internet is a sharp illustration of how a process design combined with the appropriate organizational design generates impressive innovations. However, imitators should think carefully about the type of innovation they are trying to create and should assemble the components of their innovation machine with the desired output clearly in mind.

28

ACHIEVING BEST FIT

Judith M. Bardwick, Ph.D.

$\mathbb{A}$ t the dawn of the 21st century, we find a much broader range of organizational characteristics, a wider range of people's attributes, and a greater insistence on individuality than we have seen before. As a result, the tasks of management in the 21st century will be much more complicated and customized than they were in the 20th.

While many fundamental economic conditions are changing, they are changing at different rates in different places and in different industries. The result is a range of basic economic circumstances. Because of the diversity of fundamental conditions, there is also a broad range of basic practices, values, and expectations among different organizations. This broadened range of economic and institutional conditions increases the importance of another change: There is a far broader range in people's key motives and personal characteristics than we've seen in the past.

The people issues of the 21st century are more complicated than they were in the 20th century, when virtually every person and every organization were fundamentally alike. In the 21st century, management must pay far more attention to individuals. The core differences between individuals will require that organizations customize many practices in order to engage, satisfy, and motivate people. Management now needs great listening skills, because they must relate to and lead people whose views and priorities are different from their own.

Because of the widened range of attributes of organizations and of people, the key to success in the 21st century is achieving a best fit between the priorities and characteristics of the people who are invited to join an organization and those of the institution.

STABLE AND BORDERLESS

The earth's tectonic plates are shifting; economies, governments, and social values are changing. Extraordinary advances in technology, especially, have created a worldwide economy, and that has created the conditions of permanent turbulence that I call *borderless*. Increasing numbers of organizations and people, everywhere, face ever-increasing competition and accelerating change.

There are, though, still some nations, industries, and organizations that remain largely on a *stable* path; in other words, they change slowly, they offer some level of job security, and they honor seniority. Universities, unionized organizations, many governments, civil service, and the core business of utilities come to mind.

A second group of organizations, which includes the majority of large and mature businesses, have found it necessary to transform themselves over roughly the past 15 years. They've had to change from the calm, slow-moving gait of stability to something significantly faster, flexible, and friskier. Those organizations have been striving for and achieving some fundamental changes in their culture, strategies, and practices. Total change is so difficult that a total transformation is exceedingly rare. That's why organizations that set out on the path of transformation generally continue on that path permanently.

The third and smallest group of organizations was founded in the past 20 years and especially in the 1990s. Since these companies were established in borderless conditions, they take ever-increasing requirements for innovation, adaptability, and speed for granted.

While it's always been true that different people have different priorities, today we have far greater differences in priorities between people than we ever had before. The e-conomy or borderless conditions have greatly broadened both the conditions of work and the possible payoffs of work. The largest differences are between stable and borderless organizations and the people who are attracted to one or the other of them.

There are three basic kinds of organizations: stable, transitional, and borderless. People can also be clustered into the same three groups.

Just a decade or two ago, virtually every employee in every organization was a *stable employee*: a person whose key goal was first to achieve security and then to achieve some reasonable level of success and a comfortable and predictable life. Stable people are still the largest, but they're not the most important group in the population.

Depression-impacted, stable people are security seekers. While the great majority are far too young to have lived through the Great Depression, they learned the lesson of putting security first from their parents or grandparents...or they saw the local factory closed, putting a town out of work...or they were let go and discovered their skills had little value.

Because all security seekers are Depression-impacted and share the fear of financial disaster, people in this group are far more alike than they are individuals. In the 20th century, when achieving security was the core goal for almost everyone, organizations were able to effectively deal with stable people as members of a group. Operationally, this meant that fairness was defined as identical treatment and outcomes for everyone. It meant that identical compensation and lock-step promotions were "fair," and those outcomes that reflected individual merit and contributions were "unfair."

A second, small but important group of people has emerged, that of the *borderless warriors*. These people are fundamentally different from stable security seekers. They thrive on risk, change, and unpredictability; they see more opportunity than threat in those conditions.

Borderless warriors are the first group of people since the Great Depression who bear no Depression scars. They've lived through bad economic times as well as good, and their innate optimism is tempered by a strong sense of reality. Honed by hard times during which they still achieved success, these people are genuinely confident. Borderless warriors are not deterred by lay-offs and the demise of the dotcoms; they find these times exciting and fun.

This small group is disproportionately important, because these people are the natural leaders in borderless organizations. Wherever conditions require that things be done significantly better, faster, and cheaper, these people need to be at the helm. People who prefer borderless conditions are far more likely to succeed during these times, because they inspire confidence and hope in the organization's people who are not borderless warriors.

The third group of people is the most difficult cluster to understand and motivate. They look and talk like borderless warriors, but while a few become courageous and entrepreneurial, the great majority do not develop the required confidence and personal strength.

This group is made up of two subgroups: One cluster includes young people, especially fairly recent college graduates, who have no memory of the last severe recession, which occurred in 1981–1982, and who have never seen a prolonged bear market. Growing up during two decades of good times, even after the stock market tumbled in 2000 and the economy stumbled into very slow growth, this group continues to say they expect to achieve major success, within—at the most—5 years. But their confidence and optimism are illusory. Without the experience of hard times, courage and tenacity are untested and therefore undeveloped. We can't know what this group's long-term attitudes and expectations will be, because they will be largely dependent upon what happens in the economy during the next 5 or so years.

The other people in this third group initially chose *stable* careers. They joined General Motors, IBM, or 3M, or they became accountants or lawyers. These people moved to borderless companies in the second half of the 1990s, either because the potential rewards were so breathtaking and/or because their self-esteem required that they join borderless startups to assure themselves that they, too, had what it took to be a borderless warrior.

When the bubble burst and the good times ended, the great majority of these people went back to the kinds of organizations and careers they had originally selected.

We might call the third group *transitional:* people who want to be borderless warriors and aren't; young people who are still in the process of developing strengths and confidence; and the very small number of stable people who discover that borderless conditions are exhilarating.

BEST FIT

Borderless and stable organizations (see Table 28.1) are very different in terms of the experiences they offer, their priorities and values, the amount of compensation people might earn, their levels of risk or job security, and the opportunities they offer for making a difference: creativity and leadership. People who flourish in borderless organizations are very different from those who succeed in stable organizations.

Different behaviors are required in different times, and many behaviors that are common in stable times are barriers to success in borderless times when fast, effective innovation is critical (see Table 28.2). In stable times, for example, leaders are expected to demonstrate authority by issuing orders, and subordinates are expected to do what they're told and

TABLE 28.1 Characteristics of Stable and Borderless Organizations

STABLE	BORDERLESS
Calm and deliberate	Fast and decisive
Quiet and cautious	Intense hum
Quiet and comfortable	Exciting
Hierarchical	Collegial
Competitive	Collaborative
Professional orientation	Business-driven
Low to medium risk	High risk
Work is often instrumental	Work satisfaction critical
Psychology of employees	Psychology of owners
Salaried	Shareholders
Good soldiers	Entrepreneurs
Seniority	Meritocracy
Report up	Initiate
Fun!	Fun! And fun*
Polite	Direct
Standardized	Customized

* Fun! Means extraordinary achievement and fun means having a good time.

TABLE 28.2 Stable Behaviors and Borderless Behaviors

STABLE BEHAVIORS	BORDERLESS BEHAVIORS
Give orders, tell, control, and require*	Share power, delegate, listen, and inspire
Follow procedures and rules, bureaucratic caution, delay decisions	Innovate, use judgment, initiate, make decisions
Narcissistic, hoard knowledge and resources, competitive, judgmental fiefdoms	Collaborate, share knowledge and resources, teach others, cohesive, borderless
Deferent, ask permission, salute up	Creatively confront, challenge up
Prefers non-confrontation and phony "consensus."	Prefers a diversity of views, spirited debate, and real consensus.

* For clarity, characteristics have been described as opposites. In reality, leaders have to use their judgment as to when to give orders and when to share decision-making power.

keep on saluting. That's both slow and a waste of subordinate's knowledge. Even worse, that style precludes innovation.

There are two very different populations: While some people love unpredictability, risk, and autonomy, other people like to know their place and get their orders. One group perceives itself as Ferraris and the other group is content to be Fords. People who prefer to be in stable organizations prefer merry-go-rounds. Those in borderless organizations choose roller coasters.

The greater range of organizational conditions and the newly desired behaviors that are critical to the success of borderless organizations means there are no longer "best companies" or "best practices." There's no longer one size that fits all. Instead, there's *best fit*—a match between an individual's values, priorities, and behaviors and those of an organization.

Organizations in the 21st century will succeed by achieving best fit. They will select people who have the personal characteristics that are likely to result in their being successful within the organization as it is or will be, and whose most important needs and desires can be met. Ideal outcomes are achieved when there is a best fit between the requirements and opportunities of the organization and the capacities and priorities of the employee.

Best fit, compatibility between what the organization requires and what the employee desires, leads to high motivation, comfort, and success. A bad fit leads to discomfort, high stress, and failure. Without best fit, the chances for success and retention plummet; with best fit, the chances for success soar.

STRATEGY FOR THE 21ST CENTURY: PORTFOLIO IS BACK

Maurice Saias and Olivier Tabatoni

Mechanistic strategic approaches are gone. Since the first oil crisis, turbulence has become the rule, leading to a drastic questioning of both our ways of thinking and our managerial practices. Most managers expect that sooner or later their own organization will experience some kind of discontinuous change. In these uncertain times, businesses that take nothing for granted will have an edge. It is time to reexamine how we anticipate and prepare for the future, given that the strategic toolboxes, which were developed in the 1960s and 1970s, are almost totally obsolete.

Nowadays, it is very hard to be a credible strategist, and the quest for the right moves is a waste of time and energy. Does this mean that strategy has become irrelevant for business? That the 21st century will be so erratic that pure opportunism is the only possible strategic behavior? Definitely not, but our perspectives on strategy must change. Instead of considering just strategic maneuvering, we must now take into account *strategic mindsets*—competition dealing as much with the approach to strategy as its content. For the winning organizations committed to creating their own future, the challenge is open.

In this chapter, we develop three points: What is strategy today? What kinds of discontinuities do corporations face? What are possible strategic responses?

WHAT IS STRATEGY TODAY?

The debates about the nature of strategy have never been so intense. Questions being raised include:

- Is strategy about anticipating, forecasting, and reacting, or is it about creating, influencing, and shaping?
- Is it about positioning in an industry or redrawing industrial boundaries?
- Is strategy about sustaining a competitive advantage or creating next advantages?
- Are we talking about limits to value and market creation or capabilities?
- Is it luck that differentiates the winners from the losers, Darwinism that determines the survivors, or is it purpose?

We can clarify these debates by clustering the characteristics of strategy into six broad categories.

CHANGE

During the 30 glorious years when changes were less frequent, doing consistently better was sufficient, and mechanistic models were effective; the capacity to take small or big steps made the difference in the race toward increased market share and profit. Incremental models were more than adequate. However, since the first oil shock, we have witnessed a permanent reallocation of the best cards. Turbulence, which replaced linearity, has been replaced by discontinuities. We have entered a world in which forecasting and planning are pure divination. This has made strategic planning an oxymoron. In a world in which constant change is the only thing that is predictable, the ability to question what is being done and the nature and reasons for past and present success, as well as a readiness to change the rules of the game, are indispensable strategic ingredients.

CREATIVITY

To become and stay a leader in today's fast-paced world requires a great deal of creativity. Destabilizing an entrenched competitor requires more than following the leader. For example, Toyota confronted the best car manufacturers of the West by challenging widely accepted production processes and traditional ways of managing assets. Komatsu used the new possibilities offered by fast transportation and delivery to shake up the competitive advantages of Caterpillar. The key is to systematically challenge established and accepted rules of success.

To change the game and refuse to imitate are good signs of creativity. To choose a direction and to stick with it demands imagination.

CHOICES

To say that resources are limited and that strategy means making choices is trivial. Strategy is associated with resource allocation and is therefore a political process. But, the conditions around these choices are new. First, speed and complexity have increased dramatically; second, costs are extremely high. Each decision is risky and costly. In this sense, strategy resembles gambling at a casino: Nobody knows which table to play at, given that the games change constantly. Furthermore, chips are astronomically expensive and returning to a table after having refused to play or having left is seldom possible. To watch is to not take part, and not participating means rejecting the possibility to win.

COURAGE

The more creative and surprising a strategy is, the higher its potential reward. However, as the reward increases, the risk increases. Therefore, decision makers must have courage. Indeed, unlike a few years ago when economic growth and a permissive environment eradicated mistakes, a strategic mistake today is likely to lead to a financial disaster.

Many CEOs, concerned with how they will fare in the business history books, find risk-taking less than appealing. However, success breeds failure. Strategy involves having the courage to challenge what we are and what we have been, to go against broadly accepted thinking and widely spread practices.

COHERENCE

Choices must be consistent not only among, but also with, the processes in use and with those that will be adopted or modified. We are not concerned here with coherence in time, but with consistency between strategy and the systems and processes that lead to action. The following two examples illustrate this point:

- A medium-sized successful enterprise has crafted a vision stating its intent to become the innovative leader in its industry. All the necessary ingredients are in place: communication, vision, objectives, and lines of conduct. The short-term actions are well designed, packaged, and interrelated. However, the first person to try something dramatically innovative failed and was subsequently fired. In that instant, the vision of becoming an innovative leader lost its backing.
- Another corporation had to change from selling products to providing systems and solutions. Top management

realized that in order to succeed, the different business units needed to cooperate. However, they refused to change the reward system entirely, which was based on individual business-unit performance. Team effort across business units was not taken into account and resulted in the multiplication of conflicts, a lack of cooperation, and customer dissatisfaction.

This coherence imperative is difficult to achieve, because it is risky to modify systems and processes that represent the administrative core of the corporation too frequently.

CAPACITY TO DEAL WITH COMPLEXITY

Strategists have long used simple models and paradigms to spread their approaches across their organizations. They have relied upon reduction mindsets to make choices look clear and unambiguous. For example, a company might compete either on cost, quality, size, speed, or flexibility. Unfortunately, these simple binary options have become irrelevant under the pressure of more complex demands. Financial markets demand increasing quarterly results over the long term: They record quarterly profits while asking for social and societal responsibility. Corporations must be big, fast, and flexible; centralized and decentralized; global and local; combative and consensual.

Strategy, then, is the art of carving a path in this paradoxical world; however, the culture and education of most western leaders has prepared them to think in alternative terms and to search for the "right" answer. Thus, confronting increasing ambiguity and complexity is not an easy management task.

WHERE ARE THE MAJOR DISCONTINUITIES?

In this perpetually changing world, where are the major sources of discontinuity, which, beyond technological or political revolutions, represent the highest stakes? About 10 have a systematic impact on most businesses. For simplicity's sake, we present each one separately, but it is their interrelationships that make them so complex and difficult to grasp.

GLOBALIZATION

Although globalization has its advocates and opponents, it is a reality. The question then becomes, How long will the reasons that incite corporations to globalize last? Some reasons to globalize include the following:

- The explosion of fixed cost that unavoidably lead to the quest for higher volume.
- The search for growth through geographic expansion, especially when domestic markets seem to be maturing.
- The fall of regulatory and legal barriers; faster, better transportation and communication facilities, which have accelerated the worldwide harmonization of tastes and lifestyles.
- The search for balance between political and economic risks.
- The spread of financial and human resources across the world with an overly underutilized potential of highly qualified labor force.
- The global customer base.
- The globalization of suppliers.
- The globally competitive environment that leads to the necessity to develop retaliatory capabilities.

DEREGULATION AND PRIVATIZATION

Deregulation and privatization are taking place all over the world, even in the most hostile political environments. A few widely publicized counterexamples, such as the incoherent deregulation of power generation in California or the situation of railroad transportation in the United Kingdom, cannot conceal the benefits of deregulation and privatization, especially for consumers. Deregulation and privatization have been used to correct decisions made for ideological reasons rather than economic or managerial ones. Moreover, they have become a source of government funding in difficult times.

VOLATILITY

"Volatility in the 21st Century," a special issue of *Business Week,* contributed to the popularization of this concept. In summary, it looks as if linearity has disappeared and economic cycles will be shorter, with much higher peaks and deeper troughs. Rigid assets no longer meet the flexibility imperative; likewise for unyielding human assets and mindsets.

CONVERGENCE

The impact of convergence is more visible in the high-tech arenas, such as information, communication, entertainment industries, leisure, and consumer electronics converging. However, it does stretch to the more traditional industries, such as the automotive industry, which is converging in the areas of mechanical technology, electronics, software, and new intelligent materials. Financial services are impacted by convergence; banking, insurance, mass retail distributors, the automotive industry, and large industrial conglomerates, as well as telecom operators converge and compete.

INDUSTRIAL FRONTIERS

As a consequence of convergence, industrial borders blur or disappear entirely. It becomes harder to identify competitors as companies get involved in new domains with drastically different approaches and unorthodox business methods. By doing so, they multiply the possible migration paths, and the nature of competition is modified. Competition deals as much with migration paths as it does with endgames themselves. A second type of border is disappearing. The frontiers between suppliers, customers, and competitors are being replaced by alliances and partnerships, which is accelerating the development of what is referred to as *co-opetition.*

STANDARDS

Battles for standards have always existed; however, globalization presents a new dimension. Standards give considerable commercial power to those companies who have successfully imposed theirs on the industry, as is exemplified in the use of VHS for JVC, Windows for Microsoft, and GSM for UMTS. The role of alliances, partnerships, *co-opetition*, and *complementors* is crucial for the adoption and expansion of standards. Real coalitions develop and fight for their common standards. The battles that follow often overshadow the fight for profit among the members of the coalition at least until one set of standards prevails.

DISINTERMEDIATION

The distance between producers and end users is becoming shorter and shorter. The cascade of distributors can be reduced to one step through new ways of getting in touch with the user. Charles Schwab, Dell or Gateway, and Amazon have challenged the traditional distribution value chain. The overflow of information to the user does not guarantee the quality of his or her decision. In order to help him or her, a new intermediary has emerged: the expert. The expert's role is to check the quality and the price and to make recommendations, thus helping potential customers find their way into the jungle of direct offers. Disintermediation influences the cost and the assets structure. In the medium and long run, it changes the business model.

ECOSENSITIVITY

Today, ecology is perceived as a set of rules and regulations imposed on business. The pressures are initiated by various groups whose objectives are not always clear. In the future, ecosensitivity could be a major creator of new activities.

DEMOGRAPHY

The following numbers reveal expected demographic trends. Between 2000 and 2050, the world population will grow from 6 billion to 9 billion. In the developed world, population will stabilize at about 1 billion. Life expectancy, with a few exceptions, has increased dramatically; since 1975, adding .25 per year in the developed world. Fifty percent of girls born in 2000 will live to be 100 years old. Within the next 30 years or so in the United States, WASPs will no longer be the majority, while the population of Hispanics will grow rapidly. The United States could then become the largest bilingual country in the Western world. Demographic trends impact upon markets as well as upon political, economic, and financial decisions.

FINANCIAL MARKETS

The growing power of financial markets has not stopped since the early 1960s. Beginning in the United States, followed by the United Kingdom, and then extending to most of Western Europe and the rest of the world, the last bastions of the so-called *patient capitalism* have fallen one by one. Value creation for shareholders has become the unavoidable leitmotiv. Currently, the markets react as much to the financial results, EVA, and other measurements of a corporation's economic profit as they do to their growth. Investors have been tempted by the pursuit of fantastic growth at the expense of profitability, but it did not last long. The two imperatives are again balanced in the investors' minds.

WHAT KINDS OF STRATEGIC RESPONSES?

In most cases, revolutionary strategic decisions are made while one's "back is against the wall." Usually, fundamental changes of direction and in-depth questioning of current business practices take place in desperate situations and/or with the arrival of a new leader.

This pattern begs the questions, Is the only possible route to strategic decision making apparent in discontinuous times? Is strategic revolution the only possibility? Does evolution mean rehearsing the past? If we go beyond semantic fighting or clan-like quarrels, revolution and evolution are complementary, as shown by the strategic behavior of winners around the world. These winners demonstrated their ability to successfully manage two strategic dilemmas and to handle diversity well.

THE PROFITABLE GROWTH DILEMMA

Corporations are expected to deliver profitable growth. First, profit is evaluated through EVA, which is the difference between the return on capital employed (ROCE) and the weighted average cost of capital (WACC). This difference (ROCE–WACC) must be positive. Second, growth can take many forms. Usually, growth is generated internally (organic) or externally through mergers and acquisitions.

External Growth. Recently, markets began reacting negatively to external growth. A few years ago, these negative reactions developed several months or years after the actual operation. Today they appear immediately, almost as soon as the announcement of the merger or the acquisition is made. Financial analysts have come to realize that the outcome of mergers and acquisitions seldom meets expectations. The synergies that have been promised rarely materialize, and when they do they take the form of rationalization and restructuring, which are nothing more than cost-cutting exercises. And diminishing returns apply to cost cutting. Returns increase momentarily, but they plunge rapidly because of efficiency losses due to internal conflicts, cultural shock, undesired departures of good people, and so on. The time spent by top management to solve integration issues is not devoted to the future development of the new entity. Introduced as an offensive and a source of fantastic opportunities, most mergers and acquisitions turn defensive and troublesome. The grandiose vision translates into a succession of retrenchments and restructurings, and frequently the market capitalization of the new entity falls below the level of each of the components before the operation.

Internal Growth. Internal, or organic, growth can be generated by present or new businesses on current or new markets. Whatever the content,it may be handled in a traditional or innovative manner. Even the so-called mature markets can grow. Innovation can transform even the most mature markets, thanks to new products and services, new processes, new organizational forms, or challenging mindsets. In the 21st century, competing on the basis of mindsets is as important as competing on the basis of products and services. Unfortunately, innovation hardly meets the challenge of EVA. If innovation and external growth do not convince the markets, what can be done to deliver profitable growth?

THE EXPLOITATION/EXPLORATION DILEMMA

Corporations must manage exploitation and exploration simultaneously. Excellence in exploitation, the first requirement, means a perfect command of the following:

- *Competitive advantages*: cost, quality, speed, flexibility, and so on;
- *Core competencies*: finding and protecting them as well as preventing them from becoming core rigidities; and
- *Organizational capabilities*: innovation, knowledge management, learning, acuity, and multivalence.

When competitive bases are underdeveloped, core competencies undetermined, and organizational capabilities weak, financial results are poor or purely accidental. Under these circumstances, markets lose faith and penalize attempts at exploration. In order to explore new avenues, corporations must first prove their excellence at exploiting their present businesses. This means optimizing current activities as well as extending their domain and broadening their market basis.

Then, they will be allowed to explore fundamentally new, high-risk possibilities, which are potential sources of high-profit growth.

In order to reduce the exploration risk, managers often resort to experimentation. They try new products, services, solutions, markets, and rules in one part of the organization. Experimentation appears a more reliable basis for collecting information than market research. They also tend to resort to alliances, joint ventures, and partnerships to share the risk.

The strategic success of a corporation is dependent upon its capacity to capture a disproportionate share of the future value that will be created in the evolution of its industry. At the heart of this challenge rests the capacity to manage all kinds of diversity, not just products, markets, and core competencies. Diversity and portfolio management are again at the forefront, but with very different strategic, financial, and leadership requirements.

THE NEW MANAGEMENT OF DIVERSITY

Resource-based approaches that relay a clear vision sustain the search for flexibility, innovation, efficiency, and sharing amongst businesses and markets better than a best-fit approach. Similarly, being present on many markets—the first step toward globalization—and in many businesses helps to systematize experimentation.

A clear corporate vision based on strong core competencies and organizational capabilities and backed by flexibility and continuous innovation, should satisfy shareholders. However, the large discrepancy between strategic common sense and financial outlook results in markets that, at the same time, constrain and help strategic decision-making.

Markets are influenced more by results and the convincing power of CEOs than by the future profitability of different possible strategies. Corporate valuation results from two steps: (1) The capacity to generate future cash flows with the present assets; that is, the outcome of past investments is valued. (2) The cash flow that will be generated by the future investments is valued. This second step is a bet on the amount of future investments and their profitability. To evaluate the expected cash flows the markets take into account the capacity to optimally manage the present assets as well as the clarity of the vision, managerial capabilities, and so on. Analysts also use discount rates to take risk into account. This approach assumes that investment decisions are binary and irreversible. Whereas the approach looks acceptable in a stable environment, it may be entirely inappropriate for discontinuity.

Discontinuity supposes the possibility to postpone a decision in order to experiment and collect information; strategic flexibility increases value. Furthermore, when volatility increases (i.e., investments and potential cash flows increase), so does the value of flexibility. With higher volatility, the ability to postpone a decision will prevent large, unprofitable investments in case of downturn, while providing much higher returns if a peak materializes. These conclusions are drawn from the financial option model developed by Black-Scholes and Merton for the financial markets. Researchers have attempted to extend that model from the financial to the physical world without much success, except in the case of natural resources. Today, most strategy consultants, academics, and financial experts are developing models that would be relevant for real options; therefore, increasing the probability of possible extensions from the field of finance to the industrial field in the near future. The strategic implications would be amazing: Financial markets would improve the quality of strategic decision making by providing the tools and thinking that are missing today. Instead of minimizing the risk among investments showing the same expected results, much riskier projects could be selected. Increased corporate value results from blockbuster investments instead of from the optimization of more clearly defined projects.

The key issue in valuing a flexible investment is to know how much time is available before an irreversible decision must be made. This period of time is called *maturity of flexibility*. If the maturity is nil, then the project is irreversible. Good strategies try to increase that maturity in order to accumulate knowledge.

At this stage, the strategic relevance of learning capabilities and speed becomes obvious. Indeed, if too much time is necessary to reach the final decision, competitors will move in and reap the benefits of the project, including the anticipated cash flows. To prevent that from happening, corporations send signals to convince their competitors that they are irreversibly committed; they try to develop projects that are hard to imitate; they work to lower competitive pressures by looking for strategic alliances, fighting for standards, and buying out competitors with similar projects.

At the appropriate time, managers must also make sure that they have enough financial resources to transform the exploratory adventure into a successful exploitation. Two kinds of risk endanger the corporation with insufficient financial resources:

- Rushing to a final decision, thus losing flexibility; and
- Inadequate resources, leading to abandonment of the project and possibly jeopardizing the corporation's future.

There is a delicate balance to be found with the financial markets. Corporations need the support of the market to mobilize the resources that will help them move from a successful exploitation to an adventurous exploration. But, they also need the markets to find the necessary resources to move from what looks like an exploration with high potential to its exploitation. This complex process requires an exchange of information between the corporation and the financial markets. Top management may not be in a position to fully communicate to the market the highly sensitive, strategic information. On the other hand, the markets may have a hard time grasping the complexity of the exploration activities, especially if the activity is risky and its business model innovative.

In short, the typical role of financial markets is to fund exploitation and not exploration. Therefore, exploration must be financed through internally generated funds. This implies the following:

- Sophisticated management of cash cycles, which in turn means

- The coexistence of several well-balanced cash cycles connected to a portfolio of strategically well-related businesses (the sharing); and
- A sound profitability of the core business along with an exploration activity designed as a portfolio of real options. A high profitability makes the liquidation of the corporation less optimal

- Evaluation of financial performance must not rely solely on profit, since it does not take into account exploration activities. Indeed, the most profitable activities are privileged, even if they do not generate enough cash to support the exploration. It is essential to favor high cash-generating activities that help fund exploration and are a large part of the future value created. The cash flow return on investment (CFROI) takes into account the free cash flows, what is left after financing the development of the present activities; the cash value added (CVA) measures the residual cash, what is left after financing development and remunerating capital employed. Boeing, General Dynamics, and EADS use these criteria to make their strategic choices. These companies must balance exploitation businesses with the exploration of long-cycle, cash-consuming activities.
- A new type of corporate communication with the financial analysts. Today, the financial world demands that unused cash is returned to the shareholders as dividends or share buybacks. It is compulsory to convince the analysts that part of that unused cash must be retained in order to be invested in extremely uncertain activities. The only chance to be credible and backed by the shareholders is to build a capital of trust and confidence based on past and present performance of exploitation and past record as an explorer.

Organizations must be able and willing to accept new ventures and to use resources needed to feed exploration activities, whether human, financial, or otherwise. Because these conditions are seldom met, it is difficult for the incumbent exploitation leaders to be simultaneously good explorers.

CONCLUSION

The bottom line for executives in a world of constant and rapid change, and of increasing ambiguity and complexity, is a dynamic of the courage, creativity, and flexibility to balance the enhanced risks with the greater rewards if their corporation is to embody the paradoxes of being big yet fast, centralized yet decentralized, global and local, combative and consensual. The awareness and willingness to reinvent the rules will be at the heart of the strategic approaches by successful decision makers.

30 Organizing for Strategic Flexibility

Homa Bahrami and Stuart Evans

T he key challenge facing organizational architects is to design structural configurations that are truly flexible—that have the capacity to expand and contract at short notice, to rapidly change course, and to be quickly repositioned as new realities unfold. This may be an unattainable goal. However, there are examples of dynamic ecosystems in which enterprises do exhibit some of the building blocks and the recipes of this emerging organizational order.

The ebb and flow of success in the Silicon Valley has prompted many entrepreneurs to structure their enterprises for real flexibility. The name of the game is constant change—focusing at one time on innovation, changing the rules, and reinventing the future, while at another time pruning excess to survive and consolidating in the face of a major downturn. The perpetual challenge is to grasp short-lived opportunities, innovate continuously, and compete globally. Effective organizational architectures are about harnessing kaleidoscopic change.

This chapter describes how high-technology enterprises in the Silicon Valley are organized to address the challenges of meteoric growth on the one hand and sudden downturns on the other. How do they provide anchors of stability for expectant knowledge workers, but stay flexible enough for the ups and downs of the business cycle and innovation loops? With widely dispersed global teams, how is a sense of cohesion, identity, and community achieved? How do they stay robust and resilient, while becoming agile and versatile?

THE BUILDING BLOCKS

Three core dimensions coalesce to form the architecture of the flexible enterprise.

1. *The organizational dimension* is about the traditional challenges of differentiation: how to break up the entity into manageable work nodes, projects, and teams, and focus the talent pool on targeted assignments. This task requires balancing the needs for flexibility on the one hand and stability on the other.

2. *The connective dimension* is about harnessing synergies and creating linkages. Linkages are largely about integration: how to coordinate globally dispersed work nodes by sharing codified knowledge through core processes and an efficient information and communications infrastructure.

3. *The cohesive dimension* is about binding together the various components. A blend of the hard and the soft—it is the physical, the intellectual, the financial, and the emotional glue that keeps the enterprise together.

THE ORGANIZATIONAL DIMENSION: BLENDING BASE UNITS AND PROJECT TEAMS

The organizational systems of many high-technology companies are in a continuous state of flux, yet formal structures do exist in the sense of clear reporting relationships, grouping of skills, and concise assignment of responsibility, authority, and accountability. Many firms strive to be structured yet flexible and disciplined, while creative. They have evolved dualistic work nodes that seek to strike a dynamic balance between stability and flexibility comprising base units and project teams.[1]

Base Units. Base units are the relatively stable component. They are the formal mechanism for grouping skills, clustering activities, and assigning reporting relationships. They refer to functional departments, product divisions, sales offices, manufacturing sites, and research centers. They are used to compartmentalize work, provide focus, assign accountabilities, and generate a sense of shared identity.

Project Teams. Project teams are the variable arm or the rapid deployment capability. These teams enable a firm to focus on critical assignments without causing major disruptions to the base units. Knowledge workers from various base units can be pooled together at short notice, put to work on new assignments, and disbanded once their task has been accomplished. In some cases the project teams may evolve and become the foundation of a new base unit, depending on critical mass and business scope. Consider the reflections of a senior executive of a $1 billion net storage company:

> We have a functional organization...it is the most simple from a line of sight perspective...as your products become more complex and you become geographically dispersed, it starts to fall apart...so we started what we call virtual business units...they don't own any people...there'll be a virtual CEO

---

[1] Bahrami, H. (1992, Summer). "The Emerging Flexible Organization: Perspectives from Silicon Valley," *California Management Review*.

who's responsible for bringing together cross-functional teams...let's take the example of our CDBU (content delivery business unit)...it actually has three people and drives fairly significant revenue...the various functional teams participate as members of both the functional unit as well as the CDBU.

The key point is that base units are a blend of functional and product clusters, market segments, and geographic units. While they transform over time, they are effective as a platform on which project teams, such as virtual business units, are overlaid for creating short-term flexibility.

THE CONNECTIVE DIMENSION: FUSING PHYSICAL ARCHITECTURE AND TECHNOLOGY INFRASTRUCTURE

Work has to be aligned among the various base units and project teams in order to avoid each node marching to its own tune. That is where a variety of linkages are used to facilitate communication and knowledge sharing among globally dispersed work nodes. This is succinctly summed up in the comments of the co-founder and executive vice president of a telecommunications company:

> We like the idea of small, decentralized units with focused accountability...but our products have to play together. Our customers buy an integrated system...there is a major element of success that depends on coordination and close cooperation between the units.

These linkages are typically a mixture of the physical and the virtual. They utilize cross-unit meetings, the IT infrastructure, and the physical design of offices and campus-like facilities.

Ironically, while technological sophistication facilitates remote and mobile work, the setup of the physical workplace is becoming more important. Visual and symbolic norms can be conveyed through workplace design. These can nurture collaboration, ease or impede communication, and create a sense of community.

The facilities of a major global company in Menlo Park, California, like those of many others in the Silicon Valley, are intentionally designed to create a campus-like atmosphere. A key feature is a central thoroughfare, analogous to a downtown or main street, with office complexes built around. People can "bump" into each other as a matter of course. The staircases are wider than normal to allow for continuity of dialogue and conversation among teams walking to a meeting or to the cafeteria, which is located at the center of the campus. White boards are placed along the corridors to enable people to spontaneously reflect on their creative thoughts. Shared common rooms take center stage—as they provide group space—while individual cubicles and offices take on secondary importance.[2]

The administrative backbone of the enterprise has been radically impacted by *hardwired* IT, which has made it feasible for knowledge workers to become nomadic, working any time, from any location; it has given rise to the interconnected global entity, where like a relay team, tasks are passed from location to location over different time zones. By means of knowledge management, CRM, and other tools, brainpower and critical information are distributed throughout the organization, which reduces the size of the physical center. This has given real-time broadcast capability and access to unfiltered information to the dispersed knowledge workers. This was conveyed in the comments of a senior vice president of a networking company:

> [The real value of IT] is to get information to those doing the work...information that used to filter only through the hierarchy...that only managers used to have...Two thirds of our (knowledge workers) are nomadic...able to work any place, any time...they can choose when, where, and how they work...many of our meetings are really assigned phone numbers, where people call in...recently we had a meeting with five people, in different locations, calling in...but we were all looking at the same page of our intranet at the same time."

---

[2] Bahrami, H., and S. Evans. (1997, Spring). "Human Resource Leadership in Knowledge-based Entities" *Human Resource Management, 36*(1).

Naturally, the hardwired component is dynamic and will evolve in different ways. Over time, it provides the codified knowledge base of the enterprise. The important point is that there are three complementary linkages that augment one another:

1. Technology enabled linkages;
2. Physical architecture of the workplace; and
3. Personal and team communication channels.

The real challenge is to align these and evolve them on a continuous basis.

THE COHESIVE DIMENSION: WELDING CULTURAL NORMS AND FINANCIAL CONTROLS

The productivity of employees in knowledge-based enterprises depends as much on personal commitments, motivations, and relationships as it does on capabilities. There needs to be some kind of fusing mechanism to bind together the distributed nodes. While financial controls provide the "hard" control glue, cultural norms and people policies provide the motivational "soft glue." Cultural norms and core values are broad pillars and guiding principles; nonetheless, they do impact daily actions and work practices. For instance, motivation and cultural fit influence the types of people who are recruited. Cultural fit tests are used to devise assessment and reward criteria, and they influence how a firm may deal with an adverse situation. Consider the comments of the CEO of an enterprise application software company:

> One of our unwritten cultural tenets is that everyone's a sales and support person...and that we should use our own products...in putting our value tenets together, we wanted to think about "what kind of a company do we want to work for?"...the emphasis is on the company, not the management—we even do report cards on how the whole company is living up to its cultural tenets.

Additionally, while many high-tech companies are global from inception, they still have to deal with the challenge of transferring their culture out of their home base. Many firms generate more than half of their sales outside the United States, and they have a large population of non-American employees even among their founders and early employees. As summarized by the CEO of a financial software company,

> When you open an office several thousand miles away, it is difficult to export the culture of these cases. We make sure that our new employees spend a large part of their time, early on, here at the home base, so they can really experience, feel, and live our culture, and not just read about it.

Effective high-technology firms evolve a cultural mindset, which incorporates diverse assumptions and premises. This requires balancing strong corporate values—typically reflecting the home culture—with a broad perspective—accommodating the diverse viewpoints of global customers, employees, and competitors. The most critical implementation tools focus on the composition of their employee base and senior executive teams. Other mechanisms include short-term sabbaticals to projects outside the home base, job-rotation opportunities, real-time global communication forums, and global account-management systems.

Cultural glue instills bedrock values, which provide "sameness" and give emotional cohesion to a distributed organization—disseminating the critical ingredients of the genetic code. The key challenge in striking an effective balance is *figuring out what has to be the same so that everything else can be different.*

DESIGNING A VERSATILE FEDERATION

In contrast to the mechanistic, linear hierarchies of the Industrial Era, enterprises in the Silicon Valley resemble sports teams, rock bands, and film studios, in that roles and assignments continuously change; customization, flexibility, innovation, and speed are the key challenges. Organizational personalities are forged around the dominant players, giving each company a unique look and feel.

Notwithstanding the idiosyncrasies, there are also many similarities between flexible organizational architectures. The most striking is that they resemble a versatile federation—one that can accommodate opposing needs and yet have a shared mission and climate; one that can embrace true diversity and yet have a clear purpose and identity; one that can constantly evolve its trajectory and yet provide a few anchors of stability; one that has focused silos with clear accountabilities yet can leverage horizontal synergies; one that is financially disciplined and yet has a sense of community.

A federal organizational architecture is multipolar. Globally dispersed work units and project teams are typically welded together with hardwired IT and communication systems and the soft glue of cultural norms, people practices, and personal networks. The line units are interdependent, relying on one another for critical expertise and know-how. In addition, they have a peer-to-peer relationship with the center. The center's role is to orchestrate the strategic vision, develop the shared organizational and administrative infrastructure, and create the hard and the soft glue that can create synergies and ensure unity of mission and purpose. However, these tasks are undertaken together with the line units, not dictated to them. What are the success criteria in creating a flexible federation?

First and foremost, there are clear federal mandates that apply to all citizens and work units, with built-in flexibility for autonomous "state" initiatives. Consider the positioning of IT groups; in many companies, for example, the corporate or central IT group is responsible for providing the standard IT infrastructure and communication services that can be used by all the nodes, irrespective of their special needs. The "states" take the initiative in identifying their own customized application needs. Based on their unique requirements, they may use the corporate IT function as an internal vendor or go outside for sourcing the required services. The critical task in this context is to isolate the commonalities across the various zones of "federal and state" tensions—what has to be the same across all nodes so that everything else can be locally customized.

Second, while information and communication technologies provide linkages in the context of codified knowledge, individual initiative is needed to share and crosspollinate uncodified and spontaneous know-how. In a crucial yet complementary sense, this is where *hubs* come into play. Hubs are knowledge workers who connect the dispersed units, vendors, and projects and sit at the intersection of key constituencies. They may include product managers, project leaders, account representatives, and critical interface functions like marketing, IT, human resources, and business development. Hub roles are important in distributed, nodal architectures, because they provide the connectivity between critical sources of expertise. Additionally, they manage communication links to various stakeholders and are tangible sources of real-time information.

The *front-line troops* are the radars that can detect the early signals of change, while hubs provide structural connectivity. These teams and individuals are in direct contact with the market and competitive realities, and many include programmers, engineers, salespeople, account managers, and customer service staff. Since the generals, senior executives, are typically responsible for developing the enterprise strategy, it is important to establish direct communication channels between the two and minimize the role of filters and intermediaries. Indeed, to reinforce the connectivity between the strategic vision and operational realities, many senior executives have dual roles and are directly accountable for specific line operations. By fusing their strategic and operational roles, they are able to recalibrate strategies based on real-time information and realistic action plans.[3]

---

[3] For more detail on how strategic decisions in high-technology companies entail continuous recalibration, see Bahrami, H., & S. Evans, "Strategy Making in High Technology Firms," *California Management Review*, Winter 1989, and also S. Evans "Strategic Flexibility for High Technology Manœuvres," *Journal of Management Studies*, 28 (1), 1991.

LIVING WITH SHADES OF GRAY

The flexible enterprise walks a tightrope between several opposing tensions. The organizational framework is neither totally chaotic nor tightly synchronized. Utilizing the hard wire of IT and remote work protocols does not reduce the importance of soft cultural glue, personal networks, and face-to-face interaction. The focus must be on generating short-term results while not losing sight of the long-term direction. Front-line workers exercise real power and influence, but there are also clear mandates and directional guidelines from the top.

Federal organizational architectures do not fit into the either/or premises of the traditional mechanistic structures. Instead, they must embrace the traditional paradox of centralization/decentralization. On the one hand, the need for focus coupled with the coordination needs of interdependent product families and market segments push towards centralization. Maintaining the pace of innovation and generating the capacity for rapid and flexible response to market needs push towards decentralization. This is a difficult balancing act to pull off, especially in view of continued market and political volatility.

Creating a versatile federation poses a major challenge, because our existing organizational systems, managerial vocabularies, and professional mindsets have evolved to address the challenges of the Industrial Era and its inherent focus on standardization, binary thinking, and unidimensional recipes. The emerging, knowledge-based enterprise needs a versatile set of capabilities to address technological sophistication, complex innovation, short-lived opportunities, competitive intensity, and expectant knowledge workers. It needs tolerance for thinking in terms of "shades of gray," establishing tradeoffs, and continuously fine-tuning the organizational architecture. The current turbulence in the business environment offers exciting opportunities for experimentation, innovative thinking, and diversity in organizational designs, but we have to be willing to lift our organizational blindfolds and move away from simplistic cure-all, one-size-fits-all solutions.

31

COMPETITIVE DYNAMICS, STRATEGY, AND COMPETENCE DEVELOPMENT: THE RISE OF VALUE CONFEDERATIONS IN FAST-CHANGE INDUSTRIES

David Lei

O ver the past decade, much research has focused on the sources and conditions of approaches to building and sustaining competitive advantage. As companies compete in increasingly hypercompetitive environments, managers need to engage in multiple sets of activities (e.g., product development, entry into new markets, innovating new technologies), while simultaneously reducing the costs and risks associated with these strategic activities.[1]

As part of their effort to learn about evolving market trends and new technological innovations, firms are establishing closer relationships and strategic alliances with their customers and suppliers. Managers are seeking to improve coordination and information flow among internal functions, disciplines, and lines of business to enhance the search for systemwide solutions for developing new products and markets.

Findings from research and practitioner studies suggest that efforts to sustain existing sources of competitive advantage over an extended time period may well leave an organization vulnerable to challenges from new technologies, customer needs, and new rivals.[2] Building and sustaining competitive advantage is an ongoing Herculean endeavor that involves the cultivation and integration of many distinct factors, including technology investments; improved communication patterns within the firm; fostering new and diverse sources of knowledge; as well as organizational designs that promote fast-response capabilities and continuous learning.

Firms are finding that they are no longer the dominant repository of vital knowledge and competences critical to initiating and sustaining product development. In fact, over the past decade, managers have realized the need to work closely with a broad range of suppliers and distributors to build "value constellations" and "extended enterprises" to access a wider array of competences and skills.[3]

These relationships enabled firms to reduce some of the costs and risks of investing in new technologies. However, the notion of the "extended enterprise" is no longer limited to firms and their suppliers. The Internet provides low-cost information and direct communications among economic entities.

---

[1] Some of the more prominent research pieces that have addressed this trend include the following: R. E. Hoskisson and M. A. Hitt. (1994). *Downscoping: Taming the Diversified Firm.* New York: Oxford University Press; R. A. D'Aveni. (1994). *Hypercompetition: Managing the Dynamics of Strategic Maneuvering.* New York: Free Press; C. Helfat. (1997). "Know-How and Asset Complementarity and Dynamic Capability Accumulation: The Case of R&D." *Strategic Management Journal, 18,*339–360; D. Lei, M. A. Hitt, and R. A. Bettis. (1996). "Dynamic Core Competences Through Meta-Learning and Strategic Context." *Journal of Management, 22,* 549–569.

[2] See, for example, C. M. Christensen. (1997). *The Innovator's Dilemma: When New Technologies Cause Great Firms to Fail.* Boston, MA: Harvard Business School Press. W. J. Ferrier, K. G. Smith, and C. M. Grimm. (1999). "The Role of Competitive Action in Market Share Erosion and Industry Dethronement: A Study of Industry Leaders and Challengers." *Academy of Management Journal, 42,* 372–388.

Customers are becoming increasingly capable of fostering an ongoing and active forum with providers to co-develop ideas, new products, and services. In some industries, customers are becoming a primary source of future product development ideas, whereby they help educate the marketplace, fine-tune product features, and even shape market evolution and acceptance of new offerings.

As the walls and boundaries that separate organizations from their suppliers and customers erode, the nature of competition and strategy is changing as well. Firms can no longer conceive of themselves as isolated fortresses. Over the last decade, the proliferation of "value nets" or "value confederations"[4] has begun to reshape every industry. Today's industries are rapidly metamorphosing into an interwoven entity in which firms that possess a variety of different skill sets, knowledge bases, core competences, and technologies contribute

---

[3] A series of excellent accounts of this phenomenon is described in R. Normann and R. Ramirez. (1993). "From Value Chain to Value Constellation: Designing Interactive Strategy." *Harvard Business Review, 71*(4), 65–77; R. E. Miles and C. C. Snow. (1992, Summer). "Causes of Failure in Network Organizations." *California Management Review,* 53–73; and H. Bahrami. (1992, Summer). "The Emerging Flexible Organization: Perspectives from Silicon Valley." *California Management Review,* 33–52. An excellent overview of the structural components of network organizations may be found in J. Sydow and A. Windeler. (1998). "Organizing and Evaluating Interfirm Networks: A Structural Perspective on Network Processes and Effectiveness." *Organization Science, 9*(3), 265–284; as well as R. N. Osborn and J. Hagedoorn. (1997). "The Institutionalization and Evolutionary Dynamics of Interorganizational Alliances and Networks." *Academy of Management Journal, 40,* 1997,261–278.

[4] The term *value nets* has been described in a book authored by D. Bovert and J. Martha. (2000). *Value Nets.* New York: John Wiley and Sons. Their use of the term, however, is largely confined to what individual firms can do to redesign their supply chains to maximize flexibility and the ability to reach customers using e-commerce technologies. Our conception of the term *value confederation* goes beyond the notion of Bovert and Martha's value net; in fact, we use the term value confederation to capture the underlying economic and competitive web of interrelationships that enshroud a variety of different firms, each of which seeks to contribute what it thinks will be a distinctive addition to the overall value proposition.

their individual resources to shape an entirely new mode of economic competition.

A *value confederation* is a group of firms that compete against other firms or groups of firms—both within and across industries. For a growing number of industries, product development, technological innovation, and market entry are activities that require the resources, knowledge, skills, and competences of many entities. In addition to working closely with their suppliers, firms manage their product development and technology investments using customers' knowledge and skills as key ingredients for future sources of innovation. Many firms within a value confederation work with one another through formal and informal cooperative arrangements. At the same time, they also compete for new sources of knowledge and skills that will shape their future sources of competitive advantage.

This trend suggests that firms need to develop a capability to learn from a wide range of sources and to manage the knowledge-sharing interface between the company and other members of the confederation, particularly its customers. With the evolution of these value confederations, the nature of competitive strategy is also rapidly changing. In essence, as firms steadily rely on an expanding array of suppliers, customers, and other firms to participate in key value-adding activities, the growth and acceptance of new products and technologies will increasingly be beyond the control of any single firm. A multitude of technological and organizational factors are converging to redefine the context of strategy and competitive advantage in the value confederation. As new technologies enable firms to interactively share real-time data and information with their suppliers and customers, many economic activities will increasingly occur on a virtual basis within the value confederation, whereby design data, knowledge, insight, and even skills will be freely shared among the group of firms.

We begin with an examination of the critical features of the fast-evolving value confederation concept as it relates to promoting new forms of innovation. Next, we examine how the value confederation will likely shape the environmental context of competitive strategy for individual firms. Last, we examine what firms need to consider when investing their resources to compete and cooperate within the value confederation simultaneously.

CHARACTERISTICS OF THE EMERGING VALUE CONFEDERATION

As individual firms become part of a larger economic network, or confederation of companies, the nature of product development will change markedly to reflect the economic imperatives and conditions that shape the confederation's evolution. A *value confederation* is a network of companies that use a shared product architecture or technological platform to create and develop an overall value proposition that grows stronger as more firms enter the set. A key characteristic of the value confederation is that each firm within the confederation focuses on creating and delivering a specific, distinctive, economic contribution, such as a component, skill, or stage of production activity. Each firm concentrates its efforts on a specific activity that is mutually dependent upon the efforts and output of the other participants. While firms within the confederation may engage in formal strategic alliances and collaborative arrangements with each other, the value confederation may include numerous independent participants that operate without explicit alliance relationships. Arenas in which value confederations have proliferated in recent years include personal computers, storage devices, healthcare, defense products, semiconductors, multimedia, and online services.

Value confederations occur in those industries in which exist strong dynamics for increasing returns from network-based economics.[5] A key characteristic of increasing returns is that the more suppliers, firms, and customers join the confederation, the stronger it becomes. This propensity for mutual

---

[5] See P. B. Evans and T. S. Wurster. (1997, Sept.). "Strategy and the New Economics of Information." *Harvard Business Review,* 71–82. On a related note, also see K. P. Coyne and R. Dye. (1998, Jan.). "The Competitive Dynamics of Network-Based Business." *Harvard Business Review,* 99–111.

dependence among various economic entities that accompanies increasing returns gives rise to conditions whereby firms in the network are connected to one another through common architectural standards, technological platforms, or even through common information-based infrastructures. Participating members of the confederation can change over time, and in many cases, firms will often become members of multiple and even competing value confederations. Within a given value confederation, each firm focuses almost exclusively on a given activity, building a strong base of firm-specific knowledge and skills. Each firm develops and provides a distinctive contribution to the confederation's value proposition. The overall impact of this specialization is that innovation and product development activities become correspondingly dispersed among a growing number of firms, thus necessitating a high level of technological and organizational coordination among product and process platforms.

Specialization and focus on a given economic activity, however, does not preclude competition among members within the value confederation. Paradoxically, members of a value confederation will often cooperate and compete at the same time, thus engaging in what has been described as *co-opetition*.[6] As each firm contributes its distinctive offerings and value to the confederation, it also competes for preferred position within the confederation in order to capture a dominant share of the overall value-creation opportunity. Firms that are able to innovate faster generate new forms of knowledge or have greater access to a given market—for example, they may position themselves to gain significant competitive advantage and leverage over the entire confederation. Thus, each participating firm has two competitive objectives: (1) to create a distinctive source of value that enhances the overall value proposition of the confederation, and (2) to capture a disproportionate share of total confederation rents as possible. The confluence of these two economic objectives means that each firm's internal strategy effort must anticipate how best to

---

[6] See A. M. Brandenburger and B. Nalebuff. (1996). *Co-Opetition: A Revolutionary Mindset that Combines Competition and Cooperation.* New York: Doubleday.

innovate and to assimilate the latest technology or value-added offerings into its products in advance of what competitors' innovations and customers' needs may be.

STRATEGIC IMPACT OF THE VALUE CONFEDERATION

The emergence of value confederations has provided insight into how firms will likely build sources of competitive advantage in the future. Even though value confederations have become particularly well established in those competitive environments in which common architectures and technological platforms exist, these same environments also exhibit a high level of investment risk and the frequent occurrence of potentially disruptive technologies. Consequently, an innovation that markedly changes the confederation's value proposition has collateral effects on each firm's individual sources of competitive advantage. On the one hand, firms feel the need to establish leadership in a key architecture or platform to establish industry and customer lock-in; yet, other firms may seek to redefine or even challenge the confederation's value proposition through disruptive innovations that fundamentally alter the nature of product design, process design, or buyers' needs (e.g., the rise of Sun Microsystems's Java architecture to challenge Microsoft's operating systems). Thus, within a confederation, firms must compete for those skills that enable them to secure a strong share of the confederation's overall value proposition, while understanding and perhaps investing in potentially competing technologies that could disrupt the existing value proposition in the future.

Accelerate Adoption of Core Technology Platforms. Firms within the value confederation must compete with one another to identify the best source of distinctive value, but competition must occur along a key technology platform or architecture. The essence of the value confederation depends upon cultivating a platform that establishes customer lock-in through high switching costs. Examples of platforms that create lock-in include operating systems for computers, algorithms that power wireless communication networks, technical standards for the transmission of audio and video streaming over the Internet, and the physical configuration of products for consumer electronics (e.g., VHS, DVD, CD standards). However, firms active in shaping the technology platform must look for ways to accelerate its adoption among other firms that seek to enter the confederation. By providing the technology platform to an expanding number of participants (often through low pricing, preferred access to new prototype designs, software code, or generous licensing arrangements), firms harness the power of increasing returns deterring outside firms from joining competing value confederations. Moreover, the stronger the lock-in that is established among member firms and customers, the greater the entry barriers for the entire confederation. The faster the confederation membership grows and the faster the technology platform or architecture becomes the standard, the greater the confederation's competitive position.

During the 1980s, Matsushita Electric of Japan cemented its dominance in the technological architecture for consumer-based VCRs by freely licensing its VHS format system to both its competitors and to content-based firms that produced films and other programming. Matsushita's strategy to create a dominant VHS standard by expanding its confederation to any firm willing to manufacture VCRs enabled it to outflank Sony. Eventually, Sony was forced to abandon its competing Beta standard as customers flocked to the VHS standard.

Compete for Share Within the Confederation. Product and/or process innovation become key for firms as they seek to capture and dominate a larger share of the confederation's overall value proposition. Often, competing within the confederation means investing in some key component or skill to support the technology platform or seeking a key competitive position within a critical market. A unique resource or asset that provides strategic leverage in a focused, value-adding area (e.g., manufacturing competence, software application, reputation, brand equity) enhances the firm's bargaining power within the confederation. Thus, competitive strategy within a value confederation requires firms to conceive how they can build on a distinctive contribution that simultaneously enhances and protects their bargaining power vis-à-vis other firms. In some cases, firms specialize in such a way as to exploit superior economies of scale or knowledge building a highly defensible position within the confederation. By dominating the "high ground," firms can establish a crucial foothold that enables them to carve out a core part of the overall value proposition.

Within the healthcare field, Impath has become well known for providing specialized cancer-related diagnostic support to physicians. Impath works with a broad array of hospitals, laboratories, and pharmaceutical firms to investigate and develop new diagnostic tools that help physicians better understand the different cancer treatment options that become available. This sharp focus enables Impath to become the knowledge hub for the entire medical community when it comes to modeling and understanding the progress of cancer treatment.

Invest in the Unknown. Members in the value confederation can seek to diversify their skill and competence sets by investing and learning about potentially disruptive technologies that could redefine the confederation's long-term competitive position, as well as each firm's relative competitive stance within the confederation. Small investments in cutting-edge, untested technologies might be the basis for future technology platforms. While there is no guaranteed payoff, these small investments do help the firm become more aware of potential threats. Excessive commitment to existing process technologies and product development routines may lead to inertia that makes rapid response to competitor developments all but impossible in fast-changing environments. Under ideal circumstances, investing across a range of different technologies and projects can help the firm to ensure that its knowledge base remains dynamic and permeable to ideas and innovations from partners, suppliers, and customers.

For example, Agilent Technologies (a recent spin-off of Hewlett-Packard) excels in the development of micro-array technology that is the basis for future DNA research, biocircuitry, and biotechnology. Already, many firms in the biotechnology industry are using Agilent's lithography-based approach to develop cutting-edge "gene chips" that are the basis for medical testing. However, Agilent's technology, while considered initially very promising, is not yet seen as the dominant technology platform for this emerging business. In order to hedge its investment risk, Agilent has invested in alternative micro-array technologies that utilize different process technologies in order to maximize its learning about competitive offerings. By understanding the alternative technologies that could give rise to newer micro-array technologies, Agilent can position itself to invest in new opportunities should they unfold.

In addition, firms may also directly invest in firms that possess the sources of disruptive technologies as a "hedge" in case the existing confederation's competitive position is challenged or deteriorates. Pharmaceutical firms, such as Merck, Pfizer, Bristol-Myers Squibb, and Pharmacia, have invested heavily in scores of biotechnology firms not only to learn about new genetic engineering technologies, but also to participate in shaping the possible evolution of new medicines and drug delivery systems. These investments enable each large pharmaceutical firm to broaden its network of relationships and to expand its scope of learning, while simultaneously limiting the financial and organizational risks from undertaking all of these initiatives internally.

An even bolder step in this direction is to participate in multiple, competing value confederations to diversify technology and confederation-based risk. For example, IBM has invested considerable resources with many software providers. It has made small investments in such companies as Siebel Systems, Ariba, and I2 Technologies, in order to see how its customers will use various software applications and new business exchange platforms.

IMPACT ON STRATEGY DEVELOPMENT AND GROWTH INITIATIVES

The rise of value confederations across many industries has distinct ramifications for strategy development and innovation for growth. In fact, these imperatives are likely to change quite significantly as firms design new approaches to create value while competing within the confederation. A core driver of building competitive advantage within the confederation relates to how well the firm can position itself to capture a larger share of confederation value. As a result, core activities such as developing new product and process technologies must increasingly be coordinated among many entities within the confederation; no single firm can seek to control every aspect of product and process innovation. As the value confederation grows, the tendency for each firm to specialize in a focused activity will increase as well. Consequently, managing a parallel (and often competing) set of investment initiatives, while constructing effective knowledge-sharing interfaces among cooperating firms, will itself become a new organizational competence. Devising the architecture to coordinate these initiatives among the confederation's members entails a variety of new skills and approaches.

Competition and cooperation within the value confederation will compel firms to invest in core competences, resources, and skills that will enable them to exert a growing (and ideally, disproportionate) degree of influence over member firms within the confederation. Managing this duality of competition and cooperation (also known as co-opetition) requires a different strategic lens on how best to invest and allocate resources. On the one hand, each firm needs the other member firms to contribute their distinctive assets to fulfill the overall value proposition. On the other hand, each firm competes with the same exact set of firms to learn new skills and insights, to develop new products and processes, and to capture a greater share of confederation rents. The nature of this behavior gives rise to a set of strategic conundrums that will place a great premium on each firm's ability to reinvent itself in a number of different dimensions.

An Emphasis on Seeking Modularity. A focus on utilizing core competences and resources to make products, services, and technologies more modular can substantially increase the firm's bargaining power within the confederation. *Modularity* refers to the economic concept in which product/service and component designs are sufficiently flexible to provide a range of variation in their final configuration or use without entailing a fundamental change in the basic design or layout.[7]

As the confederation's overall value proposition is unbundled among a growing number of member confederation firms, modularity becomes an important driver of product development in particular. Modularity offers a high level of what might be termed *embedded coordination,* since product components, skills, and technologies share a common set of standardized interfaces that allow for mixing and matching among the confederation's member firms' value contributions. Within each firm, product development needs to focus on maximizing the creation and use of self-contained modules (e.g., components, software, system drivers) that can quickly and seamlessly fit the offerings of other confederation firms. Product modularity thus enhances the mutual interdependence among firms. The greater the modularity of a firm's offering, the greater its economic usefulness to other members in the confederation. Consequently, a focus on enhancing modularity in product development will encourage firms to innovate in such a way that product architectures and technology platforms are distributed as broadly as possible so as to maximize the economic reach (and also the barriers to entry) of the entire value confederation.

As product designs become more modular, it is important for the knowledge base and core competencies of the firm to assimilate new technologies, insights, and skills. Ideally, intrafirm investment should be oriented towards making the firm's core competence more modular, so that the underlying technological, organizational, or knowledge-based components allow for an increase in its capacity to learn, internalize, and

---

[7] The concept of modularity as it applies to economic systems is presented in an excellent work by M. A Schilling. (2000). "Toward A General Modular Systems Theory and Its Application to Interfirm Product Modularity." *Academy of Management Review, 25,* 312–335. Also see R. Sanchez and J. Mahoney. (1996). "Modularity, Flexibility and Knowledge Management in Product and Organizational Design." *Strategic Management Journal, 17,* 63–76.

apply new skills to future product ideas. A *modular core competence* is one that accommodates and allows for a growing range of insights into the development process. As product designs become more modular, so should be the firm's approach to building its competence base. Over time, firms will likely race one another to develop both modular core competences and modular product designs in their ongoing attempts to capture a disproportionate share of value-creating activities in the value confederation.

The consumer electronics, personal computer (PC), and related multimedia industries already exhibit a growing degree of modularity-based strategies pursued by firms competing in these arenas. New products, such as MP3 players, CD burners, advanced computer platforms, videogame players, and software upgrades increasingly must be compatible with both previous as well as future design configurations. More importantly, offerings, while remaining distinctive in performance characteristics and appeal (e.g., Intel microprocessors, Apple Macintosh computers, Microsoft Windows platforms, Sony Playstation game boxes), are becoming increasingly modular in their consumer applications. Product technologies originally conceived for a narrowly defined application (e.g., computing or videogames) must now be easily configured for use in previously unforeseen arenas. For example, Sony's Playstation systems now feature not only advanced software and video graphics, but also Internet connectivity and DVD players that allow users to capture much of the benefits of earlier generation PCs. As Sony's Playstation line of videogames incorporate state-of-the-art microprocessors from IBM, Toshiba, and other firms, it is widely anticipated that the Playstation architecture could become an important competitor to next generation DVD-driven applications for both PCs and the consumer television markets. Conversely, Apple's Macintosh computers now feature desktop publishing that allows users to create their own full-motion video films and presentations, communicate on the Internet, and connect to a whole range of new digitally-driven consumer electronics applications that are still in the works.

ENHANCING FAST INNOVATION CAPABILITIES

Each firm within the value confederation focuses on its own source of distinctive value. As confederation members become mutually interdependent, product innovations occurring in one firm can dramatically impact the nature of product development in another. Within the confederation, firms jockey for a stronger competitive position by creating new skills and assimilating new sources of knowledge. The cumulative impact of such intraconfederation competitive behavior suggests that power and influence within the confederation will likely accrue to the firm that is able to innovate the fastest. While specialization by individual firms remains key, the capability to lead the confederation in pioneering new designs, process technologies, and entry into new markets enables the innovating firm to command significant influence, if even for a short time. As such, one major driver of intrafirm investment for member firms will be choosing a particular attribute or element of the overall value proposition and allocating sufficient resources to dominate it as much as possible. Under the most ideal conditions, the value-creating skills and insights possessed by any given firm should be inimitable, while the final product or service offering itself leads the confederation in terms of modularity and knowledge contribution in advance of other firms.

COMBINING DISPARATE SOURCES OF KNOWLEDGE

A new type of organizational competence may take root for some firms within the value confederation—orchestrating the technological standards, architectures, and product development activities of individual firms. Firms may specialize in this orchestration role by combining the distinctive offerings and skills of member confederation firms into a larger value proposition. Thus, by identifying emerging market trends, planning the format of future technical standards and products, and encouraging member firms to work more closely together on such initiatives, firms may serve a vital integrative role.

Japanese companies, in particular, have been practitioners of such orchestration strategies through their complex alliances and cross-holdings in suppliers and other firms. This *keiretsu* arrangement, while substantially different from our notion of a value confederation, seeks to share knowledge and technologies among key members who provide design, production, and other technology expertise.[8]

Other firms may create technological breakthroughs and become "industry statesmen," promulgating the new standards or designs among competitors in the arena. One linchpin to this approach is the simultaneous dominance and low-cost proliferation of a given technology or architectural standard that enables both suppliers and competitors to become disseminating agents of the core platform. It is imperative that the firm retains control over its intellectual property and continues to invest in the core platform to sustain dominance, while encouraging likely competitors to utilize its architectural standard, core platform, or underlying technology. The duality of this strategy requires that the innovating firm capture high profitability and competitive advantage through the increasing returns that accompany higher adoption both within and beyond the industry. Winning these "architectural wars" requires the innovating firm to ensure that its technology vision is rapidly adopted by firms likely to become important future competitors. As the technology or architecture becomes the de facto industry standard, increasing returns encourages greater usage, member participation in the value confederation, and adoption of the firm's innovation to potentially new and unforeseen applications.

In pursuing an orchestration-based strategy, firms will need highly integrative skills that can manage product development approaches concurrently among multiple firms. Strategic orchestration and architecture creation demand a higher level of meta-learning and dynamic routines that encompass intrafirm creativity and innovation that spans across other firms. This orchestration-based strategy to product development could well represent another type of compe-

---

[8] See F. Kodama. (1995). *Emerging Patterns of Innovation.* Boston, MA: Harvard Business School Press.

tence set, since the skills required for integrating different product designs and features call for an exceptional insight into technology, competitor trajectories, and customer needs.

Although high-technology hardware and software industries exhibit many firms attempting to set the standard for their respective offering, the concept of providing a common architecture to set the rules for competition are found in many other industries as well. For example, highly innovative firms in the automobile industry not only produce and assemble their own cars, but also provide a central linchpin around which dozens of specialized design firms submit their ideas and styles for consideration throughout the confederation. Honda and Toyota lead not only in continuous product improvement, but also in upgrading each car's overall "product integrity," whereby individual components work together to improve ergonomics and driver comfort as well. As other member companies supply next-generation components to Honda and Toyota, they also become implementers of new technological advances that redefine cars' functionality and features. In the networking industry, Cisco Systems serves as a prime example of this orchestration role. The company manages its own internal product development efforts with those of chip suppliers, software developers, fiber optic firms, and other component suppliers to ensure that all providers are designing their offerings along a common, modular standard. Cisco even encourages its competitors to share in the technology that is developed over time, since product design compatibility among a wide range of competitors encourages customers to upgrade their equipment needs without an overriding fear that technical standards will not be compatible from different vendors.

COMPETING ON THE CUTTING-EDGE: RENEWING ADVANTAGE VIA LEARNING

As the value confederation form of competition grows, firms will face renewed and heightened pressure to continue to invest in future products, technologies, skills, and markets.

This trend suggests that firms will need to steadily invest in creating new sources of knowledge, both within and external to the organization. Each firm will face a growing, unprecedented degree of interdependence with other firms, including competitors, suppliers, and even customers. This interdependence means that each firm must not only invest sufficiently to build and refine its own sources of innovation and competitive advantage, but also to stay ahead of likely competitors who may have similar corporate ambitions and growth trajectories.

As we enter the new millennium, it is clear that firms of all sizes face complex and even contradictory signals from the competitive environment. In some arenas, firms are downsizing and shedding businesses that no longer fit their core competence. In other arenas, companies are aggressively acquiring their rivals and investing ever-higher sums into new and often unproven technologies. While the competitive environment appears to exhibit signs of economic entropy, much of this innovation and change-driven "chaos" is actually an accelerated process of "creative destruction," whereby new technologies and products are rapidly displacing those of established firms. Thus, a key strategic imperative for any firm is to find the right balance between investing in existing products and markets (mostly profitable activities) and devoting resources to investigating and learning new skills and knowledge (decisions that are often subject to considerable internal debate). Competition is certain to hasten these economic convulsions. Moreover, any given firm within a value confederation will face continued challenges from similarly endowed (if not better) competitors seeking to drive innovation and value creation. As we have already seen from numerous corporate experiences over the past decade (e.g., Eastman Kodak), firms that were slow to grapple with change and to embrace cutting-edge products and technologies face an agonizing process of decline. However, firms that are able to navigate and even participate in shaping the future of their respective value confederations will not only win a disproportionate share of profitability, but also will set the pace for future technology-driven investments and customer expectations.

For senior managers, perhaps the most compelling strategic consideration is not to focus excessively on sustaining existing sources of competitive advantage, but rather to learn and build renewable sources of advantage for the future, such as investments in core skills and knowledge that can be easily adapted to fast-changing technologies and markets; more often than not, renewable advantage emanates from a "social fabric" that promotes experimentation, risk-taking, and knowledge-sharing across multiple lines of business and products. Equally important, managers need to inculcate within their organizations a diverse base of insight and experience to build a portfolio of talents, since there is no way to predict how competitive strategies (and the skills required to support them) are likely to evolve over the long-term.

NEW MEASURES OF PROSPERITY

Thomas Monahan
and Stephen A. Stumpf

DEFINING AND MEASURING ECONOMIC VALUE

There is little debate over the need to enhance measurement systems to better capture "value" when analyzing firms. Recent innovations in economic value measurement, such as value-based management or Economic Value Added (EVA) systems, focus on using past financial performance data to forecast future cash flows (or adjusted profit tied to a firm's operations). These measurement systems define capital in financial terms alone. Defining capital in this way has enormous consequences on the reported, and hence perceived, value of an organization. These measures also highlight what the organization's leadership should focus on to develop its internal performance measurement systems. Consequently, these performance measurement issues impact both internal and external reporting for firms.

The failure of many companies in the digital (dotcom) industry has put pressure on organizations and the investment community to better understand, define, and measure the elements of economic value. This pressure adds to the existing demand for measurement systems to more accurately assess the value of organizations in industries that require few physical assets to function successfully, such as software, knowledge, and professional service firms that predate the digital industry by decades.

The efficacy of basing value on management systems that rely on financial capital alone is coming under increased scrutiny. Many business leaders agree that a better understanding of the root causes of value creation is needed and the factors considered as part of the performance measurement system need to change. This is supported by the significant growth in firms that are using some form of Kaplan and Norton's Balanced Scorecard approach to measurement.[1]

Given the growth in a service- and knowledge-based economy, four kinds of capital are critical to understanding value creation: financial capital, human capital, intellectual capital, and social capital.

FINANCIAL CAPITAL

Financial capital is defined as the financial strength of a firm in providing assets (physical and intangible) to generate future cash flows for investors. In this measure, value (future cash flows or operating profits) is tied to the level of asset investment and past financial performance of the firm. For an agriculturally based economy or one in the early stages of industrialization, assets and cash flows are generally tied to the physical nature of property (land, plant, equipment, inventories). In this environment, a measurement system that focus-

---

[1] Kaplan, Robert S., and David P. Norton. (1993, Oct.). "Putting the Balanced Scorecard to Work." 90 *Harvard Business Review,* 134–147.

es on financial capital works well, since the survival of the business is often predicated on raising sufficient resources to acquire or control productive assets that lead to cash flow. Given the evolution of the world economy over the past few decades, the primary and overarching focus on financial measures of economic value is disturbing.

HUMAN CAPITAL

Human capital is the competencies and capabilities of the workforce (employees, managers, and executives). Organizations seek the highest quality of human talent they can afford, and they often invest in it to maintain and improve the capability of that talent. Individuals try to improve the value of their human capital through education, practice, and work experiences. The "war for talent" experienced by many firms in the late 1990s epitomizes the value that employers and prospective employees place on human capital.[2]

This change in focus, however, has not led to important changes in the measurement and analysis systems used to report a firm's economic value. For example, as industries shifted to more complicated manufacturing processes in the 1960s, the development of people was considered a key to success— more emphasis was placed on training employees and the development of the organization's human capital. This contributed to a movement by behavioral scientists to move the expenses for wages to an asset account, since human capital was considered a key to future value and therefore met the definition for being classified as an asset. It was thought that for business to value human capital appropriately, it would have to be reclassified on financial statements and measured accordingly. This change in accounting treatment never came to pass due to the uncertainty surrounding the benefit period from human capital. Many behavioral scientists still consider this omission to be a major flaw in U.S. corporate reporting systems.

---

[2] Stumpf, Stephen A., and Walter Tymon. (2001). "Consultant or Entrepreneur?: Demystifying the 'War for Talent.'" *Career Development International,* 6(1),48–55.

INTELLECTUAL CAPITAL

As business became more sophisticated and moved into complicated financial, technological, and service arrangements, the importance of *intellectual capital* (ideas) moved to the forefront. Intellectual capital existed previously (just as human capital existed before it became a common business term), but it was not frequently talked about as part of the capital of a business to be measured and reported to investors and other stakeholders.

Proprietary technologies, copyrights, patents, and trade secrets are intellectual capital, just as books, libraries, and other electronic depositories are guardians of intellectual capital. Intellectual capital has increased in importance as the knowledge needed to conduct business has deepened and as the intellectual prowess and technology necessary to solve complex business problems has increased. To the extent that one can sell intellectual capital (e.g., sell a patent to a competitor or sell ideas to a client), it is an asset of the firm. As industries embrace the internal changes necessary to make contributions in a knowledge and service economy, the creation of intellectual capital takes on significant importance. Knowing which ideas to value and selecting them from large volumes of information available to everyone via the Web is critical.

Companies with minimal assets and a relatively small workforce, such as Microsoft, use their intellectual prowess to develop ideas that lead to significant cash flow. Industries with heavy investments in assets, such as pharmaceuticals, are relying more on their pipeline of ideas for generating future value than on the size of their asset base or number of employees.

SOCIAL CAPITAL

A fourth form of capital, *social capital,* consists of the breadth, interconnectedness, and diversity of those with which one or the organization has meaningful relationships. Wayne Baker[3]

---

[3] Baker, Wayne. (2000). *Achieving Success Through Social Capital: Tapping the Hidden Resources in Your Personal and Business Networks.* San Francisco: Jossey-Bass.

puts forth a series of arguments that focus on achieving success in business through developing and leveraging social capital. He argues that it is not what you know, but whom you know that is critical in a knowledge and service economy. Social capital involves the development and leverage of relationships in the conducting of business.

The driving force behind the value creation may shift from intellectual capital to social capital for industries dependent on relationships between firms. How does one determine the value of a professional services firm? Certainly not by its financial assets. Even cash flow is close to meaningless as clients this year may not be clients next year. The ability to sustain a flow of clients is based on relationships more so than any other form of capital. Most firms have difficulty measuring this internally and it certainly is rarely reported to external constituencies.

FOUR FORMS OF CAPITAL

Clearly new and broader value drivers are emerging and our measurement systems are struggling to adjust to this changing environment. Examples abound where knowledge based firms in consulting, software creation, and financial services are focusing on developing human, intellectual, and social capital as ways of creating value for their customers and clients. Think of how professional service firms maintain relations with past employees (alumni) through formal network channels, or how universities work intently on developing close relations with alumni.

TOWARD INTERDISCIPLINARY AND INTEGRATED MEASURES

While we have an understanding of what is meant by human, intellectual, and social capital, difficulties involved with developing measurement systems to capture the value of these

Higher Education and Religious Institutions Do It Differently— Successfully

Why is it that some institutions (e.g., universities and religious organizations) that we normally do not associate with "quality management" have survived and prospered for centuries? Few institutes of higher education or religions have gone out of business or been merged into other entities so as to lose their identity. Yet, most of the Fortune 1000 companies of 50 years ago do not exist today. The premier universities and oldest religions are often the wealthiest organizations in existence. Even some newer religions (e.g., Baptists, Mormons) have expanded at rates inconceivable to most CEOs.

When isolating the unique aspects of these institutions, a few characteristics become apparent. First, both have focused on maintaining relationships with their customers over their customers' lifetimes—not just at the "point of sale." Second, both have generated significant financial strength not tied to earned income. Customers give back not for personal gain, but to support the institution. Although the traditional financial measurement systems of these institutions are often underdeveloped, they have focused on some areas of measurement in creating value that may be underutilized by corporations. A key question for corporations is, What is the fundamental value construct in this nonconventional approach to value creation that can be transferred to a profit-seeking institution?

In academia and religious institutions there is a tremendous investment in employee development. Human capital has always been viewed as a key competitive advantage, and the development process is intense in both environments. Standard measurement systems have been developed to insure that "employees" are well versed in the culture and goals of the organization. Think of the process of obtaining tenure in a university or becoming ordained in a religious order. Both are extremely time-intensive, and the commitment to development is strong. In these institutions, human capital development has contributed to a powerful feeling of community, low turnover, and an environment in which intellectual development is viewed as being critical to the organization.

Formal measurement systems have been created to monitor performance in both the human and social capital areas. Years of schooling or degrees, number and quality of publications or translations of biblical works, and dollar donations by customers are all closely monitored. These institutions recognized early on that a most difficult area to quantify—social capital—was an important area to be nurtured, valued, and measured. Religious orders maintained these relationships through networks of members across the world well before being "global" was trend. Academic institutions have built off their base of alumni to create value for future students. Maintaining relationships with past customers (alumni) has become the key value-creating strategy at many schools, even surpassing the importance of tuition or operating revenue. Their relationships are lifelong, not transaction based. Something formal and important is going on that businesses can learn from to help affect change in their operations.

investments remain. Yet, being able to measure and effectively manage these forms of capital in the future can provide a huge competitive advantage to firms. There have been recent attempts to isolate social capital by focusing on these types of relationships in developing new measurement systems. For example, activity-based management (ABM) is an attempt to measure cross-functional processes in attempting to identify and manage cost drivers across functional areas. The Balanced Scorecard is an attempt to help businesses focus on the relationships among customers, processes, financial, and innovation measures in managing their operations. Enterprise resource planning (ERP) focuses on managing operations across functions to efficiently allocate resources across the firm. Customer relationship management (CRM) focuses on managing the business-to-customer relationships in an attempt to highlight the importance of this aspect of the firm's capital. Many organizations are realizing that measuring and managing staff development, idea generation, and relationships will be an essential element of their future success. These same firms have been frustrated by the resistance experienced from many employees when implementing systems that focus on new forms of measurement.

In order to aggressively implement new performance measurement systems that emphasize process (relationships) rather than functions or outcome measures, two initiatives must take place. First, major efforts must be undertaken that focus on *unlearning* principles that employees have worked with for years. Second, employee development programs must be drastically altered to focus on the importance of relationships and social capital in cross-functional decision making as compared with functionally focused decision making. When this happens, different measurement systems can then be adopted to support interdisciplinary approaches to decision making. These systems will be able to focus more on the importance of human, intellectual, and social capital and a firm's ability to measure and manage relationships that help contribute to firm value.

LEARNING AND UNLEARNING: THE NEED FOR BOTH

Following the publication of Peter Senge's book *The Fifth Discipline*, much has been written about the learning organization. A recent guide for managers highlights what organizations can do to put learning into action.[4] Based on David Garvin's work, we define a *learning system* as one that creates, acquires, interprets, transfers, and retains knowledge, and is purposeful in modifying its behavior to reflect new knowledge and insights. Systems need to learn quickly in a knowledge-based society. Garvin's "litmus tests" of a learning organization are that the organization can say yes to the following questions (taken from his book *Learning in Action: A Guide to Putting the Learning Organization to Work*) and provide meaningful examples in support of each yes.

- Does the organization have a defined learning agenda?
- Is the organization open to discordant information?
- Does the organization avoid repeated mistakes?
- Does the organization lose critical knowledge when key people leave?
- Does the organization act on what it knows?

The heavy focus on learning (akin to a heavy focus on financial capital) can lead to unintended consequences. Just as it is unlikely for an organization to believe that it doesn't want to earn more money, it is difficult for the organization to believe that it doesn't want more learning. More is always better. Yet, sometimes, less is more. Libraries, disk space, digital files, and Web sites expand at rates well beyond an organization's capability to use, manage, or service the information. Systems need to be able to unlearn just as they need to be able to learn. Early organizational change theorists referred to this as *unfreezing*. Current ideas and structures need to be dis-

---

[4] Garvin, David A. (2000). *Learning in Action: A Guide to Putting the Learning Organization to Work.* Boston: HBS Press (pp. 13–15).

mantled to create an environment ready for new ideas and change initiatives.

To unlearn, a system must destroy, dispose of, ignore, hide, or replace some of the knowledge that has been learned, and purposefully modify its behavior to reflect that of which it has let go. Our litmus tests for an unlearning system follow:

- Does the system have a defined unlearning agenda? (Products to be de-marketed, information to be expunged, key players to be replaced, MIS indices to be changed, business models to disregard, consultants to terminate, bankers to replace.)
- Is the system open to unlearning some of its accepted concepts, frameworks, and premises? (What ways of thinking no longer apply that need to be expunged? What old paradigms might be discarded? What is highly successful today that will be an inhibitor to change tomorrow?)
- Does the system use repeated mistakes to diagnose underlying learnings so as to unlearn them? (If we continue to do this, what is it that we must unlearn to stop doing it?)
- Does the organization derive benefit from the knowledge it loses when key people leave? (Now that "they" are gone, what "idea space" has been freed up? What can we do differently now that a "barrier" has been removed)?
- Does the organization act on what it destroys, disposes of, ignores, hides, and replaces? (Having let something go, does the organization eliminate costs and burdens?)

FUNCTIONAL OR INTERDISCIPLINARY: A TIME FOR CHANGE

There is a "battle" taking place in companies that is centered on an interdisciplinary and relationship orientation versus a functional or departmental perspective in measuring performance. Built upon the need for specialization and division of labor techniques required in industry over the last century, the functional or departmental perspective to decision making has served industry well.

Academics have contributed to this functional focus in business by developing a level of expertise in functional areas that was extremely useful to solving business problems. Academic research thus supported tremendous growth in commerce. Journal articles became so specialized and discipline-focused that few academics had interest in reading, never mind conducting, research across disciplines. Having deep knowledge in a narrow specialization became the "ticket" to gaining prominence in one's field and gaining exposure in the most respected academic journals.

Business appreciated and benefited from the sophisticated functional research produced by the academic community as it helped them deal with the complex issues being addressed in the finance, accounting, strategy, and marketing functions. In recent years, however, businesses have begun to change their approach to decision making. Understanding processes that go across functional areas is becoming critical to implementing quality programs. Interdisciplinary approaches to management decision making require a different mode of thinking. Industry is changing the basic techniques it uses to conduct business, yet performance measurement systems remain unchanged. It is clear that capturing the richness of relationships among processes, functions, people, and customer groups is critical in creating value for firms and that our traditional measurement systems are not focused on capturing this type of information.

Businesses are investing billions of dollars in new systems to support interdisciplinary decision making. These systems require massive changes in the way employees use data to manage their sub-businesses—requirements that will not be met unless these managers are willing and able to unlearn much of what they believe is the foundation of their success. In making these investments, firms have underestimated the degree of commitment employees have to the functional models they have used for years. This continues to be reinforced in the practitioner literature and many executive education programs. For example, the authors reviewed the curricula of the top-ranked MBA programs in the United States and Europe and found that although there are many individual efforts aimed at increasing the cross-functionality of curricula, the majority of courses are based on a functional excellence model. Many academics believe that moving toward a more interdisciplinary model undermines functional excellence. Consequently, the basic educational structure to which future business leaders are exposed is still tied to functional knowledge and delivery rather than to interdisciplinary decision making. While functional excellence will remain important to a firm's success, the functional area managers must be able to embrace interdisciplinary perspectives, since most strategic decisions involve elements across functional areas. Even when using materials that are multidisciplinary, such as case studies or simulations, the discussion is influenced by the instructor's functional background. Team-based instruction using faculty with different functional backgrounds rarely takes place in business schools or executive education classrooms.

The difficulty involved with driving this different approach into the education of future leaders cannot be overemphasized. It will take a huge "unlearning" initiative within business schools to enable this new decision-making process to take hold. It will also require dramatic changes to the measurement systems used in industry to evaluate and reward employees.

PERFORMANCE MEASUREMENT PROGRAMS FOR TODAY (THE FUTURE IS TOO LATE)

Many companies have begun to move towards relationship-based reporting through initiatives such as ABM, Balanced Scorecards, and ERP systems. Many of these initiatives have failed; others have progressed more slowly than anticipated. We propose the following reasons for the limited success of initiatives whose intention is to offer a more thorough measurement and valuation system. We also offer recommendations to increase the probability of future success.

First, in many of these implementations firms have not directly addressed the unlearning process, which has undermined their ability to create change. Formally applying the litmus test for unlearning and following the implied recommendations in these questions will help firms address this shortcoming.

Second, it is imperative that firms change their evaluation and reward systems when they move toward focusing on other forms of capital, particularly relationship management (i.e., social capital). If firms continue to tie their evaluation and reward systems to functional-focused performance measures, employees will continue to complain that they need the "same information" in order to run their business. Educate employees as to why the four forms of capital (with emphasis on relationship management in service industries) are so critical to value creation, and then reward employees for supporting progress towards creating value along each of the four capital types. Part of this education system must involve a formal process to help employees understand the unlearning process. Without this, firms will continue to experience a lack of success with change management programs.

Third, more measures must be developed to capture the essence of human, intellectual, and social capital, and these must be included in a firm's reports, as required by the Securities and Exchange Commission (SEC) and the Financial Accounting Standards Board (FASB). Human capital measures might include educational level, training and development expenditures, library and digital knowledge resources, and e-learning opportunities. Knowledge measures might include copyrights, patents, software development, knowledge-online systems, e-learning capability, and various presentations and distributions of what has been learned and unlearned. Relationship measures might include customer and employee retention; alumni networks; meetings and conferences attended that are designed for relationship building; and collaborations and partnerships with suppliers, buyers, and other stakeholders.

Human capital, intellectual capital, and social capital are as critical to the future value of an organization as are its profits, yet these forms of capital are not meaningfully captured in current external reporting requirements. Granted, these measures are less objective (in many cases) than dollar estimates, yet they can provide analysts with a more complete picture of value drivers than what we currently require in GAAP reporting. Kaplan and Norton's Balanced Scorecard provides an effective framework to begin experimenting with a new form of reporting of these social capital measures.

Fourth, major curricula revisions must be implemented in business schools and executive education programs to better prepare participants for the interdisciplinary world they will be facing. The unlearning element of change can be significantly streamlined if business executives begin their careers open to opportunities for creating firm value through adaptive problem solving that uses interdisciplinary methods and leveraging relationships, as opposed to a near total focus on functional and financial excellence.

33

A WORLD
OF FLEAS
AND ELEPHANTS

Charles Handy

T he world of organizations is fast dividing itself into fleas and elephants. The elephants are the large organizations of business and government; the fleas are the technological start-ups and the new dotcoms. Fleas are the small consultancies and professional firms, the self-employed experts, and the specialty suppliers that service the elephants. On a humbler scale, the fleas include the little businesses that pepper our main streets with restaurants, family-run stores, hairdressing salons, and real estate agencies, not to mention the hundreds of thousands of small not-for-profit organizations as well as all our local schools and churches.

The elephants get all the attention, from academics as well as from the press, but most people have always worked in fleas. The elephants consolidate, but new ideas often come from the fleas. The elephants, particularly those that are multinational and global, matter. They fertilize the world with their ideas and their technology; they amass the piles of resources that are necessary to develop oilfields, build aircrafts, research new drugs, and spread their brands around the world. They apply the advantages of scale and the clout of size to promoting efficiency and to reducing costs to the consumer. To an elephant, in fact, size is crucial. In pursuit of ever greater size, we have, in recent years, seen elephants swallowing elephants, or, as they would no doubt prefer to put it, marrying elephants in what they call "strategic mergers."

Once married or swallowed, the elephants go on a slimming diet, shedding jobs by the thousands in pursuit of efficiency. They are addicted to a productivity formula of $1/2 \times 2 \times 3$, or an objective of having half as many people employed in, say, 5 years' time, working twice as hard and producing three times as much. Fine for the stockholders, no doubt, but not so good for the half that is downloaded. Don't, therefore, look to elephants for new jobs; they have to come from fleas. This is a lesson that America learned long ago, one with which Europe is only slowly coming to terms.

Nor should we look to the elephants for imaginative new ideas. Efficiency is, in many ways, the enemy of creativity. Efficiency abhors waste, is uneasy with experiments that might go wrong, finds nonconformity uncomfortable, and prefers predictability to risk. Elephants prefer to pick up innovations once they have been proved to work. They can then develop them, give them scale and mass, promote them, and deliver them at an acceptable price. The new ideas come from fleas, often from fleas that arrive out of a clear blue sky, from outside the industry altogether, the Amazon.coms of our new world. The trouble is that fleas tend to live on the backs of elephants, not inside their bodies. When elephants buy up the product of a flea to develop it, they will spit out the original flea as soon as they can.

Fleas, therefore, provide the new challenges for leadership at all levels in society. What sort of leadership does a flea organization require, particularly an innovative flea? What are the characteristics of successful flea organizations? Can they, should they, grow into elephants? How can elephants grow fleas, or at least encourage them; tolerate their irritation; and make use of their creativity?

The pressures of a global world, which demands an increased degree of scale, added to an unprecedented pace of innovation requiring constant invention and reinvention, means that every society needs a mixture of both inventive fleas and efficient elephants. The questions above are therefore of some urgency if we are all going to benefit from the new frontiers opened up to us by technology.

THE CHARACTERISTICS
OF CREATIVE FLEAS

At the heart of every flea organization, at least at its beginnings, lies a creative individual. In 1999, the author and his wife, a portrait photographer, conducted a study of 29 such individuals in London, England, individuals whom they called the "new alchemists," meaning that they had created something from nothing, or from the metaphorical equivalent of base metal. The flea organizations that they had created or transformed ranged from businesses of various sorts to arts or community ventures, including a school and a church.[1]

The sample was small and could not therefore be definitive, but it did provide some clues to the nature of these leaders and the organizations that they had created, all of which were successful in their own terms. The one defining and common characteristic was *passion*. These individuals were passionate about what they were doing, whether they were building new airlines (Richard Branson), new eateries in New York and London (Terence Conran), new theater companies (Declan Donnellan with Cheek by Jowl), Britain's first and only private Anorexic Clinic (Dee Dawson), or Britain's first Healthy Living Center built around a rundown church in the east end of

---

[1] The study is reported fully in Charles Handy and Elizabeth Handy. (1999). *The New Alchemists*. London: Hutchinson.

London (Andrew Mawson). If the venture was a business, money was the outcome of success but was not the reason for the passion. Richard Branson says that he turns his frustrations as a customer into businesses to "improve a bit of the world."

This passion for what they did enabled them to endure anything—the long hours necessitated in starting a venture; the failures and mistakes that inevitably occur, and which they speak of as "lessons learned" rather than failures; and even the relative poverty that many experienced until the venture started to develop. The passion was often neither logical nor reasonable. Business plans would have looked wildly optimistic at the beginning, but none of them relied on outside financing at the start. Passion, not reason, provided the driving force. These individuals were mavericks. They were determined to make a difference. That determination fueled their energy. Dedication, difference, and doggedness, therefore, were the hallmarks of the alchemists.

Their passion infected their organizations. By recruiting like-minded enthusiasts, albeit with diverse talents, the leader created a family in his or her own image. These families were "chaordic" to use Dee Hock's description of the mixture of chaos and order that seems to be characteristic of the new fast-moving businesses. Because they were small and like-minded, they could rely on empathy for much of their communication, a sense of "what would Richard (or Lucy) do?" governed their lives. Meetings were frequent, but snappy. One alchemist had his boardroom table made 5 feet high to ensure that all meetings took place standing up. Success was shared either by formal profit-sharing schemes or by joint celebrations in the case of the non-profits. They keep the cores of their organizations tiny in order to reinforce the sense of empathy at the center and to create trust.

In many respects, therefore, they were typical of a family firm—only it was their colleagues who were the family. They were not interested in creating a dynasty or a way of life for their heirs. Their passion was to make a difference to the world as quickly as they could. It was what gave their organizations energy and excitement, the sense of being on a shared voyage of discovery. What was unclear was where the voyage would end. Would they turn into elephants themselves, or would they die when the founder left?

Elephants were all fleas once, just as oaks start from acorns—but not all acorns become oaks and most flea organizations do not develop into elephants. Acorns and fleas both seem subject to nature's law of abundance: There are so many of them that enough survive, even if most fail. In Britain last year, there were almost as many small business failures as there were new startups.

To move from flea to elephant requires a change of style. Infection and empathy are no longer enough when an organization becomes large and geographically dispersed. In most cases the change of style means a change of leader. Jim Clark, the founder of Silicon Graphics, Netscape, and Healtheon, and supreme among business alchemists, could never adjust to running the businesses he created. Michael Lewis, in his book *The New New Thing*, talks of the "Serious American Executive," who would move in to run the operations that Clark had created, but could not manage.

As often as not, once the new business reaches a significant size, it is bought by an existing elephant who then immediately or in due course gets rid of the pioneering flea leader. The elephant then takes the flea under its wing and introduces the techniques of efficiency, growing the business, but in the process, destroying much of the original excitement.

CAN ELEPHANTS HARBOR FLEAS?

It would be better by far if the elephant were able to grow its own fleas. This, however, requires a particular sort of leadership and structure. What is clear is that personality is as important to the leadership of an elephant as it is in a flea. Jack Welch will be remembered as much for the way he expressed the purpose of General Electric in his own behavior and passion as for the strategic choices that he made. Percy Barnevik, when CEO of ARB, managed to infect that huge federal organization with his own enthusiasm and zeal. One CEO of a multinational described his job as a mixture of missionary and teacher, in which he was constantly communicating his message to his people.

Yet, it is not enough for leaders at the top to exhibit passion and enthusiasm for their work. That enthusiasm, that sense of vocation or passion, must be possible right through the organization. That requires space, space for any would-be fleas to express themselves in their work, space to experiment, space to fail, and enough space to correct the failures before too much damage is done or too many people notice. It won't be possible to create those spaces in an excessively tidy organization. Elephants have to be loose-limbed if there is to be room for fleas at all levels.

One answer lies in federalism. Federalism was conceived as a way of combining the independent and the collective, of being both big and small, the same but different. Americans and Germans, Australians and Canadians, Spaniards and Swiss have all got federal constitutions designed to allow independence within a union, but even these do not always see the sense in applying the same principles to their businesses. To the British, *federalism* is the F-word, a dirty word that implies a loss of control to the center. This serious misunderstanding of the principles of federalism will be a handicap in the future development of both its constitution and its economy.

This is not the place for a detailed discussion of federalism. The principles are spelled out in an article by the writer for the *Harvard Business Review,* "Balancing Corporate Power: A New Federalist Paper."[2] Suffice it here to say that federalism is a mixture of both centralization and decentralization, centralizing only those things that everyone agrees it would be crazy not to centralize and leaving as much autonomy as is possible to the various states or business groups—the space for fleas.

Federalism is messy and political. There are disputes over the allocation of resources. Information is guarded when it should flow freely. There are boundary disputes, necessary

---

[2] Handy, Charles. "Balancing Corporate Power: A New Federalist Paper." *Harvard Business Review,* (Reprint No. 92604).

compromises, and competing lines of accountability. To make it work requires an active understanding of *twin citizenship*—the idea that one can have at least two loyalties, to one's own group and to the larger collective, one can be both a Texan and an American. The lesser loyalty is easy; it is the larger one that requires work, because without it compromise is hard to obtain—why give up on local priorities for the greater good if you have no interest in the greater good? Hence the critical importance of the talk of "vision" and "values," and the necessity for the top leader to accentuate these in his or her own words and actions. Some distribution of the spoils of success from the center to the states also helps to reinforce the idea of a common good.

Properly done, however, federalism allows room for the fleas inside the elephant. ABB tries to restrict the size of its business groups to 50 persons in order to recreate that sense of a small enterprise, personally led and motivated. In a world of hi-tech, hi-touch (to use Naisbit's evocative terms) can easily be neglected. Yet, fleas rely on trust in those with whom they work, and trust needs touch. Technology communicates facts but not feelings. Fleas need both for trust to flourish. Few of us know more than 50 people well enough to gauge their feelings or to know whether or not they can be relied upon. The alchemists instinctively know this, which is one reason they are reluctant to grow too big.

Federalism offers a way forward, but it is neither easy nor tidy. Small wonder, perhaps, that many leaders of elephants shrink from it. There are alternatives. One alternative is to run an internal venture capital bank, backing innovative proposals, either from internal groups or from individuals who want to move outside. Gary Hamel describes one experiment of this type.[3] In London, a young woman called Eva Pascoe was e-commerce director for Arcadia, a fashion retailer. A typical flea, she became irritated by the restrictions of the elephant and decided that she wanted to start her own Internet fashion store, Zoom.com. Arcadia agreed to back her, taking 60 per-

---

[3]Hamel, Gary. (1999, Sept.–Oct.). "Bringing Silicon Valley Inside." *Harvard Business Review.*

cent of the shares. That way they ensure that they have access not only to any appreciation in the shares, but more importantly, to her innovations.

Some prefer to cultivate their own private flea gardens, a la Xerox Parc. Although the fleas often thrive in such corporate gardens, there is a problem in bringing them or their ideas back into the mainstream. History is littered with examples of good ideas ignored by the same elephants that paid for them to be cultivated. It is simpler, perhaps, to go flea hunting, buying up innovative companies once they have proved themselves, dumping the bad or irritating bits, and keeping the essential intellectual property.

INDEX

8 reasons why you should read the Financial Times for 4 weeks RISK-FREE!

To help you stay current with significant
developments in the world economy ...
and to assist you to make informed business
decisions — the Financial Times brings you:

❶ Fast, meaningful overviews of international affairs ... plus daily briefings on major world news.

❷ Perceptive coverage of economic, business, financial and political developments with special focus on emerging markets.

❸ More international business news than any other publication.

❹ Sophisticated financial analysis and commentary on world market activity plus stock quotes from over 30 countries.

❺ Reports on international companies and a section on global investing.

❻ Specialized pages on management, marketing, advertising and technological innovations from all parts of the world.

❼ Highly valued single-topic special reports (over 200 annually) on countries, industries, investment opportunities, technology and more.

❽ The Saturday Weekend FT section — a globetrotter's guide to leisure-time activities around the world: the arts, fine dining, travel, sports and more.

FT FINANCIAL TIMES
World business newspaper

The *Financial Times* delivers a world of business news.

Use the Risk-Free Trial Voucher below!

To stay ahead in today's business world you need to be well-informed on a daily basis. And not just on the national level. You need a news source that closely monitors the entire world of business, and then delivers it in a concise, quick-read format.

With the *Financial Times* you get the major stories from every region of the world. Reports found nowhere else. You get business, management, politics, economics, technology and more.

Now you can try the *Financial Times* for 4 weeks, absolutely risk free. And better yet, if you wish to continue receiving the *Financial Times* you'll get great savings off the regular subscription rate. Just use the voucher below.

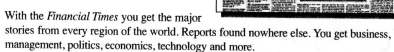

4 Week Risk-Free Trial Voucher

Yes! Please send me the *Financial Times* for 4 weeks (Monday through Saturday) Risk-Free, and details of special subscription rates in my country.

Name_____

Company_____

Address_____ ❑ Business or ❑ Home Address

Apt./Suite/Floor _____City _____State/Province_____

Zip/Postal Code_____Country _____

Phone (optional) _____E-mail (optional)_____

Limited time offer good for new subscribers in FT delivery areas only.
To order contact Financial Times Customer Service in your area (mention offer SAB01A).

The Americas: Tel 800-628-8088 Fax 845-566-8220 E-mail: uscirculation@ft.com

Europe: Tel 44 20 7873 4200 Fax 44 20 7873 3428 E-mail: fte.subs@ft.com

Japan: Tel 0120 341-468 Fax 0120 593-146 E-mail: circulation.fttokyo@ft.com

Korea: E-mail: sungho.yang@ft.com

S.E. Asia: Tel 852 2905 5555 Fax 852 2905 5590 E-mail: subseasia@ft.com

www.ft.com

FT **FINANCIAL TIMES**
World business newspaper